Tapping into Mathematics

WITH THE

TI-83 Graphics Calculator

Tapping into Mathematics

WITH THE

TI-83 Graphics Calculator

Edited by

BARRIE GALPIN AND ALAN GRAHAM

ADDISON-WESLEY

Harlow, England • Reading, Massachusetts • Menlo Park, California
New York • Don Mills, Ontario • Amsterdam • Bonn • Sydney • Singapore
Tokyo • Madrid • San Juan • Milan • Mexico City • Seoul • Taipei

The programs in this book have been included for their instructional value. They have been tested with care but are not guaranteed for any particular purpose. The publisher does not offer any warranties or representations nor does it accept any liabilities with respect to the programs.

Many of the designations used by manufacturers and sellers to distinguish their products are claimed as trademarks. Pearson Education Limited has made every attempt to supply trademark information about manufacturers and their products mentioned in this book.

Cover designed by Designers and Partners, Oxford, UK
and printed by Alden Press Ltd, Oxford
Cover photograph by permission of Texas Instruments, Inc.
Typeset by 34
Printed in Great Britain by Alden Press Ltd, Oxford.

First printed 1997
Reprinted 1999, 2001

ISBN 0-201-17547-9

British Library Cataloguing-in-Publication Data

A catalogue record for this book is available from the British Library

Library of Congress Cataloging-in-Publication Data is available

1.2

Contributors

The following people at The Open University contributed original material to this book: Mike Crampin, Chris Dillon, Judy Ekins, Barrie Galpin, Alan Graham, Gillian Iossif and David Pimm.

The necessary conversions for the TI-83 version of the book were carried out by Ruth Graham.

Acknowledgements

The publishers wish to thank the following for permission to reproduce the material listed below in this book:

Table 2.3: Central Statistical Office (1994) *Social Trends*, **24**; © Crown Copyright, reproduced with the permission of the Controller of Her Majesty's Stationery Office.

Tables 5.1 and 5.2: D. J. Hand *et al.* (eds) (1994) *A Handbook of Small Data Sets*, Chapman & Hall.

Figure 6.1: © Crown Copyright, reproduced from the 1995 Ordnance Survey 1:25000 Outdoor Leisure Map with the permission of the Controller of Her Majesty's Stationery Office.

Exercises 13.3 and 13.4: data from *The Highway Code* (1995); © Crown Copyright, reproduced with the permission of the Controller of Her Majesty's Stationery Office.

Contents

Introduction

There are two aims of this book. One is to teach you to use a graphics calculator – the Texas Instruments TI-83 – and you will need to obtain this machine if the book is to be of any use to you. By the time you get to the end of the book you will know how to use most of the facilities of this powerful calculator.

The other aim of the book is to teach you some mathematics. Some of this mathematics you will have met before, and some will almost certainly be new to you. If your previous experience of mathematics has mainly been based on pen and paper, you will find that having access to a graphics calculator opens up fresh and exciting ways of looking at familiar topics.

A tool for mathematics

The graphics calculator is one of a long line of calculating devices which have provided ever more powerful tools for doing mathematics. People have used piles of stones, the abacus, slide rules, logarithm tables and mechanical calculators which were worked by turning a handle. In recent years, simple electronic calculators appeared, followed quickly by more advanced 'scientific' calculators. The TI-83, like other graphics calculators, is able not only to carry out calculations of various sorts, but also to draw graphs and other diagrams, to process large amounts of statistical data, and to carry out pre-programmed sequences of instructions. It is certainly more powerful than the calculating aids that preceded it, but like them it is no more than a tool which, in the hands of a skilled operator, can assist in doing mathematics.

This book is designed to help you to acquire skill at exploiting the power of this machine. As with any machine, to become a skilled user you need to know not only *how* to use it but also *when* it is likely to be useful. Although some people use a food processor to chop up food, they are not likely to use it if they are making a single tomato sandwich. In the same way, just because the TI-83 will carry out calculations, it does not mean that you will always need or want to use it, particularly if you are faced with a calculation that you can do in your head or more quickly on paper. However, the more you find out about the various advanced processes that the calculator can handle, the more you should find that mathematics itself becomes accessible to you.

For example, if you know *how* to work out what the pound in your purse might be worth in ten years' time if inflation continues at present levels, you are more likely to be able to make informed judgements when planning your future needs. In this way, the calculator is an empowering tool for carrying out mathematics in the real world.

Similarly, once you know *how* to produce sequences of numbers, you may find yourself gaining satisfaction and enjoyment from looking for patterns in those sequences. So as well as supporting the solving of practical problems, the calculator is also an empowering tool for exploring mathematics for its own sake.

The book's structure

Unless you have used a graphics calculator previously, you would be best advised to work through the chapters in the order that they appear.

Chapter 1 deals with the basic functions of the calculator and covers some basic arithmetic in everyday concepts.

Chapters 2–5 cover using your calculator to handle quantities of data: once data are entered into the calculator's memory, averages and other statistics can be calculated and the data displayed in ways which provide greater insights into what the data represent.

In Chapters 6–9 the graphical features of the calculator are introduced, set in various real-world contexts – maps, speeds and (perhaps surprisingly) music. It is in this section of the book that algebra begins to be used as a means of describing graphical forms.

Chapters 10–13 link the two previous themes of handling data and drawing graphs by considering 'mathematical modelling'. Various types of graph are studied, and you see how they can be used to analyse data collected from many types of real-world situation.

Programming the calculator plays an increasingly important part in the book, and this is particularly true in Chapters 14–16. You will see how to write short programs to (among other things) produce a perspective drawing, evaluate frequently used formulas and draw various wave-forms. The final chapter encourages you to adapt your mathematical tool for your future personal use.

Using the book

When you are working through the book you will always need to have the TI-83 calculator to hand. When you are asked to press a button and look at what appears we hope that you will do just that. Becoming skilled in using this device involves doing, not just reading about it.

We suggest that you also have pencil and paper to hand and make short notes for yourself as you work. This sort of approach will often help you to think about a task, as well as being a record of your progress. You may also want to write notes in this book or highlight particular features which seem important.

You will find a number of exercises to try out with your calculator: we suggest that you try these as you come to them. Comments and solutions to calculations are given at the back of the book, starting on p. 267, but you will find it most effective if you work through and think about each exercise before you turn to read the comments. Sometimes there are further comments in the text immediately following the exercise. The exercises are essential, so you should try them all.

You will also find some challenging puzzles and investigations: which are labelled 'Brain stretchers'. Some of these take the form of investigations designed to stimulate you to explore on your own. Some invite you to explore the calculator itself, while others invite you to explore some mathematics using the calculator as a tool. The puzzles are often deliberately worded in a fairly broad way in order to encourage you to define your own problem within the context suggested in the text. There are no answers or comments provided – perhaps you will want to write your own! We hope that you will try as many of the Brain stretchers as you have time for – although they are not essential if you run out of time.

Since this book was originally published, the TI-83 Plus calculator has become available, and some readers may be using this later model. There are a number of small differences between the two models. Where these differences affect the use of this book, additional text has been included for users of the TI-83 Plus. There are very few occasions where this has been necessary, and most occur in Chapters 1 and 16.

Some of the most obvious differences on the TI-83 Plus are on the keyboard of the calculator. Compared with the picture of the basic TI-83 on the front cover of the book, the number keys on the TI-83 Plus are very pale grey – these keys will be referred to as being 'grey' throughout this book.

In addition, the MATRX key on the basic TI-83 is replaced by a blue APPS key on the TI-83 Plus, which has MATRX above the x⁻¹ key in place of [FINANCE] on the basic TI-83. As the MATRX, APPS and [FINANCE] facilities of the TI-83 are not covered in this book, these differences won't affect your use of this book at all.

TI-83 Plus users may find that some of the page references in this book to the *TI-83 Guidebook* are not quite accurate; this particularly occurs in Chapter 16 of this book.

Chapter 1 Exploring your calculator

1.1 Setting up the TI-83

Slide off the cover of your TI-83 and have a look at the keyboard. Some of the main features are described below.

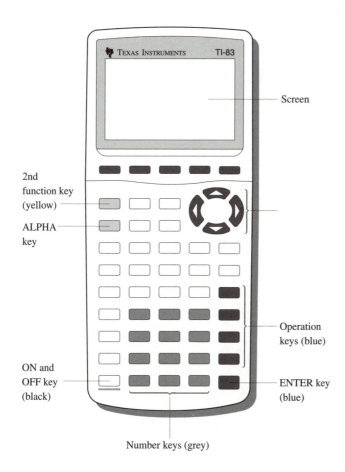

First, notice the screen (also called the **display**) at the top. This is where calculations, graphs and so on are displayed. The remainder of the calculator, where the various keys are located, is called the **keyboard**.

display

keyboard

The **number keys** are in the bottom part of the keyboard and are coloured grey. To the right of the number keys are the four **operation keys**. These are blue in colour and are marked ⊞, ⊟, ⊠ and ⊡.

number keys

operation keys

Below the operation keys, also in blue, is an important key marked ENTER which is used to complete calculations and to confirm other instructions to the calculator.

In the top row of the keyboard, coloured blue, are the keys which are used to draw graphs on your calculator.

cursor keys Near the top right-hand corner of the keyboard are the four blue **cursor keys** marked with arrow heads, as shown above. The cursor keys enable you to move around the screen of the calculator.

main function Now, notice that almost every key has more than one different purpose or function. The **main function** is written directly on the key: for example, the key in the bottom left-hand corner of the keyboard is the ON key. But notice that

second function written above this key in yellow is the word OFF. This is the **second function** for that key and is activated by first pressing and releasing the yellow second-function key [2nd] near the top left-hand corner of the keyboard (pressing the ON key then turns the calculator off).

Some keys also have third functions, written in green above them. Most of these allow you to type letters of the alphabet by first pressing the green key marked [ALPHA].

◇ To switch on the calculator, press [ON].

◇ To switch off the calculator, press [2nd], release this yellow key and then press [OFF].

Try this now.

This book uses the same notation as that used in the *TI-83 Guidebook*. The main function keys, like [ON], are written inside a box, whereas second function keys, like [OFF], are written inside square brackets. The grey number keys and alphabetic symbols are not written inside boxes but are always in bold type: for example, **8**.

Press the [ON] key once more.

You should be able to see a flashing rectangle in the top left-hand corner of the screen. If the rectangle is not there, or if it is indistinct, you may need to adjust the display contrast to make it dimmer or brighter. Press and release [2nd] and then hold down either the [▼] cursor key to make the screen lighter or [▲] to make it darker. (This is explained in Section 1-3 of the *TI-83 Guidebook*.)

To make sure that the calculator is set up correctly, you should first reset the memory by pressing [2nd] [MEM].

MEM is the second function of the blue operation key marked [+], in the bottom right-hand corner of the keyboard.

menu What is displayed on the screen is known as the MEMORY **menu**. It is so called because it offers you a number of options to choose from. This particular menu offers five options (the MEMORY menu on the TI-83 Plus offers eight options).

Press **5** to select the **Reset** option (for the TI-83 Plus press **7** to select the **Reset** option). The RESET secondary menu is then displayed. Press **2** to select the **Defaults** option.

This displays another menu, the RESET DEFAULTS menu.

Then go ahead and press **2** to select RESET.

The screen should now show the words **Defaults set**.

The TI-83 provides you with several different screens for menus, drawing graphs, writing programs and so on. The most important screen, where calculations are carried out, is called the **Home screen**. After clearing the memory, you are automatically returned to the Home screen. If you should find yourself trapped on another screen, the 'panic' buttons to return 'home' are one or other of the following:

CLEAR or [2nd] [QUIT]

Home screen

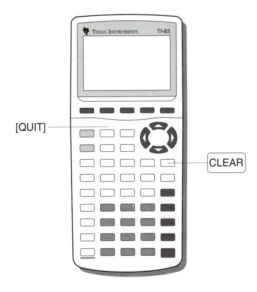

If you are already on the Home screen, CLEAR also erases entries on that screen. Press CLEAR now to erase the **Defaults set** message. Your calculator is now set up and ready for action!

1.2 Using your calculator for basic arithmetic

The four rules of arithmetic

You are now going to use the four blue operation keys on the bottom right-hand side of the keyboard:

$$\boxed{+} \quad \boxed{-} \quad \boxed{\times} \quad \boxed{\div}$$

and the blue cursor keys at the top right-hand side:

$$\boxed{\blacktriangle} \quad \boxed{\blacktriangledown} \quad \boxed{\blacktriangleleft} \quad \boxed{\blacktriangleright}$$

You will also need the grey number keys and the blue key marked $\boxed{\text{ENTER}}$, which is in the bottom right-hand corner of the keyboard.

Exercise 1.1   *Press and see the operation keys*

Press the first of the key sequences below and check that the results were what you expected. Next, look carefully at what the display shows. What is revealed about how your calculator displays information? Note down your comments.

Repeat this procedure for the other key sequences.

Press	See
(a) **5** $\boxed{+}$ **7** $\boxed{\text{ENTER}}$	5+7 12
(b) **5** $\boxed{+}$ **7** $\boxed{\blacktriangleleft}\boxed{\blacktriangleleft}\boxed{\blacktriangleleft}$ **6** $\boxed{\text{ENTER}}$	6+7 13
(c) **5** $\boxed{-}$ **7** $\boxed{\text{ENTER}}$	5-7 -2
(d) **5** $\boxed{\times}$ **7** $\boxed{\text{ENTER}}$	5*7 35
(e) **5** $\boxed{\div}$ **7** $\boxed{\text{ENTER}}$	5/7 .7142857143

(f) $\boxed{\times}$ **7** $\boxed{\text{ENTER}}$	5/7
	   .7142857143
	Ans*7
	    5

There are quite a few points to note.

◇ Notice that the entries appear on the left of the screen and the results of a calculation on the right, one line lower.

◇ Key sequence (b) shows how to edit a key sequence – if, for example, you press the wrong key at some point, you can use the cursor keys to reach the entry you want to correct and then simply re-type it.

◇ The 'minus' sign, '⁻', for the answer '⁻2', is shorter and slightly higher than the subtract sign '−' in the entry '5 − 7'. There are, in fact, two separate 'minus' keys. The one which means 'do the operation subtract' is the blue key marked [−]. The key which you must use to enter 'minus numbers' (that is, negative numbers) is the grey key on the bottom row, marked [(-)]. So, if you wish to calculate 5 × ⁻3, press **5** [×] [(-)] **3** [ENTER] to produce the result ⁻15.

◇ The division sign, which is marked [÷] on the keyboard, is displayed on the screen as **/** and the multiplication sign, marked [×], is displayed on the screen as *****.

◇ Decimal numbers less than 1 are displayed without the zero to the left of the decimal point. Note also that the 'true' decimal value for the fraction $\frac{5}{7}$ goes on for ever. (Try using pencil and paper division to divide 5 by 7 if you aren't convinced about this!) Notice, therefore, that your calculator is capable of displaying results to a maximum of 10 digits.

◇ Key sequences (e) and (f) show what happens when you complete a calculation and then continue with the answer you have just calculated. The calculator signals you have done this with the abbreviation **Ans** shown at the beginning of the next calculation.

◇ Notice also that key sequences (e) and (f) show a division by 7, followed by a multiplication by 7. This has resulted in the same answer to (f), namely the value 5, as you started with in (e). This demonstrates the mathematical relationship between the two operations of multiplication and division, namely that either one is the **inverse** of the other. In other words, what one does, the other undoes. Two other operations which are inverses of each other are addition and subtraction.

inverse

◇ Finally (and you would have to have been extremely eagle-eyed to have spotted this), your calculator will round answers where appropriate. This can be deduced from the answer to sequence (e). If you had divided 5 by 7 using pencil and paper and gone on beyond 10 digits of accuracy, you would have got an answer like this:

$$0.71428571428571\ldots$$
$$7\overline{)5.00000000000000\ldots}$$

However, because the calculator can display only the first 10 digits, it must make a sensible decision about how the final (tenth) digit, the 2, is displayed. The first 10 digits in the answer are marked in bold below.

this 2 becomes a 3...   *...because this is 5 or more*

.7142857142 8571...

5

Exercise 1.1 revealed that the 'factory setting' of your calculator is fixed to display results to an accuracy of up to 10 digits. The next subsection shows how to reset the number of decimal places to something different, depending on the sort of calculation you wish to do. For example, calculations involving money are likely to produce answers giving pounds and pence (or dollars and cents, francs and centimes, and so on). Most currencies display money to two decimal places: £3.67, $16.50, 45.52Fr and so on, so it is useful to fix the number of decimal places to two for such calculations.

Incidentally, at this point if you have not used your calculator for five minutes you will have found that it has switched itself off in order to conserve the battery. Do not panic! All you need to do is to press [ON] again and you will see the display as it was.

Setting the number of decimal places

You have already seen the MEMORY and RESET MEMORY menus. Now you will need to use another menu, by pressing the key marked [MODE], which is just to the right of the yellow [2nd] key. You will also need the four cursor keys. The [MODE] key allows you to alter some of the basic settings of the calculator, while the cursor keys enable you to move the flashing cursor around the screen.

Carry out each step in the following table.

Press	See	Explanation
[MODE]	Normal Sci Eng Float 0123456789 Radian Degree Func Par Pol Seq Connected Dot Sequential Simul Real a+bi re^θi Full Horiz G-T	Select the MODE menu. Notice that on each line there are options, one of which is highlighted to show the current settings.
[▼] [▶] [▶] [▶]	Normal Sci Eng Float 01■3456789 Radian Degree Func Par Pol Seq Connected Dot Sequential Simul Real a+bi re^θi Full Horiz G-T	Move the flashing cursor to *select* the 2 on the second row of the menu. This means you are choosing '2 decimal places'.
[ENTER]	Normal Sci Eng Float 01▨3456789 Radian Degree Func Par Pol Seq Connected Dot Sequential Simul Real a+bi re^θi Full Horiz G-T	*Confirm* the choice by pressing [ENTER].

CLEAR   This returns you to the Home
                                     screen.

5 ÷ 7 ENTER |5/7   The answer is now displayed to two
                              .71| decimal places only.

You may well need some practice at changing the number of decimal places. Try using the MODE menu to set the number of decimal places to 4 and again enter the sequence

> 5 ÷ 7 ENTER

Check that the result is .7143. Note that the final digit has been rounded up (from a 2 to a 3) because the fifth digit is 5 or more.

What answer would you expect when you press the following?

> 3 × 5 ENTER

Try it and see if you were right.

Spend a few minutes now exploring this feature of your calculator.

When you feel confident that you can fix the number of decimal places displayed by the calculator, press MODE once more and set the number of places to **Float**. This will return your calculator to its original setting, allowing it to display up to 10 digits.

You might like to make some notes at this point about how to change the number of decimal places displayed by the calculator.

Some calculator conventions

Your calculator will interpret in a particular way the order in which you press the keys. For example, if you enter the key sequence:

> 2 × 3 + 4 ENTER

the calculator will first multiply 2 by 3 and then add 4 to the result to give the answer 10. On the other hand, you might be surprised to find that if you enter:

> 2 + 3 × 4 ENTER

you will get the answer 14 because the calculator first multiplies 3 by 4 and then adds 2.

The order in which the calculator handles the calculation depends upon the operations involved. Multiplications and divisions are handled before additions and subtractions.

Suppose you enter the following, more complicated, sequence:

> 4 × 2 − 7 + 9 ÷ 3 ENTER

Since this contains multiplications as well as divisions, and additions as well as subtractions, the calculator must have a rule about what to do first. The procedure built into the calculator is first to perform the multiplications and divisions working from left to right – first multiplying 4 by 2 (to give 8) and then dividing 9 by 3 (to give 3). The calculation is set out below in a way that should show this more clearly.

$$4 \times 2 - 7 + 9 \div 3$$

that is,

$$8 \quad -7 + \quad 3$$

The calculator's next step is to perform the additions and subtractions, again working from left to right – first subtracting 7 from 8 (to give 1) and then adding 3 to give the answer 4. Try it for yourself on your calculator and confirm that you get the answer 4.

bracket keys

A way of forcing your calculator to perform a calculation in a different order is to use the **bracket keys**. For example, press the following sequence:

7 ⊞ 2 ⊠ 4 [ENTER]

This sequence produces the answer 15. The reason for getting the answer 15 is that the calculator performs the multiplication (2 × 4) before the addition (7 + 8). Now, suppose you wish to perform the addition before the multiplication. The way to override the calculator's pre-programmed choice to do multiplication before addition is to place the addition part of the sequence in brackets. You need to use the black bracket keys, which are just above the grey number keys. Press:

⊞ 7 ⊞ 2 ⊟ ⊠ 4 [ENTER]

This gives the answer 36 (that is, 9 × 4).

bracket what you want the calculator to perform 1st otherwise see highlights.

Other calculator keys allow you to recall and change or 'edit' what you have entered. Suppose in tackling one of the above calculations you entered the following, by mistake:

4 ⊠ 5 ⊟ 7 ⊞ 9 ÷ 3

Pressing [ENTER] will give the answer 16, which is not what you were expecting. Then you spot the mistake, which was that 5 was entered instead of 2. To recall your entry press:

[2nd] [ENTRY]

Note that [ENTRY] is the second function of [ENTER] and notice again the notation: the main function [ENTER] is written inside a box, whereas the second-function key [ENTRY] is written inside square brackets.

The original entry appears followed by a flashing cursor. Now use the blue cursor key ◄ to move the cursor back over your entry until it lies over the 5. Press **2** to overwrite the 5. You do not have to return the cursor to the end of the line; just press [ENTER] and the calculator will show the correct answer, 4.

To get the feel of this, try the next exercise.

Exercise 1.2 *Guess 'n' press*

Look at the first key sequence in the following table. Write down in the 'Guess' column what answer you would expect it to produce on the calculator's display.

Only then press the sequence and write down under 'Press' the result you actually got. Think about the key sequence and note down any comments about how your calculator functions or about some related mathematical idea.

Clear the display and repeat for each of the key sequences in turn.

Key sequence	Guess	Press	Comment
(a) 2 + 3 ◄ 4 ENTER	6	6	✓
(b) 2 + ◄ − 3 ENTER	−1	−1	✓
(c) 2 + (-) 3 ENTER	−1	−1	✓ OK once I'd found (-) symbol
(d) 3 + 4 × 5 ENTER	23	23	because I remembered what I read.
(e) 4 + 6 ÷ 2 ENTER	7	7	✓
(f) 3 − 4 ÷ 2 + 1 × 9 ENTER	12	10	3−2+9 = 10 bad calculation in head
(g) 2nd [ENTRY] ENTER		10	? — recalls last entry (even if cleared)
(h) 2nd [ENTRY] 2nd [ENTRY] 2nd [ENTRY] ENTER		7	? — has recalled (e)
(i) × 6 ENTER		42	OK 6×7 = 42
(j) 4 ÷ 0 ENTER	0	error	? actually correct in a way.

The final key sequence is worth considering further. First, an **error message** was produced, because division by zero is not possible in mathematics. The problem now is how to respond to the error message. In fact, what you see on the screen is another menu, with two choices labelled **Quit** and **Goto**.

Selecting **Quit**, by pressing **1** or ENTER, will cause your current calculation to be abandoned, and you will be returned to a fresh line on the calculator's Home screen.

Selecting **Goto**, by pressing **2**, takes you back to the line containing the sequence which caused the error, which in this case was **4** ÷ **0**. If you wish, you can now edit or remove the error.

You may care to investigate by making some deliberate mistakes now. For example, what happens if you use the − key rather than (-) in part (c)?

error message

1.3 Some calculator puzzles

If you would like some more calculator practice, try your hand at the following puzzles. No answers are given because most of these activities have no single numerical answer. You may like to try them out with friends – or make up some of your own.

Brain stretcher   *Doing it with your eyes closed!*

Look at your calculator for about one minute. Now turn it over and see how many of the keys you can draw in their correct position.

Why are the keys laid out as they are?

Can you classify the keys into four or five useful headings?

Brain stretcher   *Is it true?*

Here are some mathematical statements for you to explore with your calculator. Are they true? If not, why not? Can you modify them so that they are true?

◇   You can't take bigger from smaller.   F

◇   Multiplying makes numbers bigger.   F

◇   The ÷ key is the 'divide into' key.   l

◇   The more digits a number has, the bigger it is.   F

◇   There are two 'minus' keys, one marked − and the other (-).   T

Brain stretcher   *Missing keys*

Can you make all the numbers from 0 to 9 using just these keys?

4   +   −   ÷   ENTER

You can use any of them more than once and you need not use them all in a given sequence.

Write down key sequences for each number, trying to use as few key presses as possible.

For example, 5 could be   4   ÷   4   +   4   ENTER .

Brain stretcher — Big sum, small sum

Use the digits 1, 2, 3, 4 and 5 just once in any order to form two numbers; for example, 123 and 54.

Which numbers have:

◇ the greatest sum?

◇ the least sum?

◇ the greatest difference?

◇ the least difference?

Brain stretcher — Big product, small product

Use the digits 1, 2, 3, 4 and 5 just once to form two numbers so that:

◇ their product is greatest

◇ their product is least (the product of two numbers is what you get when they are multiplied together)

Try extending the problem by using six digits, seven digits and so on.

Brain stretcher — 1089 and all that

Take a three-digit number, say 417.

Reverse the digits and subtract whichever number is the smaller from the bigger:

$714 - 417 = 297$

Reverse the digits of the answer and add to the previous answer:

$792 + 297 = 1089$

Try this process for other three-digit numbers. Do you always get 1089? Which numbers does it not work for?

What if you start with a four-digit or a two-digit number?

What if …?

Brain stretcher — Puzzling behaviour

Type any number in your calculator and press [ENTER].

Now press [÷] 5 [+] 2 [ENTER].

Keep on pressing [ENTER] many times.

What is going on?

Try other starting numbers.

Try changing the 5 and/or the 2.

1.4 Squares and other powers

squaring   Multiplying a number by itself is called **squaring** the number, and there is a key on the calculator that does this for you. It is a black key on the left-hand side of the keyboard and is marked x^2. Try using it for these examples now.

Press	See	Comments

3 $\boxed{x^2}$ $\boxed{\text{ENTER}}$
 	
. 1 $\boxed{x^2}$ $\boxed{\text{ENTER}}$
	3^2
	        9
	$.1^2$
	        .01
	■	

$\boxed{\text{(-)}}$ **4** $\boxed{x^2}$ $\boxed{\text{ENTER}}$	-4^2 -16 _	Did you expect this answer?
$\boxed{(}$ $\boxed{\text{(-)}}$ **4** $\boxed{)}$ $\boxed{x^2}$ $\boxed{\text{ENTER}}$	$(-4)^2$ 16	You need brackets if you wish to square a negative number.

3 $\boxed{÷}$ **2** $\boxed{x^2}$ $\boxed{\text{ENTER}}$
 	
$\boxed{(}$ **3** $\boxed{÷}$ **2** $\boxed{)}$ $\boxed{x^2}$ $\boxed{\text{ENTER}}$
	$3/2^2$
	        .75
	$(3/2)^2$
	      2.25
	■
		Fractions can be squared too, but brackets are necessary.

Another way of saying 'five squared' is 'five to the power 2'. So:

      5×5 is written as 5^2 and this is said 'five to the power 2'

It would be reasonable to extend this so that:

      $5 \times 5 \times 5$ is written as 5^3 and this is said 'five to the power 3'

      $5 \times 5 \times 5 \times 5$ is written as 5^4 and this is said 'five to the power 4'

and so on.

There is a key on the calculator which can be used to carry out such calculations involving powers. It is marked $\boxed{\wedge}$ and is on the right-hand side of the keyboard, above the blue operation keys. To work out $2 \times 2 \times 2 \times 2 \times 2$ or 2^5, for example, you need to press the sequence shown in the table below. Similarly 0.6^3 is the same as $0.6 \times 0.6 \times 0.6$. Enter the sequences on your calculator to work out the values of 2^5 and 0.6^3.

Press	See	Comment
| 2 $\boxed{\wedge}$ 5 $\boxed{\text{ENTER}}$ <br><br> . 6 $\boxed{\wedge}$ 3 $\boxed{\text{ENTER}}$ | ```
2^5
              32
.6^3
            .216
``` | *2×2×2×2×2 = 32* <br><br> It does not matter whether you enter .6 or 0.6. |

Brain stretcher   *Negative powers*

What possible meaning could there be for negative powers, such as 7^{-3}?

Try using the power key to work out the value of 2^{-1}.

Does the answer look familiar? Try 2^{-2}, 2^{-3}, 2^{-4}...

Can you predict what 10^{-1}, 10^{-2}, 10^{-3}, ... might mean? Check your prediction on the calculator.

1 ÷ 7 ÷ 7 ÷ 7

10⁻³ = 0.001
1 ÷ 10 ÷ 10 ÷ 10

Brain stretcher   *Fractional powers*

Press the following:

1 6 $\boxed{\wedge}$ $\boxed{(}$ 1 $\boxed{\div}$ 2 $\boxed{)}$ $\boxed{\text{ENTER}}$

What is going on here?

Press $\boxed{\text{2nd}}$ $\boxed{\text{ENTRY}}$ and change the 16 to other numbers such as 20, 25, ...

Once you know the effect of raising to the power $\frac{1}{2}$, try other fractions such as $\frac{1}{3}$ and $\frac{2}{3}$.

$16^{1/2} = 4$
$25^{1/2} = 5$
```

1.5   Everyday calculations

This section looks at some everyday situations which invite calculation, starting with a familiar item – a till receipt from a shop.

Checking the receipt

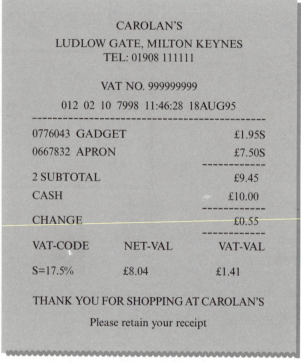

```
                    CAROLAN'S

            LUDLOW GATE, MILTON KEYNES
                 TEL: 01908 111111

              VAT NO. 999999999

        012 02 10 7998  11:46:28  18AUG95
-------------------------------------------------
0776043  GADGET                      £1.95S
0667832  APRON                       £7.50S
                                  ------------
2 SUBTOTAL                            £9.45
CASH                                £10.00
                                  ------------
CHANGE                               £0.55
                                  ------------

VAT-CODE          NET-VAL          VAT-VAL

S=17.5%           £8.04            £1.41

        THANK YOU FOR SHOPPING AT CAROLAN'S

             Please retain your receipt
```

As you can see, this shop receipt contains a great deal of information, and tells its own story about the transaction that took place. Imagine that you are asked to play detective and that your suspect was found in possession of the receipt.

Study the receipt carefully and sort out in your mind the 'where', 'when' and 'what' of the transaction. Then complete the file below.

Initial Crime Report

M   01234567

ANY TOWN POLICE

Classification of offence

We have reason to believe that the suspect entered the premises of ___CAROLAN'S___ (shop) at ___LUDLOW GATE___ ~~X~~ _____ (address) in the town of ___MILTON KEYNES___ on the morning of ___18 AUG___ in the year ___'95___. At precisely ___11:46:28___ am, ___2___ items were purchased, namely a ___GADGET___ and an ___APRON___ costing £ ___1.95___ and £ ___7.50___ respectively. An amount of £ ___10.00___ was submitted to the cashier and £ ___0.55___ in change was received.

Reported by: _____ of _____

There are other gems of information contained in this receipt. Let us now look at some of the more mathematical ones. First, we are in a position to check that the basic arithmetic is correct.

Use your calculator to check the two calculations performed by the shop till and recorded on the receipt. (You may want to use the MODE menu to set the calculator to display two decimal places as explained in Section 1.2.) Specifically:

◇   Is the subtotal correct?

◇   Is the change correct?

Value added tax (VAT) is charged on many of the goods bought in the UK. As can be seen from the receipt, at the time that these purchases were made, the rate of tax was 17.5%. This means that on every £100 net cost, the VAT charge is £17.50, bringing the total to £117.50. In other words:

$$\text{Net cost} + \text{VAT} = \text{Gross charge}$$

$$£100.00 + £17.50 = £117.50$$

This is what the customer pays.

Because you may wish to use the VAT rate frequently, it may be convenient to store it in one of the calculator's memories. All the green single alphabetic characters can be used to store numerical values. For example, you could decide to store the VAT rate in the memory labelled V.

In the figure below, notice the V above the grey **6** key; this indicates that V is the **third function** of this key. To access it you will need to press and release [ALPHA] **third function** followed by the grey **6** key. Do not do this yet.

The other key you will need is [STO▸] which is just above the [ON] key.

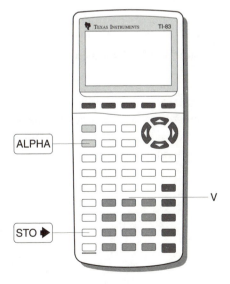

Remember that a given percentage is simply a fraction made up of that number divided by 100. To store 17.5% (or $\frac{17.5}{100}$) in V, press the following keys:

1 7 . 5 $\boxed{\div}$ **1 0 0** $\boxed{\text{STO}\blacktriangleright}$ $\boxed{\text{ALPHA}}$ **V** $\boxed{\text{ENTER}}$

When you press $\boxed{\text{ENTER}}$ you will see .18 appear on the screen. This is because you have set the calculator to display two decimal places. However, .175 has been stored in the memory.

Now you may do VAT calculations using the memory. For example, to calculate the VAT on a payment of £72, press

7 2 $\boxed{\times}$ $\boxed{\text{ALPHA}}$ **V** $\boxed{\text{ENTER}}$

If your calculator is set to two decimal places, you will see that the amount of VAT is £12.60.

The number you have stored in V will remain there ready for use, even after the calculator has been switched off.

Now have another look at the receipt, in particular the section which deals with VAT.

VAT-CODE	NET-VAL	VAT-VAL
S = 17.5%	£8.04	£1.41

These three pieces of information might be read as follows:

◇   the current VAT rate for these items is 17.5%

◇   the net value of the goods comes to £8.04

◇   based on a VAT rate of 17.5%, the VAT paid on the goods is £1.41

Use the calculator to check whether:

◇   the VAT value of the goods, based on a rate of 17.5%, really is £1.41

◇   the sum of the net value and the VAT paid equals the gross value on the receipt

Working out VAT on the calculator means working with percentages. If you are unsure about working out percentage increases or decreases, then read on and try the examples. However, if you are confident about your skills with percentages you could skip the next subsection.

Percentage increases and decreases

There is no single right way of calculating percentage increases and decreases. The next two examples show different approaches.

Example 1

A railway season ticket from my local station to London costs (at current prices) £825. Calculate the new cost if ticket prices rise by 6%.

Method 1

To find the new cost of a ticket we can find 6% of £825 and then add this amount to the original cost. Remember that a given percentage is simply a fraction made up of that number divided by 100.

So a 6% rise means a fare increase of:

$$\frac{6}{100} \times £825 = 0.06 \times £825$$
$$= £49.50$$

The new cost of the season ticket is

$$£825 + £49.50 = £874.50$$

One way of tackling this on the calculator is summarized in the following table.

Press	See	Comments
MODE ▼ ▶ ▶ ▶ ENTER	Normal **Sci** Eng Float 01**2**3456789 **Radian** Degree **Func** Par Pol Seq **Connected** Dot **Sequential** Simul **Real** a+bi re^θi **Full** Horiz G-T	This sets the calculator to two decimal places.
CLEAR		Return to the Home screen.

0 . 0 6 × 8 2 5 ENTER
 + 8 2 5 ENTER
	0.06*825
	           49.50
	 Ans+825
	        874.50
	 ■
		Calculate the price increase.
		
		 Add the increase to the original price.

Method 2

Method 1 was rather clumsy. A more elegant method works like this: think of the original cost of £825 as 100%, so increasing it by 6% is the same as working out 106% of £825. Now:

$$\frac{106}{100} = 1.06$$

Therefore, an easy way of increasing the original fare by 6% is to multiply it by 1.06. This gives:

$$1.06 \times £825 = £874.50$$

Now use the calculator (the MODE should still be set to two decimal places).

Press	See	Comments
1 . 0 6 ⊠ 8 2 5 ENTER	0.06*825 49.50 Ans+825 874.50 1.06*825 874.50	Calculates the new price directly, unlike the previous method.

Example 2

When I went into the local branch of a department store, I was offered 15% off the price of what I bought if I signed up for the company's credit card. My purchases came to £74.64; what would be the price if I took up the company's offer?

Method 1

The price reduction is 15% of £74.64, or

$$\frac{15}{100} \times £74.64 = 0.15 \times £74.64$$
$$= £11.20$$

so the new price is

$$£74.64 - £11.20 = £63.44$$

Method 2

If you think of £74.64 as 100%, then reducing the price by 15% is the same as finding $100\% - 15\% = 85\%$ of the original price. Now:

$$\frac{85}{100} = 0.85,$$

so multiplying the original price by 0.85 is the same as reducing the price by 15%. The new price is:

$$0.85 \times £74.64 = £63.44$$

Try these on your calculator.

The next exercise will give you some more practice at calculating percentage increases and decreases.

Exercise 1.3   Ups and downs

Practise calculating percentage changes by completing the table below.

Original price	Percentage change	Final price
£100	77% increase	£177.00
£2750	11% decrease	£2447.50
£100	18% decrease	£82·00
£1080	35% increase	£1458.00
£51	100% increase	£102
£2	250% increase	£7
£3	$33\frac{1}{3}$% decrease	£2

Handwritten working:
100 × 1·77
2750 × 0.11 = 302.50
2750 − 302.50
100 × 0.18 = 18·00
100 − 18·00 = (82·00)
1080 × 1·35
51 × 2 !!
2 × 3.5 !!
3 × 0.333 = 1
3 − 1 = (2)

Comparing price rises

While reading a newspaper article, I noticed some examples of how prices changed in the 10 years from 1984 to 1994. The table below shows the typical prices that you would have expected to pay in 1984 and in 1994 for a pint of milk and a Ford Fiesta motor car.

	Price in 1984	Price in 1994
Pint of milk	21 pence	36 pence
New Ford Fiesta	£4704	£7990

I was interested to see whether the price of milk had increased more than the price of Ford Fiestas. One approach might be to subtract the 1984 price from the 1994 price to give the price increase. This reveals that milk rose in price by 15 pence (36 pence − 21 pence) while Ford Fiestas rose in price by £3286 (£7990 − £4704). However, this is not a very helpful result, as I am not comparing like with like. A more useful approach is to calculate the percentage price increases of each item over the ten-year period. Here are two possible ways of calculating the percentage price increase of a pint of milk.

Method 1

The increase in price of a pint of milk was 36p − 21p = 15p. Now this increase can be expressed as a percentage by writing it as a fraction of the original price and multiplying by 100:

$$\frac{\text{increase in price}}{\text{original price}} \times 100 = \frac{15}{21} \times 100 = 71$$

Method 2

You can work out the new price as a percentage of the original price by expressing the new price as a fraction of the old price and multiplying by 100:

$$\frac{\text{new price}}{\text{original price}} \times 100 = \frac{36}{21} \times 100 = 171\%$$

Since the original price is 100%, the percentage price increase is

$$171\% - 100\% = 71\%.$$

So whichever way you calculate it, milk prices went up by 71% over the ten-year period.

Exercise 1.4   Pinta or Fiesta?

Make sure that you understand how the above calculations were done.

(a) Use your calculator to work out the percentage price increase of a Ford Fiesta.

(b) Which of the two items, milk or a Ford Fiesta, has shown the greater percentage price rise?

An investigation

In the introduction to this book, a distinction was drawn between the exercises on the one hand and brain stretchers on the other. Most of the exercises are designed to help you practise your calculator skills. The puzzles and investigations invite you to use the mathematics you have been learning to find out more about a particular situation.

Investigations are usually much more open-ended than exercises. With an investigation you often need to stop and think about what information you will need to tackle the task, and how you should interpret the results of your calculations.

This section contains an account of a short investigation on the theme of saving public money. It is included here as an example of how an investigation might be tackled, with the calculator being used simply as a mathematical tool. In the account of the investigation there are two exercises for you to carry out – please do not give in to the temptation to miss these out.

The investigation arose as a result of a comment made by a politician in a radio interview. He claimed: 'A hospital could save more money in one week by fixing a dripping tap than it spends in a week on a nurse's wages'.

Handwritten annotations:

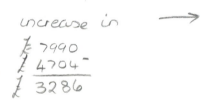

% price increase of a pint of milk.

increase in →

£ 7990
£ 4704 −
£ 3286

① $\frac{3286}{4704} \times 100$

= 69.86%

② $\frac{7990}{4704} \times 100$

= 169.86%

169.86% − 100%

= 69.86%

rounded up − 70%

Spend a few minutes thinking about the politician's statement. It is a serious claim and implies that significant sums of public money are wasted by ignoring apparently trivial items such as dripping taps. There is also, perhaps, a hint that if hospitals were more efficient about tackling problems like this they would have more money to spend on nurses' salaries.

Why do you think the statement might have been made? Do you think it is likely to be true? Do you think the politician made a calculation to come up with this comparison? Most people actually take such remarks at face value without questioning or challenging them. How could *you* check it out now?

There are two main aspects to think about.

◇ How much water would be lost in one week? What would this mean in everyday terms?

◇ Could you confirm or deny the politician's claim that a dripping tap costs a hospital more in a week than one nurse's wages?

Exercise 1.5   *Water, water everywhere*

Before reading on, spend a few minutes making some notes about what information you would need to check the claim and how you would go about getting the information.

Write down what needs to be calculated, and how you would do the calculations.

Also, try to get a feel for the quantities involved. Start by asking yourself questions such as just how much water is likely to be lost if a tap drips for a week – would it be enough to fill a jug, a bucket, a bath or a swimming pool? How much does water cost, approximately? How much do nurses cost? How could you find out?

There is no single right way of tackling this investigation, but here is the approach of some of the authors.

Before tackling this question, it is a good idea to know roughly what quantities are being dealt with. We found that water is charged to hospitals in units of cubic metres (written as m³). That is quite a lot of water – 1 m³ of water is equivalent to 1000 litres. For comparison, a lavatory flush uses about 9 litres of water and an average bath uses roughly 90 litres. If you are more used to thinking in gallons, then one cubic metre of water is equivalent to about 220 imperial gallons, or about 90 household buckets.

Here are some other basic facts we decided we needed.

◇ What is a typical annual salary for a nurse? At the time of writing this is about £12 000. The annual cost (including pension costs and National Insurance) to a hospital of employing a nurse would be around £15 000.

◇ How fast does a tap drip? We started by assuming that the tap drips roughly once per second.

water drips at a
rate of 1 drip/second
∴ 1 minute - 60 drips
1 hour - 60 × 60 = 360 d
1 day - 60 × 60 × 24
= 86,400 drips
1 wk = " × 7
= 604,800 drips.
360 drips = 1 mug?
∴ 360 √604,800
= 1680 mugs?
= 1 bath full?
or 840 litres?
cost of water
1p / litre
∴ 840 pennies
or 8.40 in one wk.

Handwritten notes (left margin):

- 1 drop / second.
- 12 drops = 5ml.
∴ 12s = 5ml.
60s in 1m
how many 12s in 1 min? ⑤
∴ 5 × 5ml = 25ml in 1 min
60m in 1hr
∴ 25ml × 60m = 1500ml/hr
24hr in 1 day
∴ 24 × 1500ml = 36000ml/day
7 days 1 wk
∴ 36000ml × 7
= 252000ml in 1 wk
1000ml = 1L
∴ 252L / wk ⓐ

average bath 90L
∴ 2.80 baths
nearly 3 baths ⓑ
1000L = 1m³
∴ water lost is
0.25m³ @ a cost
of £0.91/m³
0.25m³ × £0.91 = 23p ⟶ ⓒ
water
£15000 ÷ 52 = £288.46p ⟶ ⓒ
nurse.

ⓓ unlikely

agrees with ans in back

◇ What volume of water is this? To get a measure of the volume of water going down the drain we carried out a small experiment. We set a tap dripping and found that it took about 12 drops to fill a teaspoon. According to most cookery books, a teaspoon holds about 5 millilitres of liquid.

◇ How much does water cost? This is a hard question because it depends how it is being costed and indeed on who is paying for it. One local water authority suggested that, for a typical hospital in their region, a figure of about £0.91per m^3 would be appropriate.

◇ There are 1000 millilitres in 1 litre of water and 1000 litres in 1 cubic metre of water.

Exercise 1.6   *Nor any drop to drink*

On the basis of these figures and assumptions, calculate the following, using your calculator where appropriate.

(a) How many litres of water are lost in one week?

(b) How many baths or buckets is this?

(c) Compare the costs of employing a nurse for a week with the cost of the water wasted.

(d) How likely does the politician's claim seem now?

Of course, we made some assumptions in reaching this conclusion. First, we assumed a drip rate of one per second. Let us be daring now and make the assumption that the tap is dripping at a rate of 10 drops per second. Using this assumption, the weekly cost of water you have just calculated should be multiplied by 10.

Also, our method of measurement was, at best, rather rough and ready. However, if we had decided that it took only, say, six drops rather than 12 to fill a teaspoon, the cost of the water would still only be doubled.

We also assumed that the water wasted was cold. But even if the hospital had been losing water which it had paid to heat, it is still unlikely that one bath (or even 10 baths or 20 baths) full of hot water would cost anything like the cost of employing a nurse.

The point of the calculation was not to produce an exact answer – the accuracy of the input data we used would not warrant that – but rather to check whether the order of magnitude of the politician's claim was reasonable. The results suggest that the claim does not stand up to investigation. Our check did not require much in the way of complicated mathematics, just a few facts and figures and one or two fairly straightforward calculations.

Next time you come across similar claims don't automatically assume that they are true. Do your own short investigation and check them out for yourself, with your mathematical tool (the calculator) ready at hand.

1.6 Large and small numbers

Understanding how the calculator displays and handles very large and very small numbers is important if you are to interpret the results of calculations correctly. This section focuses on a way of representing numbers known as **scientific notation**.

scientific notation

Before you start, make sure you return your calculator to its 'factory setting' so that it can display up to 10 figures. The procedure is as follows:

◇ Press MODE.

◇ Move the cursor to the second line of the MODE menu and select **Float**.

◇ Press ENTER to confirm your selection.

◇ Finally, press CLEAR to return to the Home screen.

Scientific notation

What answer would you expect if you multiplied 20 million by itself; that is, 20 000 000 squared? How many zeros should the answer have? If you used pencil and paper to do this (and kept track of all the zeros) you would probably end up with the answer 400 000 000 000 000; in other words, 4 followed by 14 zeros. Let us see now how your calculator copes with this calculation.

Press	See	Explanation
2 0 0 0 0 0 0 0 $\boxed{x^2}$	20000000²	2 followed by seven zeros. The calculator is ready to perform the multiplication 20 000 000 × 20 000 000.
ENTER	20000000² 4E14	The calculator is restricted to displaying a maximum of 10 digits. It has therefore switched to scientific notation.

The notation E14 should be read as '10 to the power 14' (mathematicians usually just say '10 to the 14') which means fourteen 10s multiplied together.

So the calculator display 4E14 means 4 times 10 to the power 14.

It is written 4×10^{14} and is short for 400 000 000 000 000.

The number 14 (the power of 10) is also called the **exponent** and means the number of 10s, in this case, that are multiplied together. This explains why the letter E is used in the calculator display: E is for 'exponent.'

exponent

Now, instead of 20 million squared, what would 90 million squared be? What answer would you expect?

Since 20 million squared $= 4 \times 10^{14}$, you might expect that 90 million squared $= 81 \times 10^{14}$.

However, the calculator shows a different answer. Try it and see.

The calculator's answer of 8.1E15 or 8.1×10^{15} is in fact the same number as 81×10^{14}, and both are short for 8 100 000 000 000 000.

However, when a number is written using scientific notation the convention is to use a number between 1 and 10 before the exponent. So here, instead of 81×10^{14}, the number 8.1 is used with an extra power of 10.

Another way of interpreting 8.1×10^{15} is to imagine that the decimal point in the number 8.1 should be moved 15 places to the right, filling in as many zeros as necessary.

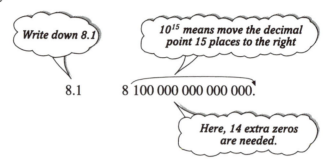

Exercise 1.7   *The sky's the limit*

(a) The speed of light, measured in metres per second, is about 300 million (300 000 000) metres per second. What is this number in scientific notation?

(b) Einstein's famous equation says that $E = mc^2$, the energy E (in joules) associated with a mass of m kilograms is equal to m multiplied by c squared, where c is the speed of light (in metres per second). Using the value of c given in your answer to part (a), work out the value of E in scientific notation for a mass of 1 kilogram.

(c) The distance from the Earth to the Sun is about 149 million kilometres. What is this number in scientific notation?

(d) What is the largest number your calculator can handle? For example, enter any number and keep squaring. How far can you go before the calculator displays an error message?

Small numbers very close to zero can also be expressed in scientific notation. For example, enter a simple starting value such as 4.3 and then repeatedly divide by 10. This can be done by pressing

   4 . 3 [ENTER]

   [÷] **1 0** [ENTER] [ENTER] [ENTER] [ENTER]

and so on.

Watch carefully how the answers go: 4.3,   .43, .043,   .0043. After the next division by 10, the display suddenly jumps into scientific notation and you see 4.3 E^-4, as shown on the right.

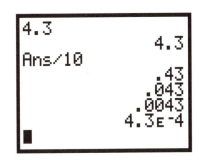

The E^-4 part means that the decimal point in the number 4.3 should be moved four places to the left. which requires the insertion of some additional zeros.

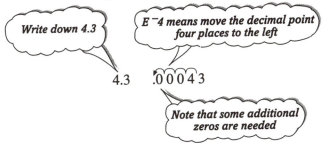

What happens to the result if you keep dividing by 10? You should see the exponent change from $^-4$ to $^-5$ to $^-6$, and so on. As the negative exponent gets larger, the corresponding decimal number gets smaller.

As with large numbers, the notation E^-4 should be read as '10 to the power $^-4$' (or simply '10 to the minus 4').

Do not worry about negative powers of 10 for the moment. Just think of the notation as a way of writing down small numbers where the negative sign reminds you that the decimal point must be moved to the left. Here is another example.

The calculator display 3.75 E^-6 means the same as 3.75×10^{-6}.

So the procedure is as follows.

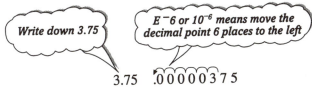

The smallest number above zero that the calculator can handle is 1.0 E^-99. Any smaller numbers are simply recorded as zero on your calculator. However, even though your calculator cannot handle numbers smaller than 1.0 E^-99 (that is, 10^{-99}), you can imagine numbers as small as you like.

Exercise 1.8   *Small is...?*

(a) What are the following numbers in scientific notation?
0.1   0.0045   0.0000006 1.0×10^{-1} 4.5×10^{-3} 6.0×10^{-7}

(b) Convert these numbers back to conventional decimal form.
3.78×10^{-4} 8.91E$^-7$ 0.7×10^{-3} 0.000378   0.00000089l   0.0007

> ### Brain stretcher $\quad\quad\quad\quad\quad\quad\quad\quad 1+1 = 2\,E\,0$
>
> Using the MODE menu, change the setting in the top line from **Normal** to **Sci**.
>
> Carry out a range of different calculations.
>
> When would this calculator setting be helpful for you?
>
> (Do not forget to return to the **Normal** setting when you have finished exploring this question.)

when using large nos & small nos (sci. not. is already done)

Now imagine that all the numbers which your calculator is capable of displaying are set out in order in a line. A version of what the calculator number line might look like is shown in Figure 1.1, but note that it is not drawn to scale.

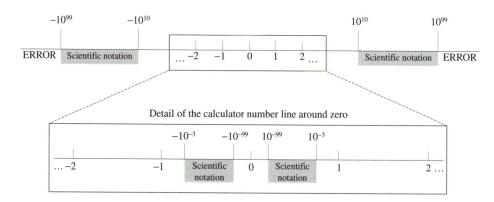

Figure 1.1 *The calculator number line.*

Zero is at the centre of the line. To the right of zero lie all the positive numbers up to 10^{99}. To the left of zero lie all the negative numbers up to $^{-}10^{99}$. Around zero are all the numbers between $^{-}10^{-99}$ and 10^{-99}, which the calculator treats as zero. It is worthwhile spending some time studying Figure 1.1 and being clear about what it means.

Consider the following questions and try to answer them for yourself before reading the comment.

◇ What is the distinction between the numbers $^{-}10^{99}$ and 10^{-99}?

◇ This number line has not been drawn anything like to scale. What might it look like if it were? If the interval on the number line between 0 and 1 000 000 000 occupied, say, 3 cm on the page, how far away would you have to place the value 10^{99} using the same scale? Would you expect an answer in metres, kilometres or in astronomical numbers such as the distance from the Earth to the Sun?

It is important to recognize the difference between negative numbers and numbers with negative powers. For example, $^{-}10^{99}$ is a very large negative number (written out fully it would be $^{-}1$ followed by 99 zeros) which lies a long way to the left of zero on the number line. In contrast 10^{-99} is a very small positive number which is very close to zero (this time the full version would look like 0.000000...00001, with 98 zeros between the decimal point and the 1). This tiny number would lie just to the right of zero on the number line.

Very small and very large numbers can be difficult to comprehend. Nothing in our everyday experience helps us to get a good feel for them. For example, numbers such as 10^{99} are so big that if Figure 1.1 were drawn to scale you would be dealing in enormous distances. But how big is big?

First, express $1\,000\,000\,000$ in scientific notation as 10^9. Next, to find out how many times bigger 10^{99} is, the calculator can be used to divide 10^{99} by 10^9. This involves entering the calculation $10^{99} \div 10^9$, as follows.

The numbers can be entered directly in scientific notation using the [2nd] [EE] key sequence. The [EE] key is the second function of the black [,] key, shown below.

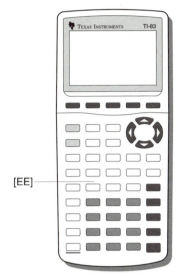

[EE]

The procedure is as follows.

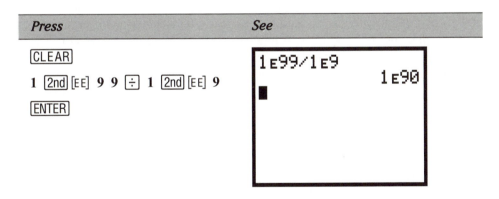

Press	See
[CLEAR]	`1E99/1E9`
1 [2nd] [EE] 9 9 [÷] 1 [2nd] [EE] 9	`1E90`
[ENTER]	

The result of the division is 1E90 or 10^{90}. In other words 10^{99} is 10^{90} times bigger than 10^9. So if 10^9 is represented by a distance of 3 cm on the diagram then, to the same scale, 10^{99} should be represented by a distance of 3×10^{90} cm. How far is that?

There are 100 centimetres in a metre and 1000 metres in a kilometre. So there are

$$1000 \times 100 = 100\,000 \text{ cm}$$
$$= 10^5 \text{ cm in a kilometre}$$

To convert the distance from centimetres to kilometres, divide 3×10^{90} by 10^5 using the same procedure as before. Try it; you should find it gives an answer of 3×10^{85} km. So how far is that? It turns out that it is unimaginably further than the most distant galaxy in the universe. These are truly **BIG** numbers!

The next exercise gives you some calculator practice with big numbers.

Exercise 1.9   *Pieces of gold*

Imagine that in exchange for this magic calculating device that you are holding in your hand, Queen Calcula of Sumwhere offers you either:

23652000 →

(a) as many gold pieces as the number of minutes you have been alive;

or

98010 →

(b) as many gold pieces as the largest number you can get on your calculator using just five key presses; 2nd EE 99 Enter

→ 1.00E99 ?? Ans say 10E99!

or

465. ✗ →

(c) one gold piece on the first day of this month, two on the second, four on the third, eight on the fourth, and so on, ending on the last day of the month.

Which should you accept and why?   Ans says Enter 2³¹ - 1

gives 2147 483 647

or 2.147483647 ×10⁹.

don't get this !!!

More short investigations

Here are two short investigations involving large numbers for you to try. Please do not turn to the comments on these exercises until you have made some notes and had a go yourself.

Exercise 1.10   *Where did I come from?*

Family trees can be fascinating things. On the principle that everyone has biological parents, extending a family tree back in time shows that everyone has an increasing number of ancestors the further back you go. So it seems that every generation of your direct ancestors must have contained twice the number of people as the generation which followed it: you have two parents, four grandparents, eight great-grandparents, 16 great-great-grandparents and so on.

If you went back, say, 30 generations, how many ancestors should each person have? And where did they all come from?

Exercise 1.11   *A colossal cash cache*

A newspaper report in 1994 revealed that the former Philippines ruler, Ferdinand Marcos, had stashed away around 1240 tons of gold during his 21-year dictatorship. At that time it was reputedly sitting in an airport warehouse in Switzerland. A question that may come to mind on reading the article is to see just how much 1240 tons of gold is worth: thousands of pounds, or millions, or billions? Spend a few minutes deciding what further information you would require to answer this question before reading on.

There is an issue here about where such information might come from, because not everyone has a comprehensive reference library on their doorstep. Firstly, what is the price of gold? The financial page of the same newspaper from which the article was taken stated that gold was selling at $391.25 per ounce. You will also need to know the rate of conversion between ounces and tons. A dictionary or an encyclopaedia could supply the information that there are 16 ounces in 1 pound and 2240 pounds in 1 ton.

Finally, the rate of conversion between dollars and pounds sterling (again from the financial page of the newspaper) was given as 1.497 dollars to the pound sterling.

Use the information provided above to make an estimate of Ferdinand Marcos' purported fortune in 1994.

Handwritten notes:

$1240 T \times 2240$
$= 2777600$ pounds
$\times 16$
$= 44441600$ ounces.
$\$/oz = \$391.25$
44441600×391.25
$= \$1.74 \times 10^{10}$
$\$1.74 \times 10^{10}$
convert to £
£1 - \$1.497
$\$1.74 \times 10^{10}$
$= £1.16 \times 10^{10}$

1.7 Mathematical functions

As you have probably already observed, there are very many mathematical functions on your calculator, and most people will need to use only a few of them regularly. However, here is an opportunity for you to be introduced informally to some more of the useful ones. The most commonly used functions are visible directly on the keyboard, but there are others contained within the MATH menu.

This section is designed to take you on a whistle-stop tour of some of the special features of your calculator. It is important to note that you are not expected to have an understanding of all the mathematical features that your calculator provides after working through this section. Rather, the aim is to give you an idea of what some of the keys on the calculator do. In later chapters, most of these features will be explained more fully and you will be able to build on what has been introduced here.

The best way to explore a new calculator button is to try it out using very simple numbers. Some examples are included to get you started. Note down any insights you uncover about what these keys do. Also, do not forget to practise saying the names of the functions – it is important to be able to talk mathematics as well as write it.

You may have noticed some mathematical jargon in the preceding pages; terms like the 'square' of a number and an 'exponent'. Learning mathematical language is an important part of learning mathematics. The word 'function', in particular, is a much-used word in mathematics and it is worth thinking about for a few moments before moving on.

One way of thinking about a mathematical function is to imagine a processor with an input and an output, perhaps rather like the one shown in Figure 1.2.

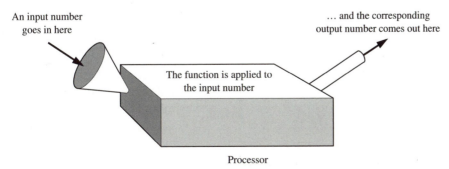

Figure 1.2 A function represented as an input–output machine.

A number is supplied to the input of the processor. Inside the processor it is converted to another number (do not worry for the moment about how this is done), and this new number is then delivered to the output. The function itself is the relationship between the input number and the output number.

In a sense, this is how the calculator operates. When a number is entered, it is displayed on the calculator's screen and treated as an input. You then select the particular processor you want by pressing the appropriate keys.

Pressing, say, **7** $\boxed{x^2}$ $\boxed{\text{ENTER}}$ instructs the calculator to work out the square of the input, 7, and to display the result, 49, the output, on the screen.

Square roots

You met the 'square' function in Section 1.4 and you will know that it is necessary to press the $\boxed{x^2}$ key after the input number. For 'square roots' you need the 'second function' key located above $\boxed{x^2}$. Unlike the $\boxed{x^2}$ key, $\boxed{\text{2nd}}$ $\boxed{\sqrt{}}$ must be pressed *before* the input number, 'square root' is both written and said before the number (for example, 'the square root of 10'), whereas 'square' is written and said after the number (for example, '10 squared'). Note that when the square root key is pressed, an open bracket also appears on the screen.

Here are some examples.

Press	See
$\boxed{\text{2nd}}$ $\boxed{\sqrt{}}$ **1 0** $\boxed{)}$ $\boxed{\text{ENTER}}$	√(10) 3.16227766
$\boxed{\text{2nd}}$ $\boxed{\sqrt{}}$ **. 4 9** $\boxed{)}$ $\boxed{\text{ENTER}}$	√(.49) .7

You may have spotted that, like multiplication and division, these two keys, $\boxed{x^2}$ and $\boxed{\text{2nd}}$ $\boxed{\sqrt{}}$ are also each other's inverses. This means that if you enter a positive number, use the $\boxed{x^2}$ key to square it, and then use $\boxed{\text{2nd}}$ $\boxed{\sqrt{}}$ to find the square root of the result, you should get back to the number you started with. The table below shows a simple demonstration of this property. Enter the number 5, square it (to get 25) and then take the square root of the answer to return to the value 5.

Press	See	Explanation
5 $\boxed{x^2}$ $\boxed{\text{ENTER}}$ $\boxed{\text{2nd}}$ $\boxed{\sqrt{}}$ $\boxed{\text{2nd}}$ $\boxed{\text{ANS}}$ $\boxed{)}$ $\boxed{\text{ENTER}}$	5² 25 √(Ans) 5	[ANS] is a second-function key located at the bottom of the keyboard.

Diagrams are often useful in mathematics to illustrate relationships. Figure 1.3 shows one way of looking at the relationship between $\boxed{x^2}$ and $\boxed{\text{2nd}}$ $[\sqrt{\ }]$. Starting from a number, 5 in this case, follow the arrows via the $\boxed{x^2}$ box to the result 25. You can think of this as the 'doing' path. Now for the return journey, which can be described as the 'undoing' path. Starting from 25 you are led via its square root, $\boxed{\text{2nd}}$ $[\sqrt{\ }]$ and you return to the same starting point once more.

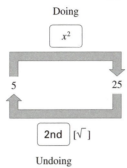

Figure 1.3   Doing and undoing.

This notion that mathematical operations often come in pairs, one doing something to a number and the other undoing it, occurs again and again in mathematics. Try to get the feel of the idea and be on the lookout for other pairs of mathematical operations that can be thought about in terms of doing and undoing. What other mathematical operations have you come across that can be described by a 'doing–undoing' diagram?

Addition and subtraction are inverses of each other, as are multiplication and division, and you may have thought of some others. Figure 1.4 shows the doing–undoing diagram for the operations of adding and subtracting 3 from a number (any number – choose one and try it). Notice that you can start the cycle at either side.

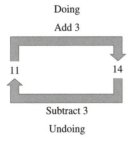

Figure 1.4   Adding and subtracting 3.

Similarly, Figure 1.5 shows the diagram for multiplying and dividing any number by 5. In each case, you can see that what one operation does, its companion inverse undoes, and again you can start with either operation.

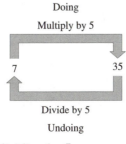

Figure 1.5   Multiplying and dividing by 5.

The earlier example of square and square root being inverses of each other seems to work either way round – if you start with a positive number, square it and then find the square root of the result, you get back to where you started, as in Figure 1.3. Similarly if you try it the other way round, as in Figure 1.6, by starting with a number, finding its square root and then squaring it you must also get back to the number you started with, surely?

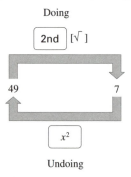

Figure 1.6   Square rooting and squaring.

Well, no, not always! It turns out that this doing–undoing cycle works only if you start with a positive number. It runs into trouble if you start with a negative number. There are two problems and which one occurs depends on which operation you try first. If you start with, say, $^-8$ and use the calculator to square it (remember that you need to use brackets here!), you get the positive number 64. Now find the square root of 64 and your calculator will display 8 rather than $^-8$, as shown in Figure 1.7.

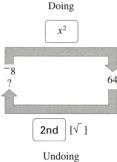

Figure 1.7   Squaring a negative number and then finding the square root.

Why is this?

Think for a moment about what happens when a positive number, say 8, is squared. Squaring 8 gives $8 \times 8 = 64$; another positive number. Finding the square root takes you back to the starting number, 8.

Now consider what happens if you start with a negative number and square it. For example, when $^-8$ is squared, the result is $^-8 \times {}^-8 = 64$. Now, when you try to return to the start by finding the square root of 64 there is no means of knowing, by looking at the 64 on its own, whether you should get back to $^-8$ or $^+8$.

When you use the calculator to find a square root of a positive number you need to be aware of this ambiguity. The calculator gives only the positive answer; *you* must decide whether it is the positive or negative value that is appropriate.

A second problem surfaces if you start with a negative number and try to find its square root. Try finding the square root of $^-4$ on your calculator by pressing [2nd] [√] [(-)] **4** [)] [ENTER].

This sequence produces an error message because no positive or negative number exists which is the square root of a negative number.

To clear the error you have a choice. Selecting **Quit** will cause your current calculation to be abandoned and you will be returned to a fresh line on the calculator's Home screen. Selecting **Goto** takes you back to the line containing $\sqrt{^-4}$ so that you can edit it to remove the error which the calculator assumes you have made.

You may be wondering why the calculator is unable to find the square root of a negative number such as $^-4$. Remember that every real number, whether positive or negative, has a positive square. Put another way, there is no positive or negative number which on squaring gives a negative answer. Therefore, as Figure 1.8 indicates, no real number exists which is the square root of a negative number.

Figure 1.8   Finding the square root of a negative number gives an error message.

So square roots must be handled with care. A central feature of doing mathematics is to be clear about when you can and when you cannot use a particular idea or procedure.

Reciprocals

The key that is used to find the reciprocal of a number is above the [x²] key on the left-hand side of the keyboard. Notice what is written on the key, [x⁻¹]; it might well be said '*x* to the power minus one', or just '*x* to the minus one'. The reciprocal of a number is the same as raising the number to the power minus one and both can be described as 'one over' the number or 1 divided by the number. For example, the reciprocal of 4 is $\frac{1}{4}$, the reciprocal of 2 is $\frac{1}{2}$, and so on. The [x⁻¹] key must be pressed *after* the input number. Here is an example.

Press	See
4 [x⁻¹] [ENTER]	
0 . 1 2 3 [x⁻¹] [ENTER]	

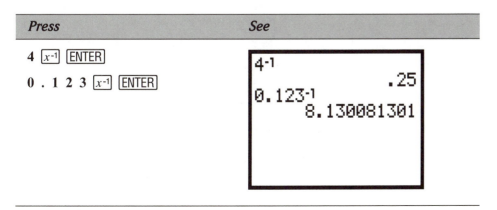

If $\boxed{x^{\text{-}1}}$ is used to find the reciprocal of a number, which key will 'undo' this operation and get back to the original number? The following two examples give a clue to this.

Press	See	Explanation
8 $\boxed{x^{\text{-}1}}$ $\boxed{\text{ENTER}}$	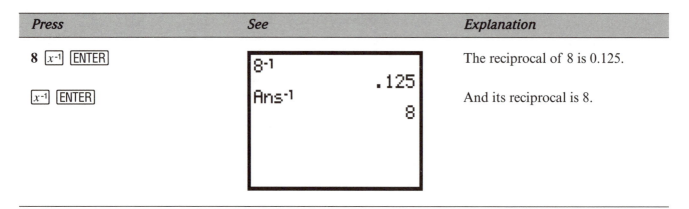	The reciprocal of 8 is 0.125.
$\boxed{x^{\text{-}1}}$ $\boxed{\text{ENTER}}$		And its reciprocal is 8.

(Screen shows:)

```
8-1
              .125
Ans-1
                 8
```

In other words, the $\boxed{x^{\text{-}1}}$ key is its own inverse – using it twice brings you back to the number you started with. Figure 1.9 shows the doing–undoing diagram for the reciprocal function.

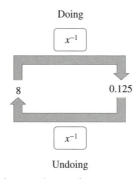

Figure 1.9   *Doing and undoing reciprocals.*

The π key

The value of the mathematical constant π, pronounced pi, is stored permanently in the calculator. The π key is the second function of the $\boxed{\wedge}$ key.

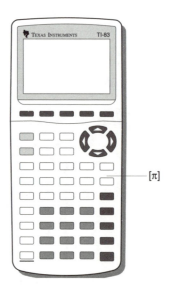

Try pressing the following key sequence now and see the value of π displayed to ten figures of accuracy.

Press	See
2nd [π] ENTER	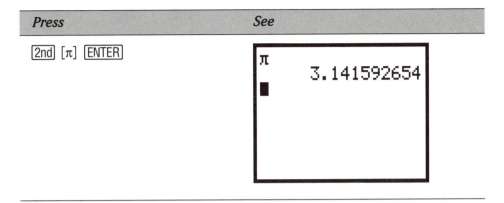

Notice the difference between this calculator key and the others described so far in this section. Whereas the square, square root and reciprocal keys are similar to input–output machines and change one number into another, π is simply a number – but a rather special one which appears in many mathematical formulas. For example, the area A of a circle of radius r is given by the formula

$$A = \pi r^2$$

So to calculate the area in square metres of a circular rose bed with radius 0.8 metres you would use the following key sequence:

2nd [π] **0 . 8** x^2 ENTER

Exercise 1.12 *Speakeasy*

This exercise is to give you practice in saying as well as doing mathematics. First, using MODE set your calculator to 4 places of decimals. Next, complete the table by noting in the second column how you would say the mathematical expressions out loud. Finally, note down their values in the third column.

Maths	Say	Value
$\sqrt{\pi}$	'the square root of pi'	1.7725
2^9		
$(2.5 \times 7.2)^{-1}$		
$\left(\dfrac{1}{\sqrt{2}}\right)^3$		
$\dfrac{^-6+\sqrt{(6^2-15)}}{2}$		

Reset your calculator mode to **Float** before continuing to the next section.

The MATH menu

We now turn to look briefly at some of the
functions stored in the MATH menu. Press
MATH and you will see that it is rather different
from the menus you have used before.

Notice that across the top of the display are the headings MATH (for
mathematical), NUM (for number), CPX (for complex) and PRB (for
probability). Each of these refers to a further submenu. Initially, the first of
these submenus, MATH is displayed. Also notice the ↓ beside the 7 at the
bottom of the screen, indicating that there are more options below, which can be
seen by scrolling downwards with the ▼ key.

Do this, and you should see the display on the
right.

Press ▼ once more and see what happens.

Now try pressing ▲.

To see the MATH NUM submenu, press the right cursor key ▶ once.

Have a look at the CPX and PRB submenus, each of which has seven
options.

To return to the MATH MATH submenu you can either press ▶ once more,
or use the left cursor key.

Most of the functions in the MATH menu will be gradually introduced as you
work through this book. You may well be able to guess the purpose of some
of them now. For example, option 3 of the MATH MATH submenu is the
cube   **cube** function. It is an alternative to using ^ 3, just as x^2 is an alternative
to ^ 2.

cube root   Option 4 is its inverse, the **cube root** function.

Check this now by following the key sequences below. You should notice that
two different methods will be used to select the functions from the menu. Before
you begin, make sure you are currently in the Home screen.

Press	See	Explanation
CLEAR		This ensures that the current line on the Home screen is cleared.
5 0 MATH 3 ENTER	50³ 125000	This is the direct way to select the third item in the menu.
MATH ▼ ▼ ▼ ENTER 2nd [ANS]) ENTER	³√(Ans) 50	An alternative (longer) way to select a menu item. The cube root of the previous answer is evaluated.

In general, then, a menu item can be selected either by pressing the number to the left of the instruction you want, or by selecting the item with the cursor using the ▼ key and then confirming it with ENTER.

Option 5 in the MATH MATH menu looks similar to the cube root function above it but the 3 has changed to x. This allows you to calculate other roots. For example, since 4 to the power 6 is 4096, it follows that the sixth root of 4096 is 4. Or, in mathematical symbols:

$$4^6 = 4096 \text{ so } \sqrt[6]{4096} = 4$$

Here are the key sequences you would need to do this using the calculator.

Press	See	Explanation
6 MATH 5	6 ˣ√■	Select the fifth item in the menu. It appears on the Home screen.
4 0 9 6 ENTER	6 ˣ√4096 4	Notice that the 'x' on the display could easily be confused with a multiplication sign.

Brain stretcher   Factorial!

Option 4 in the MATH PRB submenu is labelled with an exclamation mark.

Press 3 MATH ◄ 4 ENTER to calculate 3! (This is read as '3 factorial'.)

Try 4! and 5! and 6!, and so on.

What is going on here?

Try other numbers in front of the '!' sign.

What is the largest factorial the calculator can deal with?

Brain stretcher   *The NUM submenu*

Work out how to use the first five options in the MATH NUM submenu. For example, try entering **fPart(8/3)** or **round(π,4)**. Use the ⌑ key to enter a comma.

Try with different numbers until you feel you understand how each option works. You can check your understanding by referring to p. 2–14 of the *TI-83 Guidebook*.

Brain stretcher   *Fractional steps*

Press **0** ENTER ＋ **1** ÷ **1 2** MATH **1** ENTER ENTER ENTER . . .

What does the ▶**Frac** command do?

Can you predict each new fraction as it appears?

Try using factions other than $\frac{1}{12}$.

Try adding decimals such as 0.3.

Exercise 1.13   *Explaining to others*

Depending on your previous experience, this may have been the first time you have come across the mathematical terms 'square', 'square root', 'reciprocal' and 'power'. Do you feel you could now explain what they mean to someone else who is unfamiliar with these terms?

Using your own words, try to write a few notes on each term as if you were explaining the meanings to someone else. If you are still hazy about the meaning of the terms, then try to be clear about what it is that you do not understand.

In working through this chapter, you have started to unlock some of the power of your calculator by exploring a few of its functions. You have looked at some examples of everyday calculations, explored techniques for handling large and small numbers and started to use some mathematical ideas and language. Remember that this is only the first step, and is intended to give you an initial appreciation of the calculator as a mathematical tool.

Chapter 2 Averages

This is the first of four chapters which deal primarily with the statistical facilities of the TI-83.

In this chapter, you will learn how to enter and edit data and how to perform simple calculations on lists of numbers.

People who use calculators regularly sometimes have the experience of thinking up a clever and efficient way of carrying out some kind of calculation one day, and not being able to remember how they did it the next! If you make a practice of recording your ways for doing things well, and note warnings for yourself about making errors, you are less likely to find yourself in this predicament.

2.1 Calculating the mean and the median

In this section, you are going to enter some batches of data into the statistical registers (or lists) of your calculator and find two types of average: the mean and the median.

As you press the key sequences given, watch the display after each separate key-press and check that the information provided on the screen is what you expected.

There are three main stages involved in using the statistical keys to find the mean and the median, and you will look at them in turn. They are:

◇ checking and clearing data lists

◇ entering the data into one or more of the lists, and editing where necessary

◇ doing the calculations

These will be illustrated for the batch of data in Table 2.1.

Table 2.1 Daily temperatures at midday during June 1994, to the nearest ° Celsius

13	17	12	15	14	16	14	16	16	15	13	15	17	20	21
24	23	20	21	17	19	22	19	22	18	19	19	22	21	23

Checking and clearing data lists

Before entering new data into your calculator, it is good practice to clear away any existing data. The TI-83 provides a number of **lists** where batches of data can be entered. When you reset the calculator's memory, six list names were stored: L_1, L_2, ..., L_6 and they are called up using the second functions above the grey 1, 2, ..., 6 number keys.

lists

Some of these lists may already contain data. If so, it would be a good idea to clear them. So, begin by checking the existing data lists. This is done by means of the STAT EDIT menu. The key marked STAT, which is just to the left of the four blue cursor keys, is the route to most of the statistical functions that you need to know about.

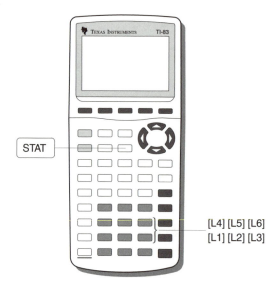

Press STAT and you will see the screen on the right.

This menu is similar to the MATH menu that you met in Chapter 1. There are three headings across the top line (EDIT, CALC and TESTS), indicating that there are three submenus. At the moment you can see the five options contained in the STAT EDIT menu. It is the first of these options, **Edit**, which enables you to examine and alter the data lists that are already stored. This option is already highlighted.

Now press **1** or ENTER to see the lists.

List screen

It is worth remembering that pressing either STAT **1** or STAT ENTER allows you to examine the data lists on what we shall call the **List screen.**

You can now see lists L_1, L_2 and L_3. In the display shown here there are some data in lists L_1 and L_2, but list L_3 is empty.

Check whether L_1, L_2 and L_3 contain any data in your calculator.

Scroll to the right using the right cursor key, ▶ and check the other three lists, L_4 to L_6.

Lists may be cleared using **ClrList**, which is option 4 in the STAT EDIT menu.

Press STAT **4**.

ClrList is pasted onto the Home screen. You must now say which list(s) you want to clear.

To clear L_1 and L_2 press 2nd [L1] , 2nd [L2].

The black . key is above the grey **7** key. Add the names of any other lists that need to be cleared, separated by commas.

Press ENTER.

Now press STAT **1** to see the List screen and check that the two lists have indeed been cleared.

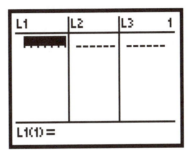

Lists can also be cleared within the List screen. This can be achieved by using the ▲ key to scroll to the top of the list required, say L_1, until the list name is highlighted at the top of the screen.

Then press CLEAR ENTER.

The cursor is in L_1, ready for you to enter data.

Notice that the bottom line of the screen reads $L1(1) =$.

The list selected is L1

The first item in the list

Entering the data

Begin to enter the data from Table 2.1 in L_1 as follows.

Press	See	Explanation
1 3 ENTER **1 7** ENTER **1 2** ENTER **1 5** ENTER **1 4** ENTER **1 6** (Do not press ENTER yet)		Enter the first five values. The last value, 16, is the sixth value in the data list (a useful check that you have entered the correct number of values).

Continue entering the data into list L_1 and check at the end that $L1(30) = 23$. For convenience, the data are repeated below.

13	17	12	15	14	16	14	16	16	15	13	15	17	20	21
24	23	20	21	17	19	22	19	22	18	19	19	22	21	23

Notice that if the completed list is now scrolled upwards using the [▲] key until L1 is highlighted, the list is displayed at the bottom of the screen in the form

$$L1 = \{13, 17, 12, 15...$$

Editing the data

If you find that you have miskeyed one or more of the data items, then it is easy to make corrections. Using the arrow keys, place the cursor on the incorrect number, type the correct number to replace it and press [ENTER] to confirm the value.

If you have left one of the data items out, use the arrow keys to place the cursor on the item following the omission. Then press [2nd] [INS] and a zero will be inserted. All the subsequent data items are moved down one place in the list. The zero can then be replaced by the missing data item.

If you have inserted an extra unwanted data item, simply place the cursor on top of it and press [DEL]. All the following items will be moved one place up in the list.

Spend a few moments now editing the data (for example, overwriting, inserting and deleting data items) to check that you can do it.

Summarizing the data

You can now find the mean and the median of the batch of data which you have entered in list L1. First, check on the List screen that what you have in list L1 corresponds to the data given above.

Once the data have been entered, the calculator is ready to provide you with various summary values. Some of these are not needed for this investigation, but they will be displayed anyway. You will need to focus on just those values that you are interested in.

You can obtain the summary values of the data by:

◇ selecting 1-Var Stats from the STAT CALC menu

◇ entering the list to which it is to be applied (in this case L1)

◇ confirming your selection

To do this follow the steps below.

Press	See	Explanation
| [STAT] [▶] | ```
EDIT CALC TESTS
1:1-Var Stats
2:2-Var Stats
3:Med-Med
4:LinReg(ax+b)
5:QuadReg
6:CubicReg
7↓QuartReg
``` | This is the STAT CALC menu. You need to select option 1: **1-Var Stats**. |
```

1

[2nd] [L1]

```
┌─────────────────────────┐
│ 1-Var Stats L1          │
│                         │
│                         │
│                         │
│                         │
│                         │
│                         │
└─────────────────────────┘
```

1-Var Stats is pasted to the Home screen.

The list to be summarized, L1, is entered.

[ENTER]

```
┌─────────────────────────┐
│ 1-Var Stats             │
│  x̄=18.1                 │
│  Σx=543                 │
│  Σx²=10161              │
│  Sx=3.387095185         │
│  σx=3.330165161         │
│ ↓n=30                   │
│ ■                       │
└─────────────────────────┘
```

The 'one-variable' summary statistics are displayed.

[▾] [▾] [▾] [▾] [▾]

```
┌─────────────────────────┐
│ 1-Var Stats             │
│ ↑n=30                   │
│  minX=12                │
│  Q₁=15                  │
│  Med=18.5               │
│  Q₃=21                  │
│  maxX=24                │
│ ■                       │
└─────────────────────────┘
```

Use the [▾] key to scroll down to see more summary statistics.

These results are explained below.

◇ $\bar{x}$ (read as 'x bar') is the **mean** of the values in the list.   **mean**

◇ Σx (read as 'sigma x') is the sum of the values. The symbol Σ is the Greek capital letter equivalent to S. It means 'the sum of'.

◇ Σx^2 is the sum of the squares of the values.

◇ Sx and σx are measures of how widely spread the data are – they will be explained in Section 4.3. σ is the lower case equivalent of Σ.

◇ n is the number of values in the list.

◇ minX and maxX are the lowest and highest values in the list.

◇ Med is the **median** – the 'middle value' when the data are sorted into   **median** ascending or descending order.

◇ Q_1 and Q_3 are known as the quartiles. They will be explained in Chapter 3.

The first figure that you need from this display is the mean value: $\bar{x} = 18.1$. There is a certain reassuring quality about observing that the other values are consistent with this information. For example, note that the mean is found by adding all the values together (in this case, $\Sigma x = 543$) and dividing this sum by the number of values (in this case, $n = 30$). You might like to check this on your calculator now by pressing **5 4 3 [÷] 3 0 [ENTER]**.

This should confirm the result that the mean is 18.1.

The median can also be read off the 1-Var Stats display; it has the value 18.5 (Med = 18.5). As you did with the mean, you can check this value from first principles, as described in the next subsection.

Checking the median from first principles

Since there is an even number of values ($n = 30$), the median is the midpoint of the two middle values when the numbers are written in ascending order. In this case, the two middle values are the fifteenth and the sixteenth values. These can be identified by using the calculator to sort the items in order of size and then simply looking at the two middle values.

To sort a data list into ascending order (that is, from smallest to largest), use the **SortA** option, which is number 2 in the STAT EDIT menu. **SortD**, which is option 3, will sort a data list into descending order (from largest to smallest).

To sort the list into ascending order, follow these steps.

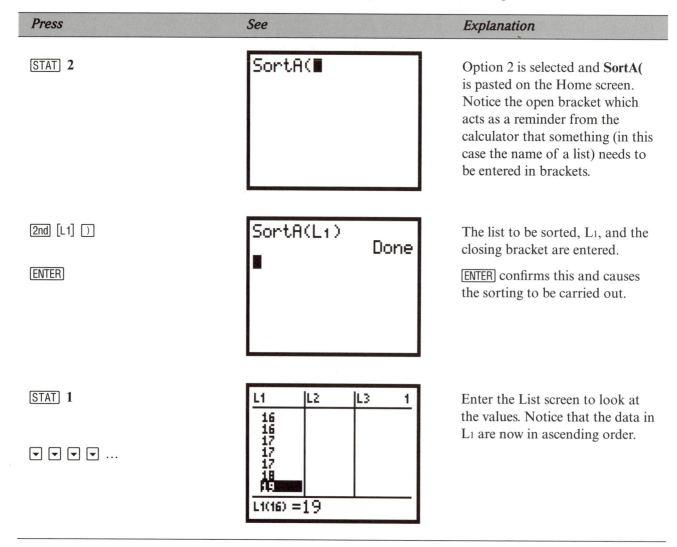

Press	See	Explanation
[STAT] 2	SortA(■	Option 2 is selected and **SortA(** is pasted on the Home screen. Notice the open bracket which acts as a reminder from the calculator that something (in this case the name of a list) needs to be entered in brackets.
[2nd] [L1] [)] [ENTER]	SortA(L1) Done ■	The list to be sorted, L1, and the closing bracket are entered. [ENTER] confirms this and causes the sorting to be carried out.
[STAT] 1 [▾] [▾] [▾] [▾] …	L1 L2 L3 1 16 16 17 17 17 18 19 L1(16) =19	Enter the List screen to look at the values. Notice that the data in L1 are now in ascending order.

Scroll through the data until you get to $L_1(16)$, the sixteenth data item. The median is the midpoint of the fifteenth and sixteenth data items. So the median is halfway between 18 and 19. That is, the median is 18.5, which confirms the value given in 1-Var Stats.

At this point you will probably need some practice at using the statistics keys to find the mean and the median. First, here is a summary of the main steps involved.

Finding the mean and the median

◇ Check the existing data lists.

◇ Clear the lists, if necessary.

◇ Enter (and, if necessary, edit) the data.

◇ From the STAT CALC menu, select **1-Var Stats**, name the list you wish to summarize, and confirm your selection; for example, press

[STAT] [▶] **1** [2nd] [L1] [ENTER]

◇ Read off the values of the mean, $\bar{x}$, and the median, **Med**.

Exercise 2.1 *Practice at finding the mean and the median*

A popular brand of calculator battery, the Duracell MN1500 Size A, is sold in packs of four. On 9 October 1993, in a particular town (Leamington Spa), a price check, made in 11 different large stores, produced the following results.

Store	Price (£)	Store	Price (£)
WH Smith	3.49	Superdrug	3.29
Woolworths	3.09	Tesco[2]	2.99
Currys	3.49	Sainsbury	3.29
Boots[1]	3.29	Great Mills	3.49
Dixons	3.39	Quick Buy	3.76
Rackhams	3.79		

[1] Additional offer – buy two, get £1 off [2] Reduced in a special offer from 3.29

Enter these 11 prices into one of the data lists of your calculator and find their mean and median.

Brain stretcher   *Below average?*

'Nine out of ten people earn below average wages', said the politician.

Can that be true? Make up 10 weekly wages and enter them as a list into your calculator. Adjust the figures until nine out of the 10 are below one of the averages.

Now, can you make up realistic figures so that nine out of 10 weekly wages are higher than average?

Brain stretcher   **What's my list?**

Make up sets of data and enter them into lists so that when 1-Var Stats are calculated the following values appear

(a) $\bar{x} = 3.25$ (b) $\bar{x} = 2$

    $n = 4$ $n = 3$

    Med = 2.5   Med = 1

2.2   Calculating the mean from frequency data

In this section, you are asked to use your calculator to find the mean from a batch of data consisting of values with associated **frequencies**.

frequencies

Here again is the batch of data, which was given in Section 2.1.

Table 2.1   Daily temperatures at midday during June 1994, to the nearest ° Celsius

13	17	12	15	14	16	14	16	16	15	13	15	17	20	21
24	23	20	21	17	19	22	19	22	18	19	19	22	21	23

In this section we shall represent these data in a slightly different way. You may have noticed that several of the data values occur more than once. In fact, there are only 13 different temperatures (12 °C to 24 °C, inclusive). Table 2.2 shows the frequencies with which each of these temperatures occurs.

Table 2.2   Frequencies of daily temperatures at midday during June 1994, to the nearest ° Celsius

Temperature (°C)	Frequency	Temperature (°C)	Frequency
12	1	19	4
13	2	20	2
14	2	21	3
15	3	22	3
16	3	23	2
17	3	24	1
18	1		

Entering frequency data into two lists

You will be asked to enter the temperature values in list L_1 and the corresponding frequencies in list L_2, so check and if necessary clear these lists, as was explained in Section 2.1.

Press STAT 1 to go to the List screen.

Press **1 2** ENTER **1 3** ENTER **1 4** ENTER and so on up to 24 to enter the various temperature values.

L1	L2	L3	1
19			
20			
21			
22			
23			
24			

L1(14) =

Press ▶ to place the cursor on L2(1), ready to enter the frequencies into L2.

L1	L2	L3	2
12		------	
13			
14			
15			
16			
17			
18			

L2(1)=

Press **1** ENTER **2** ENTER **2** ENTER… to enter the 13 frequencies into L2.

Check as you do so that the frequencies are alongside their corresponding temperatures in L1.

L1	L2	L3	2
19	4		
20	2		
21	3		
22	3		
23	2		
24	1		

L2(14) =

Finding the mean for frequency data

You now need to instruct the calculator to perform a 1-Var Stats summary of the values in L1, with corresponding frequencies in L2.

Press	See	Explanation
STAT ▶ 1 2nd [L1] , 2nd [L2]	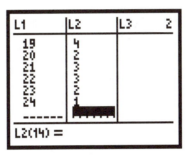 `1-Var Stats L1,L2`	Select 1-Var Stats and paste it to the Home screen. Notice the order: L1 (values) first, L2 (frequencies) second.

[ENTER]

```
1-Var Stats
 x̄=18.1
 Σx=543
 Σx²=10161
 Sx=3.387095185
 σx=3.330165161
↓n=30
```

Confirm the selection.

The summary statistics are displayed.

[▾] ...

```
1-Var Stats
↑n=30
 minX=12
 Q₁=15
 Med=18.5
 Q₃=21
 maxX=24
```

Scroll downwards to display all of the information.

Notice that this calculator display is identical to the one obtained in Section 2.1. This should not be a surprise, since the data are the same; the only difference is that instead of entering each temperature separately, the 13 different values have been entered along with their frequencies.

Here is a summary of the main steps involved in finding the mean and median for frequency data.

Finding the mean and the median for frequency data

◇ Check and, if necessary, clear the existing data lists.

◇ Enter the values into one list, say L_1, and the corresponding frequencies into another list, say L_2.

◇ From the STAT CALC menu, select **1-Var Stats**, name the two lists, separated by a comma and confirm your selection; for example, 1-Var Stats L_1, L_2.

◇ Read the values of the mean, $\bar{x}$, and the median, **Med**.

---

weighted mean

Note that calculating summaries of data with 'weights' is the same as that for data with frequencies. So, to find a **weighted mean**, enter the values in one list, enter the weights in another, and proceed as for frequency data.

The next exercise will give you practice at finding summary statistics for frequency data.

Exercise 2.2   Practice at summarizing frequency data

Table 2.3 shows the number of dwellings (thousands) by number of bedrooms built by local authorities and new towns in England and Wales in 1976 and 1992.

Table 2.3   Number of dwellings built (in thousands)

	1976	1992
1 bedroom	39.7	1.4
2 bedrooms	32.2	1.5
3 bedrooms	47.1	1.0
4 bedrooms[1]	5.0	0.0
All houses and flats	124.0	3.9

[1] This category actually includes homes with more than four bedrooms, but ignore this complication here.

Source: Social Trends 24, Table 8.5, p. 111

The most striking feature of this table is the sharp decline in local authority building that took place over the period (roughly speaking, for every thirty dwellings built in 1976, there was just one built in 1992). Another question to explore is whether local authorities were building larger or smaller homes in 1976 than in 1992. One way to check this is to calculate, and then compare, the mean number of bedrooms per dwelling built in 1976 with that for 1992.

◇   Clear lists L_1, L_2 and L_3 in your calculator.

◇   In L_1 enter the different numbers of bedrooms (the numbers 1, 2, 3 and 4).

◇   Enter into L_2 the 1976 frequencies and into L_3 the 1992 frequencies.

◇   Calculate the mean number of bedrooms per dwelling for each of the two years and compare them.

Entering sequences in lists

In Section 2.1, you learned the standard way of entering data using the List screen. Occasionally, it is easier to enter data directly from the Home screen. Suppose, for example, you wanted to enter just four numbers, 10, 20, 30 and 40, into list L_2. The list of numbers separated by commas and enclosed in curly brackets can be entered on the Home screen and then stored in a list. The curly brackets can be entered using the second function of the ordinary bracket keys, just above **8** and **9**.

To produce the list, press

[2nd] [{] 1 0 [,] 2 0 [,] 3 0 [,] 4 0 [2nd] [}]

then press [STO▸] [2nd] [L2] [ENTER] to obtain the display on the right.

```
{10,20,30,40}→L₂
       {10 20 30 40}
■
```

Pressing ⌷STAT⌷ **1** confirms that the data are stored in L2.

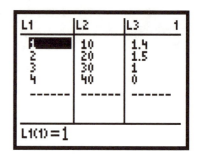

If you had wanted to enter the numbers 10, 15, 20, 25, …, 100 in steps of five, this method would certainly not be any quicker than using the List screen. However, there is a possible shortcut which uses one of the built-in features of the calculator: the **seq** or sequence function. This is the fifth option of the LIST OPS menu. Notice that ⌊LIST⌋ is the second function of the ⌷STAT⌷ key.

arguments

After **seq**, in brackets, it is necessary to enter five letters or numbers, separated by commas. These five entries are known as **arguments**. You may recall from Section 2.1 that SortA required a single argument: the name of a list.

To produce a sequence of numbers going from 10 to 100 in steps of 5, the third, fourth and fifth arguments must be 10, 100 and 5 respectively. The first two arguments have a different purpose which will become clear later: for the moment, you will need to enter **X** for both of them, using the black ⌊X,T,Θ,*n*⌋ key, which is close to the ⌷2nd⌷ key.

Return to the Home screen of the calculator, by using ⌷2nd⌷ ⌊QUIT⌋.

Press ⌷2nd⌷ ⌊LIST⌋ ⌊▶⌋ to display the LIST OPS menu.

Option 5, **seq**, is required.

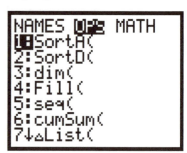

Press **5** to paste **seq(** to the Home screen.

To enter the five arguments, press

⌊X,T,Θ,*n*⌋ ⌊,⌋ ⌊X,T,Θ,*n*⌋ ⌊,⌋ **1 0** ⌊,⌋ **1 0 0** ⌊,⌋ **5** ⌊)⌋

Finally, to store the sequence in L2 press

⌊STO▶⌋ ⌷2nd⌷ ⌊L2⌋ ⌷ENTER⌷

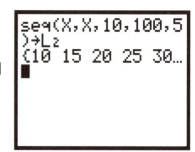

Note that the first part of the sequence has appeared on the Home screen. By holding down ⌊▶⌋ it is possible to scroll to the right, through to the end of the sequence. Alternatively, of course, you can press ⌷STAT⌷ **1** and confirm that the sequence has been stored in L2.

Very often, when entering frequency data, the values are in a regular sequence and the use of **seq** can save a lot of tedious button pressing. If you require a sequence which goes up in steps of 1, the final argument may be left out.

The TI-83 can deal with any lists containing up to 999 values.

Exercise 2.3 *Temperature sequence*

The temperatures in Table 2.2 could have been entered using **seq**. What key sequence would you need to use to enter them into list L₁?

Try this on your calculator and look on the List screen to check that the correct values have been entered.

Brain stretcher   Guess and press with *seq*

For each of the following, predict what sequence of numbers will be produced. Then enter the sequence on the calculator to see if you are right.

Remember that you do not have to enter the whole line each time. Using ⟨2nd⟩ ⟨ENTRY⟩ and then editing the previous entry will probably save you time.

◇   seq(X, X, 1, 7, 2)

◇   seq(X, X, 1, 7, 4)

◇   seq(X, X, 7, 2, ⁻1)

◇   seq(X, X, 1990, 2000)

◇   seq(X^2, X, 1, 5)

◇   seq(2X, X, 1, 5)

◇   seq(3X, X, 0, 1, 0.1)

Chapter 3 Quartiles and boxplots

As you saw in Chapter 2, various summary statistics for a batch of data are calculated and displayed using 1-Var Stats. These include the mean and the median. In fact, when 1-Var Stats is used, several other statistical values are calculated and displayed on the screen. These include the **quartiles** and the **minimum** and **maximum values**. The meaning of these values will be discussed in this chapter.

quartiles
minimum value
maximum value

You will also begin to use the graph-plotting facilities of the calculator, in particular the statistical plotting facilities, which use [STAT PLOT]. This is the second function of the Y= key in the top left-hand corner of your calculator's keyboard.

[STAT PLOT]

VARS

3.1 Quartiles

This section explains the meaning of Q_1 and Q_3, which are displayed when 1-Var Stats is used.

Table 3.1 contains data which will be used to discuss these values.

Table 3.1 The gross weekly earnings of 14 cleaners and domestics in 1993 in £

Women	137	144	226	98	172	119	183
Men	120	181	193	153	238	295	142

The main steps involved in finding the quartiles can be summarized as follows:

◇   Enter the data.

◇   Use 1-Var Stats to find summary statistics for the batch of data, including the quartiles.

Entering the data

If there are already data in the lists L1 or L2, then clear those lists first using **ClrList** from the STAT EDIT menu. This can be done by pressing

[STAT] **4** [2nd] [L1] [,] [2nd] [L2] [ENTER]

Note that, if you do not specify the list(s) to be cleared, you get an error message; in that situation, press **1** or [ENTER] to return to the Home screen, then start again.

Now enter the earnings of the female cleaners and domestics in list L1 and the earnings of the male cleaners and domestics in list L2. If you are unsure how to enter these data, look back at Section 2.1.

Finding the summary statistics

As you saw in Chapter 2, summary statistics for a batch of data can be obtained using **1-Var Stats** in the STAT CALC menu.

Press [STAT] [▶] to display the STAT CALC menu. **1-Var Stats** is Option 1 in this menu.

Press **1** to select it and then press [2nd] [L1] to select list L1.

```
1-Var Stats L1
```

Finally, press [ENTER] and scroll down to see the lower set of statistics.

The median of the women's weekly earnings, **Med**, is £144.

Also displayed on the screen are the values of Q1 and Q3.

```
1-Var Stats
↑n=7
 minX=98
 Q1=119
 Med=144
 Q3=183
 maxX=226
```

Q1 is the **lower quartile** and Q3 is the **upper quartile**.

So, for this batch of data, the lower quartile is £119 and the upper quartile is £183.

The **interquartile range** is defined as the difference between the quartiles:

$$Q_3 - Q_1$$

For the earnings of the seven female cleaners and domestics, the interquartile range is £183 − £119 = £64.

Q1, the lower quartile

Q3, the upper quartile

interquartile range

Exercise 3.1   *Practice at finding the median and quartiles*

Use your calculator to find the median and the quartiles of the earnings of the seven male cleaners and domestics in Table 3.1.

How does the TI-83 calculate quartiles?

The median and the quartiles of the earnings of the seven female and seven male cleaners and domestics are shown in Figure 3.1.

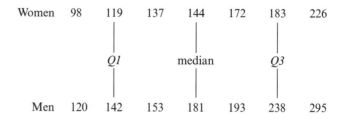

Figure 3.1 *The median and the quartiles for the cleaners' and domestics' earnings.*

Notice that the data have been written in ascending order in the figure. However, when using your calculator to find these statistics you do not need to sort the data into ascending order first. But if you are finding these statistics without the aid of a calculator, you must begin by sorting the data into ascending order. Then the median is the middle value (or the midpoint of the middle two values if there is an even number of values), and the quartiles lie *approximately* a quarter of the way into the batch from either end. The median and quartiles divide the batch into four parts, each of which contains *approximately* 25% of the values in the batch.

This description of the quartiles is rather vague; it does not say exactly how to find the quartiles. In fact, there is more than one method for selecting the quartiles of a batch of data and the different methods sometimes give slightly different answers. To find out what method the TI-83 has been programmed to use, you need to look at what the TI-83 does for batches of various sizes.

For a batch of seven values, which have been sorted into ascending order, the median is the fourth value, and the quartiles are the second and sixth values. You can see this for the cleaners' and domestics' data in Figure 3.1. In this case, the lower quartile is the middle value of the numbers below the median and the upper quartile is the middle value of the numbers above the median. The median and quartiles of a batch consisting of the values 1, 2, 3, 4, 5, 6 and 7 are shown below.

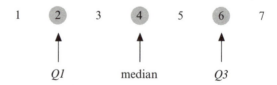

Figure 3.2 *The median and the quartiles for a batch of size seven.*

Notice that, because of the batch size, the median and quartiles are actually data values here. This will not always be the case.

What does the TI-83 do for batches of size eight or nine, or any other size? In the next exercise, you are asked to investigate the rules used by the TI-83 to find the quartiles of a batch of data. You will find it convenient to use batches of consecutive numbers: this makes it easier to see what the calculator is doing when it calculates the quartiles of a batch.

Exercise 3.2   Finding the rules for quartiles

(a) For each of the following batches of data, use your calculator to find the median and the quartiles of the batch.

   (i)   1 2 3 4 5 6 7 8

   (ii) 1 2 3 4 5 6 7 8 9

   (iii) 1 2 3 4 5 6 7 8 9 10

   For each batch, draw a diagram similar to Figure 3.2 showing the median and quartiles.

(b) What method do you think the TI-83 uses to find the quartiles? Try to explain what you think the TI-83 is doing. Write down your ideas.

(c) Using the method you described in part (b), find the quartiles of the following batch.

   1 2 3 4 5 6 7 8 9 10 11

   Now use your calculator to find the quartiles. Does it give the same answers as you got using your method? If not, then modify the method you described in part (b).

(d) Repeat part (c) for at least two more batches of data, where at least one has an even batch size and one an odd batch size. In each case, make the size of the batch different from any used so far.

3.2   Boxplots

There are three main stages involved in obtaining boxplots on your calculator:

◇   Entering the data.

◇   Setting up the plots.

◇   Displaying the plots.

You should be becoming familiar with entering and editing data by now; the process was described in detail in Section 2.1. The other two steps will be illustrated using the earnings data for 17 chefs and cooks given in Table 3.2.

Table 3.2   The gross weekly earnings including overtime for 17 chefs and cooks in 1993 in £

Women	165	210	110	235	152	128	172	136	
Men	147	275	233	188	165	330	130	200	249

Start by entering the earnings data into your calculator with the data for female chefs and cooks in L3 and for male chefs and cooks in L4.

Setting up the plots

In this subsection, you will need to use the calculator's five graphing keys, which are in the top row of the keyboard.

Setting up statistical plots is done using [STAT PLOT]. This is the second-function facility for the key marked Y= in the top left-hand corner of the keyboard.

Press 2nd [STAT PLOT] to see the STAT PLOTS menu.

You should see something similar to what is shown here: some of the details depend on what settings were used the last time a plot was done on your calculator.

There are four options shown on the screen: **Plot 1**, **Plot 2**, **Plot 3** and **PlotsOff**. There is a fifth option, **PlotsOn**, which can be seen if you use the ▼ key to scroll downwards.

The information displayed includes the current settings of plots. Up to three plots can be displayed at any one time. The details in the particular setup shown above indicate the following, and you should check them through carefully:

◇   Plot 1 is switched on and is set up to be a boxplot ( ) for the data in L1.

◇   Plot 2 and Plot 3 are switched off and are currently other types of plot: do not trouble with the details of these now – they will be explained later, when you need to use them.

You can display up to three plots at the same time. Selecting **PlotsOff** (option 4) and confirming your selection switches off all the plots; selecting **PlotsOn** (option 5) and confirming your selection switches on all the plots. Note that if you do not confirm your selection, by pressing ENTER, then your selection will not be executed.

Each time you wish to set up one or more plots, it is a good idea to begin by switching *off* all the plots; then switch *on* each plot that you wish to be displayed as you set it up.

To obtain boxplots of the earnings data in Table 3.2, two plots must be set up: Plot 1 for the women's earnings and Plot 2 for the men's earnings.

First switch off all the plots on your calculator by pressing **4** ENTER.

(Note that if you have previously produced any other graphs or drawing on the graphing screen these will also need to be removed at this stage. Ways of doing this are included in the summary in Section 5.3.)

Press 2nd [STAT PLOT] to bring the STAT PLOTS menu back on to the screen, and select option 1 by pressing either **1** or ENTER.

The screen should now look something like the one on the right.

Notice that **Plot 1** is highlighted along the top of the screen. Below this there are various rows, each of which presents different options:

◇ Using the cursor keys, you can move the flashing cursor around the screen. Move the cursor to select the **On** option with the cursor keys and confirm your choice using ENTER.

◇ The next row of options, labelled **Type**, contains six icons representing different types of statistical plot. Select the fifth icon ⊞ using the cursor keys and confirm your choice using ENTER.

◇ Press to move the cursor onto the next row alongside **Xlist**: here you require list L3, so press 2nd [L3].

◇ Move down onto the bottom row and, if necessary, alongside **Freq**: enter a 1, indicating that each of the values of L3 is to be used just once.

Before moving on, make sure that your screen has exactly the same options as the one shown above, with **On** and ⊞ highlighted.

Now, move the cursor to the top of the screen and press ▶ to select **Plot 2** and press ENTER

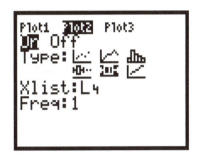

Use a similar method to the one given above to produce the display shown on the right.

The boxplots are now set up ready to be displayed.

Displaying the plots

The TI-83 will automatically display the plots so that they fill the screen sensibly. You will need to use the blue ZOOM key at the top of the keyboard.

Press ZOOM.

The ZOOM menu appears, displaying seven options, with a further three options which can be seen if you use the ▼ key to scroll downwards.

Option 9 is required, which is **ZoomStat**.

Press **9**.

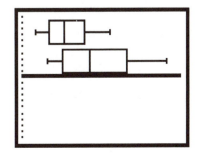

Two boxplots are displayed on the **Graphing screen**.

Graphing screen

Plot 1 is at the top of the screen and **Plot 2** beneath it. Also on the screen you can see the horizontal axis just below **Plot 2** and a line of dots on the left-hand side of the screen. The positions of these have been determined automatically by the calculator when you use **ZoomStat**.

There is another, manual, method for determining how the boxplots will be displayed, and this allows more flexibility and choice. To use this method, you must use the $\boxed{\text{WINDOW}}$ key in the top row of the keyboard.

Press $\boxed{\text{WINDOW}}$ now. The display should be similar to the one shown here.

Xmin and **Xmax** are the minimum and maximum values, corresponding to the left-hand and right-hand extremes of the screen. The **ZoomStat** option has set these to 88 and 352.

```
WINDOW
 Xmin=88
 Xmax=352
 Xscl=1
 Ymin=-10
 Ymax=10
 Yscl=1
 Xres=1
```

If you were to set the values of **Xmin** and **Xmax** by hand, you would need to choose **Xmin** a little below the smallest value in the lists and **Xmax** a little above the largest value. Looking at the data in Table 3.2, you can see that all the numbers lie between 100 and 350. So if **Xmin** is set to 100 and **Xmax** is set to 350, then the two boxplots will be neatly accommodated on the screen.

Use the cursor keys to place the flashing cursor after **Xmin**=.

Press **1 0 0** $\boxed{\text{ENTER}}$.

The flashing cursor will have moved to **Xmax**=.

Press **3 5 0** $\boxed{\text{ENTER}}$.

Press the $\boxed{\text{GRAPH}}$ key, in the top right-hand corner of the keyboard, to see the two boxplots on the Graphing screen.

Press $\boxed{\text{WINDOW}}$ again and change the **Ymin** setting to zero, to place the horizontal axis at the bottom of the screen.

Press $\boxed{\text{GRAPH}}$ to see the effect of this.

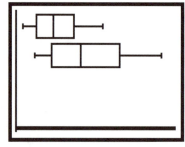

Note that, at any time after the boxplots have been set up, pressing $\boxed{\text{GRAPH}}$ will display the boxplots.

It is worth noticing that the calculator uses two rather confusing sets of notation:

◇   **Xmin** and **Xmax** are WINDOW settings.

◇   **minX** and **maxX** are the extreme values of a list.

Using TRACE with boxplots

You have now obtained boxplots on your calculator's Graphing screen. How can you transfer them to paper? You know what the boxplots should look like when you have drawn them but, as you can see, there are no numbers on the screen and five values should be marked on a boxplot: *min, Q₁, Med, Q₃* and *max*. So how should you proceed?

One possibility is to calculate the five statistics. But these numbers still have to be put in the correct positions on the boxplot. Fortunately, there is an easier way. You can make use of the TRACE facility of your calculator to find the values which should be marked on a boxplot.

If the boxplots are no longer on the Graphing screen of your calculator, press GRAPH to bring them back.

Now press the TRACE key, in the top row of the keyboard.

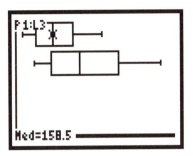

A flashing cross appears at the median of the upper boxplot.

Notice that **P1:L3** is written in the top left-hand corner of the screen, indicating that the point marked is on Plot 1 and is representing data from L3.

At the bottom of the screen is written **Med = 158.5**.

Using the right and left cursor keys you can move the cross to the quartiles and the extremes, one step at a time; at each stage, the value at that point is displayed at the bottom of the screen. Try this now.

Using the up or down cursor keys moves the cross from one boxplot to the corresponding point of the other boxplot. Note that **P1:L3** changes to **P2:L4** in the top left-hand corner of the screen as you move to the second boxplot. Then, as before, the left and right cursor keys can be used to obtain the values of *min*, Q_1, Med, Q_3 and *max*. Try this now.

It should be clear to you now how to obtain the values you need to complete a rough sketch of the boxplots. The next exercise takes you through the steps.

Exercise 3.3 *Sketching boxplots*

(a) Display the boxplots of the chefs' and cooks' earnings on your calculator's Graphing screen.

(b) Make a rough copy of the display. The boxplots should be roughly proportional to the boxplots shown on the screen. They should also be positioned one above the other as on the Graphing screen: the median of **Plot 1** should be roughly in line with the lower quartile of **Plot 2**, the lower quartile of **Plot 1** should be roughly in line with the minimum value (called **minX** by the TI-83) on **Plot 2**, and so on.

(c) Use TRACE to obtain the values you need to complete the boxplots, and add them to your sketch. Position the numbers as shown here for **Plot 2**.

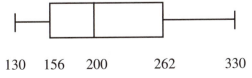

130   156   200   262   330

Figure 3.3   Boxplot of men's earnings data.

(d) Finally, check that your sketch looks like the one on the screen, and does not misrepresent the data.

The steps in the last exercise are the ones that you should go through whenever you want to draw a rough sketch of some boxplots. If an accurate diagram is required, then the rough sketch will help you to choose a sensible scale for the boxplots and will contain all the information you need. Displaying the boxplots on the Graphing screen will enable you to check that you have not made any gross errors in drawing them: you will be able to see straight away if your boxplots are not the same shape as those on the screen.

Using TRACE provides an alternative to 1-Var Stats if you need to find the five summary statistics, *min, Q₁*, median, *Q₃* and *max*.

Here is a summary of the main steps involved in drawing boxplots to find summary statistics.

Drawing boxplots and finding summary statistics

◇ Check and clear (if necessary) the data lists. Enter the data into the lists.

◇ Switch off existing plots using option 4 in the STAT PLOTS menu. Use the STAT PLOT menu again to set up **Plot 1**, **Plot 2** … as boxplots.

◇ Select option 9, **ZoomStat**, from within the ZOOM menu to display the boxplot.

◇ Use TRACE to read off the five summary statistics for each list.

◇ If desired, the values of **Xmin** and **Xmax** can be adjusted using WINDOW, and boxplot(s) can be redrawn by pressing GRAPH.

Brain stretcher   *Strange boxplots*

Are these boxplots? Can you produce them on your calculator?

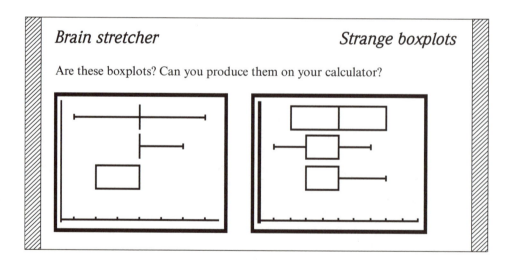

Chapter 4 Scatter plots, random numbers and measures of spread

In this chapter, you will be introduced to some more of the functions available using the MATH key, and to another statistical plot, the scatterplot. The distinction between the two statistics Sx and σx, which are displayed when using 1-Var Stats, is also explained.

4.1 Scatterplots

Table 4.1 contains data on male lung cancer death rates in 1950 and cigarette consumption in 1930 for 11 countries.

Table 4.1 Per capita cigarette consumption (1930) and male lung cancer death rates (1950)

Country	Mean cigarette consumption/annum	Male lung cancer death rate/100 000
Iceland	220	58
Norway	250	90
Sweden	310	115
Canada	510	150
Denmark	380	165
Australia	455	170
USA	1280	190
Holland	460	245
Switzerland	530	250
Finland	1115	350
Great Britain	1145	465

The activities in this section take you through the steps involved in obtaining a scatterplot for these data on your calculator. The three main stages in obtaining a scatterplot are the same as for boxplots.

◇ Entering the data.

◇ Setting up the plot.

◇ Displaying the plot.

Entering the data

Check to see whether there are already data in either of the lists L_1 and L_2. If necessary, clear the lists either by choosing option 4, **ClrList**, from the STAT EDIT menu, or by highlighting the list name on the List screen and pressing CLEAR.

paired data

Enter the cigarette consumption data in list L_1 and the male lung cancer death rates in L_2. Make sure that you enter the data in the order given in the table for both lists: these are **paired data**, so it is important to keep corresponding values in corresponding positions in the lists.

Setting up the plot

Setting up the plot is done using STAT PLOT. Press 2nd [STAT PLOT] to obtain the STAT PLOTS menu. Then switch off all the existing plots by pressing **4** to select PlotsOff and then ENTER to confirm your selection. (If the Graphing screen is displaying other graphs and drawings they will need to be cleared using the methods described in Section 5.3.)

Bring the STAT PLOTS menu back onto the screen by pressing 2nd [STAT PLOT] again.

Select **Plot 1** by pressing either **1** or ENTER.

Now use the cursor keys to select, and ENTER to confirm, the options shown here for Plot 1. The **Xlist** and **Ylist** options are selected by pressing 2nd [L1] and 2nd [L2] respectively.

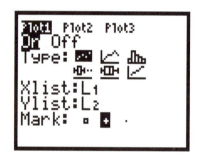

The bottom row, labelled **Mark**, allows you to choose from three possible plotting symbols.

x-axis, y-axis

Notice that the X list is set to contain the values in L_1 and the Y list to contain the values in L_2. This means that the L_1 values will be plotted on the horizontal axis (the **x-axis**) and the L_2 values on the vertical axis (the **y-axis**).

Displaying the plot

Before plotting the scatterplot, you must set the minimum and maximum values of X and Y. Again these values can be set automatically (using **ZoomStat**) or else you can set them by hand (using **WINDOW**). Both of these methods are described below.

Using **ZoomStat**, the TI-83 can set the limits of the display automatically, based on the known maximum and minimum data values of X and Y.

Press ZOOM **9**.

The scatterplot shown here is displayed.

Notice that points are marked with a cross, because of the choice made in the last line when setting up the plot.

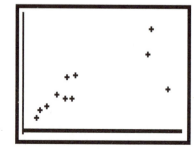

The minimum and maximum values of X and Y can also be set by hand using **WINDOW**. With small data sets such as the ones used here, these values can be found simply by inspecting the data lists. However, where the batch sizes are larger – say 20 or more – it is less easy to pick out the minimum and maximum values in the lists.

There are several ways of obtaining the minimum and maximum values in a list on your TI-83. Some of these involve using the functions **min** and **max**, which are available in different menus on the calculator. In the following sequence of instructions, the MATH NUM submenu is used.

Press MATH and you will see the screen on the right.

Four submenus are available here: MATH, NUM, CPX and PRB.

Press ▶ to reveal the NUM submenu.

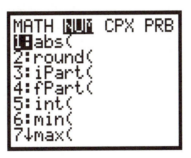

min and **max** are options 6 and 7 in this submenu. Notice that both options are followed by an opening bracket, indicating that when they are pasted to the Home screen they will require an argument. You may recall that, in Chapter 2, you met **SortA** and **SortD** which require one argument and the **seq** function which requires five arguments. **min** and **max** also require just one argument – the name of the list.

Press **6** to paste **min(** on to the Home screen.

Now it is necessary to specify which list is to be used.

Press 2nd [L1]] ENTER.

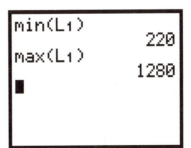

The minimum value of L_1 is 220.

Press MATH ▶ 7 2nd [L1]] ENTER.

The maximum value of L_1 is 1280.

Exercise 4.1 *Extreme values*

Use the **max** and **min** options in the MATH NUM submenu to find the extreme values of L_2.

Check these values and the extremes of L_1 by inspecting the values in the lists L_1 and L_2 on the List screen.

Now that you know the extreme values of lists L1 and L2, it is possible to decide on appropriate window settings. Recall that the L1 values are to be plotted on the horizontal or *x*-axis and L2 values on the vertical or *y*-axis.

Press [WINDOW].

The values which have been entered automatically are displayed.

Now enter the values shown here.

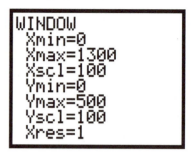

Notice that for a scatterplot, unlike for a boxplot, you need to specify **Xscl, Ymin, Ymax** and **Yscl** as well as **Xmin** and **Xmax**.

Xscl and **Yscl** specify the distance apart of the tick marks on the two axes.

Xres can be left at the default value of 1 for now.

Press [GRAPH] to see the scatterplot.

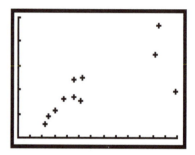

Notice the tick marks on the axes. In both cases they are 100 apart because **Xscl** and **Yscl** were set to 100. The spacing on the two axes is different because the *x*-axis was set to run from 0 to 1300 and the *y*-axis from 0 to 500.

Using TRACE with scatterplots

Compare the scatterplot on your Graphing screen with the data values in Table 4.1. It is often useful to be able to identify which mark on the scatterplot corresponds to which pair of data values. Where, for example, on the scatterplot is the mark representing the data from Canada?

Press [TRACE].

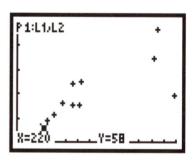

Notice that **P1:L1,L2** has appeared in the top left-hand corner of the screen. This stands for Plot 1, which displays data from lists L1 and L2.

The cigarette consumption and the lung cancer death rate for the first country (Iceland) are now shown at the bottom of the screen (X = 220, Y = 58); the plotting symbol for the corresponding point has changed to a square with a flashing cross over it.

Each time you press the right cursor key, the flashing cross moves to the point corresponding to the next country on the list, and the values for that country are displayed on the screen. Similarly, pressing the left cursor key moves the flashing cross to the point corresponding to the previous country on the list. So, to find the mark representing the Canadian data, first note the values from the table (X = 510, Y = 150) and then use the cursor keys until these values appear at the bottom of the screen. The flashing cross then indicates where the Canadian data lies on the scatterplot and this enables you to make comparisons with the data from other countries.

TRACE is very useful if you need to draw a scatterplot on paper. First, obtain the scatterplot on your calculator screen and draw similar suitable axes on your paper. Second, using TRACE, plot each point in turn, checking its position against the display on the screen. Finally, compare the pattern of the marks on the screen with that of the ones you have plotted on paper. If the patterns are not the same, use TRACE again to identify any points that look different on your plot and on the screen.

4.2 Generating random numbers

One way of thinking about the idea of random numbers is to imagine selecting numbered balls, randomly, from a bag. Although 'balls in a bag' is quite a useful model for understanding randomness, it is not a particularly common or useful scenario. In this section, something a little more realistic is considered.

Imagine a square surface which has been marked out in nine smaller squares, as shown below.

1	2	3
4	5	6
7	8	9

Now imagine an event which might occur **at random** in these small squares: that is, the event is as likely to appear in any one square as in any other – each square is equally likely. For example, if the small squares are set out in the middle of a large field, apparently random events might be the falling of a raindrop or the appearance of a daisy.

at random

It is possible to use random numbers to **simulate** the occurrences of events in these small squares. The calculator can be used for this purpose by getting it to generate a string of random digits in the range 1 to 9.

simulate

There are a number of ways of generating random numbers on your TI-83. Two of them involve the use of either **rand** or **randInt**: these are options 1 and 5, respectively, in the MATH PRB menu.

Using randInt

Press [MATH] [◄] to display this menu now.

Notice that option 5, **randInt**, unlike option 1, **rand**, has an open bracket attached to it, indicating that when it is pasted to the Home screen you are expected to enter arguments inside the brackets.

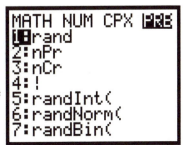

```
MATH NUM CPX PRB
1:rand
2:nPr
3:nCr
4:!
5:randInt(
6:randNorm(
7:randBin(
```

Earlier in this chapter you met **min** and **max**, both of which required a single argument, the name of a list. **randInt** requires two arguments which must be integers (whole numbers).

Select **randInt** by pressing **5**.

Then press ⁤1⁤ ⁤,⁤ ⁤6⁤ ⁤)⁤ ⁤ENTER⁤.

Your calculator should have produced an integer chosen at random in the range 1 to 6 inclusive.

Get the calculator to do this again a few times. Remember that you do not need to enter the whole command again: simply pressing ⁤ENTER⁤ repeatedly will cause the last command entered to be carried out again and again.

Your screen should look rather like the one on the right, although it would be surprising if it looked exactly the same: after all you are expecting randomly chosen numbers.

Spend a few minutes now exploring the command **randInt** with different integer arguments.

Brain stretcher   *Lottery*

Investigate what happens when you use three integer arguments for **randInt**; for example, try **randInt(1, 6, 10)**.

Use this facility to produce six random numbers between 1 and 49.

There could be a problem if you wanted to use these numbers in a lottery draw. Can you see what the problem might be? Can you think how it might be solved?

Using rand

Now think about how you might generate a string of random integers from 1 to 9 to simulate the occurrence of events in the nine squares described at the beginning of this section.

One difficulty with generating lots of random numbers in this way on a calculator is that there is no obvious way of keeping a track of how many numbers have been produced. The other command, **rand**, in the MATH PRB menu will be more helpful.

Press ⁤MATH⁤ ⁤◀⁤ **1** to select **rand** and paste it to the Home screen. There are no opening brackets so no argument is expected.

Press ⁤ENTER⁤ and repeat it a few times. This time you will see a random decimal number appear on the display each time ⁤ENTER⁤ is pressed. This number is in the range 0 to 1.

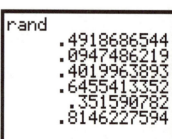

Your display should resemble the one shown here. Most of the strings contain 10 digits but occasionally, as in the fifth string here, there are fewer digits.

Exercise 4.2 *Shorter strings*

(a) Generate a sequence of about 20 random strings like these. As you do so, check to see whether each string has 10 digits. How do you account for the occasional string which has fewer than 10 digits?

(Hint: If you are unsure of the reason for this, press **0 . 2 0 0** [ENTER] and observe its result on the right of the display. It is shown as .2 with the zeros at the end not displayed.)

(b) How often, on average, do you expect there to be only nine digits?

(c) Will there ever be only eight digits? How often on average? What about seven digits, six, five, four, three, two, one?

The results from Exercise 4.2 are summarized and extended in the following table.

Number of digits in display	Number of final zeros	Occurs on average one time in	
9	1	10	$= 10^1$
8	2	100	$= 10^2$
7	3	1 000	$= 10^3$
6	4	10 000	$= 10^4$
5	5	100 000	$= 10^5$
4	6	1 000 000	$= 10^6$
3	7	10 000 000	$= 10^7$
2	8	100 000 000	$= 10^8$
1	9	1 000 000 000	$= 10^9$

So there was a small, but finite, chance that your calculator produced a display with very few digits. There are likely to be thousands of people carrying out the same activity, so there is a good chance that someone, somewhere, will have got a six-digit display or one with even fewer digits.

Now back to the simulation of raindrops falling on the nine small squares.

Use **rand** to fill the screen of your TI-83 with random numbers once again. You should produce something similar to the display below but with different numbers. Ignore all the zeros and make a **tally** of the first 60 *non-zero* digits.   **tally**

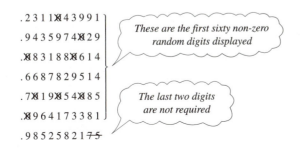

```
.2311843991
.9435974829
.8831888614
.6687829514
.7819854885
.8964173381
.9852582175
```

These are the first sixty non-zero random digits displayed

The last two digits are not required

The number of 1s, 2s, ..., 9s in the first 60 non-zero numbers were counted by doing a tally as described below. A stroke for each digit was made as it occurred, any zeros being ignored. So, for example, after working along the first three rows, the tally looked like this.

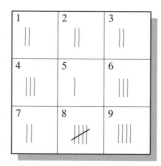

Notice that, when the fifth 3 was obtained, the fifth stroke was drawn across the first four, thus marking out a group of five. The advantage of this is that the frequencies can be counted easily when they are arranged in groups of five.

The complete tally of the first sixty non-zeros is shown here.

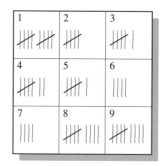

Now use your calculator to generate similar random numbers and make a tally of the first 60 non-zero digits.

Pseudo-random numbers

Data, a character from the TV series 'Star Trek: The Next Generation', is an android (though he prefers to describe himself as an artificial life form). In one of the episodes, he is asked, 'How are you, Data?' He replies, 'I am operating within established parameters, thank you.'

Unlike humans, who are capable of spontaneous action, artificial life forms like calculators, computers and androids are unable to carry out any procedure that has not been pre-programmed. How, then, is your TI-83 able to come up with a truly random number? The answer is that it cannot – it can only generate what are called 'pseudo-random' numbers. Like all similar machines, the TI-83 is pre-programmed with commands to generate the next 'random' number from the previous one. In addition a 'seed' number is used from which to generate the first 'random' number. This means that any two brand new TI-83 calculators, since they use the same seed number, will produce the same 'random' sequence of numbers from first use. When you reset your TI-83's memory, as you did in Chapter 1, the seed number was also reset. You might want to test this, but do not forget that resetting the memory will clear any data lists, settings, programs or anything else that you have stored in your calculator. A less drastic way of producing the starting sequence of 'random' numbers is to set the seed number (which happens to be 0) as follows.

Press **0** [STO▸] [MATH] [◂] **1** [ENTER].

Now press [MATH] [◂] **1** [ENTER] to produce the first 'random' number.

Press [ENTER] six more times and you should see the exact display of pseudo-random numbers shown here.

```
.9435974025
 .908318861
.1466878292
.5147019505
.4058096418
.7338123112
.0439919875
```

A moral to be drawn from this result is that the calculator's random facility must be treated with caution since, like Mr Data, it is 'operating within established parameters'. Knowing this, it may be possible for someone to predict which 'random' number your TI-83 comes up with next. They would only need to know the pre-programmed method for calculating such numbers and the last 'random' number that had been generated.

Brain stretcher   How does **randInt** work?

Try setting the seed to 0 again and then use **randInt(1,10)** five times to generate the initial five random integers between 1 and 10.

Compare with the first five decimal numbers produced by **rand**, which are shown in the screen display above. (The first one was .943....)

Can you predict what your next two integers will be? Can you work out what rule the calculator is using?

What would the re-seeded starting sequences be for:

    randInt(1,100)?

    randInt(1,5)?

    randInt(1,2)?

    randInt(1,n)?

Brain stretcher   How random?

It is easy to store random numbers in the data lists.

For example, the following would store 100 random numbers in the range 1 to 7 in list L1.

        randInt(1,7,100) → L1

If you were to draw a boxplot to show the spread of the data in L1, what would you expect it to look like?

Try it and see.

4.3 Standard deviation

In Chapters 2 and 3, you used **1-Var Stats** to find various summary statistics including the mean, the median and the quartiles of a batch of data. This short subsection, looks again at the output from **1-Var Stats** and, in particular, at the standard deviation of a data batch.

In Section 2.1 you calculated summary statistics of the following data representing daily temperature at midday during June 1994.

$$13 \quad 17 \quad 12 \quad 15 \quad 14 \quad 16 \quad 14 \quad 16 \quad 16 \quad 15 \quad 13 \quad 15 \quad 17 \quad 20 \quad 21$$
$$24 \quad 23 \quad 20 \quad 21 \quad 17 \quad 19 \quad 22 \quad 19 \quad 22 \quad 18 \quad 19 \quad 19 \quad 22 \quad 21 \quad 23$$

The data were in L_1.

You selected **1-Var Stats** by pressing $\boxed{\text{STAT}}$ $\boxed{\triangleright}$ **1**.

Pressing $\boxed{\text{2nd}}$ $\boxed{\text{L1}}$ $\boxed{\text{ENTER}}$ produced the display shown on the right.

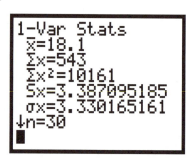

Notice the two summary statistics labelled Sx and σx (σ is the Greek lower case letter sigma: σx is read as 'sigma x'). These are the two versions of the standard deviation:

◇ Sx is the value obtained when $n - 1$ is used to calculate the standard deviation;

◇ σx is the value obtained when n is used.

The formula used in this book is:

$$\text{standard deviation} = \sqrt{\frac{\Sigma(x - \overline{x})^2}{n}}$$

and this version of the standard deviation of a batch of data is given by σx in **1-Var Stats**. Notice that σx is always smaller than Sx.

Hence the standard deviation of the June temperatures is given by

$$\text{standard deviation} = 3.330165161 \approx 3.33 \text{ (to two decimal places)}$$

Exercise 4.3 Standard deviation practice

Enter the data values 1, 2, 3, 4, 5 into list L_1 and the data values 6, 7, 8, 9, 10 into list L_2.

Use **1-Var Stats** to calculate the standard deviation of each of the two batches of data. What do you notice?

Joining lists

It would be interesting to see what happens to the standard deviation and other summary statistics when two lists are joined together. For the data from Exercise 4.3 it would be a simple matter to enter the data values 1 to 10 into another list, L_3 say. However, you may sometimes wish to join two long data lists which have already been entered. Would you really have to enter all those data values again in a third list?

There is, in fact, a short way of doing this using some of the calculator's list-handling facilities. Try this out now with the short lists in L_1 and L_2 and then look out for opportunities to use it later with longer lists.

How can you join two lists of data together into a single list? Check that you still have five items in L_1 {1, 2, 3, 4, 5} and five more in L_2 {6, 7, 8, 9, 10}. The challenge is to finish with the 10 items {1, 2, 3, 4, 5, 6, 7, 8, 9, 10} in the single list L_3. It might be tempting to think that entering $L_1 + L_2 \rightarrow L_3$ might work. Try it and see what happens.

One correct method involves creating five extra zeros at the end of L_1, five zeros at the beginning of L_2, and then storing the result of $L_1 + L_2$ in L_3. A new command, **dim** (short for dimension), is used which is option 3 on the LIST OPS menu. Return to the Home screen and carry out the following steps.

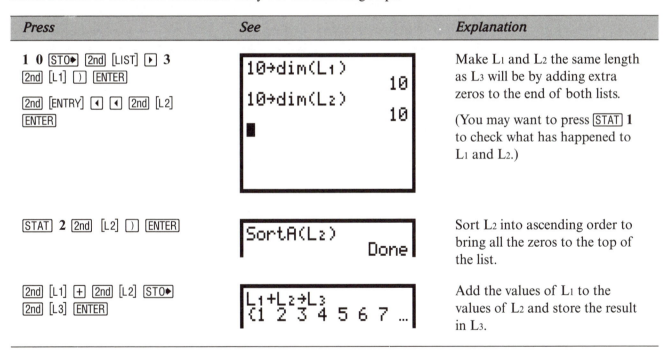

Press	See	Explanation
1 0 [STO▶] [2nd] [LIST] [▶] **3** [2nd] [L1] [)] [ENTER] [2nd] [ENTRY] [◀] [◀] [2nd] [L2] [ENTER]	10→dim(L1) 10 10→dim(L2) 10 ■	Make L_1 and L_2 the same length as L_3 will be by adding extra zeros to the end of both lists. (You may want to press [STAT] **1** to check what has happened to L_1 and L_2.)
[STAT] **2** [2nd] [L2] [)] [ENTER]	SortA(L2) Done	Sort L_2 into ascending order to bring all the zeros to the top of the list.
[2nd] [L1] [+] [2nd] [L2] [STO▶] [2nd] [L3] [ENTER]	L1+L2→L3 {1 2 3 4 5 6 7 …	Add the values of L_1 to the values of L_2 and store the result in L_3.

However, the TI-83 provides an easier way of doing this. Option 9 in the LIST OPS menu is labelled **augment** and can be used to join two lists together, or as the TI-83 Guidebook calls it, 'concatenate' them.

Try pressing:

[2nd] [LIST] [▶] **9** [2nd] [L1] [,] [2nd] [L3] [)] [STO▶] [2nd] [L4] [ENTER]

What would you expect to see in L_4? Check your guess on the List screen.

Exercise 4.4   *1-Var Stats with a joined list*

Check on the List screen that list L3 contains a combination of the data values from L1 and L2, that is the integers 1 to 10 inclusive.

How would you expect the summary statistics of data list L3 to be related to those you calculated for L1 and L2?

Use **1-Var Stats** and L3 to check your predictions.

Brain stretcher   *Changing lists – changing stats*

Enter any 10 values into the list L1.

Calculate the **1-Var Stats** and note them down.

On the Home screen enter L1 + 5 → L2 to make the L2 values 5 more than those in L1. (This way of using data in one list to produce data in a second list will be described in more detail in Section 5.8.)

Can you predict the **1-Var Stats** for list L2? Check your predictions.

What if you enter L1 × 2 → L2?

Try other similar expressions in L2.

Chapter 5 The statistical features of the TI-83

Most of the main statistical features of the TI-83 are summarized in this chapter. The chapter has two aims. Firstly, it provides you with a convenient summary of the features you have learned about in Chapters 2–4. Secondly, it will introduce you to some of the other statistical features available on the TI-83.

This chapter does not cover options 3 through to C in the STAT CALC menu, all of which deal with **regression**. You will meet these facilities in Chapters 10–13.

regression

There are no exercises in this chapter although there are several Brain stretchers, which you may wish to try.

Two data batches are used in this chapter. The data in Table 5.1 will be used to illustrate features described in Sections 5.1–5.3. Two groups of rats were provided with different diets, one a restricted diet and the other permitted free eating. A note was made of the number of days that the rats in each group lived and these data are shown in Table 5.1.

Table 5.1   Length of lives in days of rats on a restricted diet and free eating

Restricted diet	1136	901	1327	1220	789	1181	604	1085	1045	211	974
Free eating	675	791	630	731	547	768	387	702	736	836	

Source: A Handbook of small data sets (ed. D. J. Hand et al.), Chapman & Hall, 1994, p. 193

Notice that these are not paired data – there is no link between, for example, the first values in each list.

5.1   Entering and editing data

The TI-83 has six registers (called **lists**) for storing data. A list can hold up to 999 data values. Option 1 of the STAT EDIT menu takes you to the List screen, where lists can be entered and edited.

lists

Clearing existing data lists

The standard way to clear lists is using option 4 in the STAT EDIT menu. You must specify which lists you wish to clear, otherwise you get an error message.

Press	*See*	*Explanation*
STAT 4 2nd [L1] ENTER	```ClrList L₁ Done ClrList L₂,L₃ Done```	Clear list L₁
STAT 4 2nd [L2] , 2nd [L3] ENTER		To clear more than one list at a time, put a comma between the named lists.

There are other ways of clearing lists which are sometimes faster.

◇ One method uses option 4, **ClrAllLists**, in the MEM menu. You may recall using the MEM menu at the beginning of Chapter 1 to reset the calculator to its factory setting. [MEM] is the second function of the blue [+] key.

As the name suggests, the **ClrAllLists** option clears all of the data stored in all of the six lists.

Press [2nd] [MEM] **4** [ENTER].

```
ClrAllLists
              Done
```

If you look now at the list screen, you will see that all of the data has been cleared from each list.

◇ A third, very direct, method of clearing lists which can be used when you are using the List screen is as follows.

Press [STAT] **1**.

The display on the right shows the lists L1, L2 and L3 with some typical data values. As usual, the first data value in L1 is highlighted.

```
L1      L2      L3      1
9       5       6
9       6       3
5       9       3
6       8       5
8       9       8
4       5       7
9       6       5
L1(1)=9
```

Press [▲] to move the cursor over L1 at the top of the screen.

Press [CLEAR] [ENTER] and all the values in L1 disappear.

To clear L2, position the cursor over L2 at the top of the screen and again press [CLEAR] [ENTER].

Try clearing some lists using these three methods to find out which one you prefer.

Entering and editing data

Here is the standard way of entering data into lists.

◇ Press [STAT] **1**.

You should now see lists L1 and L2 displayed on the List screen. They should be empty, because they have just been cleared. The cursor is in L1, awaiting data entry.

```
L1      L2      L3      1
                        6
  ------  ------        3
                        3
                        5
                        8
                        7
                        5
L1(1)=
```

◇ Enter the restricted-diet rat data into L1, remembering to press [ENTER] after each value. When all 11 values have been entered, the cursor should be on the blank twelfth space.

To correct a miskeyed entry, move the cursor to the incorrect value and overtype it with the correct one. To remove an entry completely, move the cursor to that entry and press DEL. To insert a new value at some point in the list use 2nd [INS] and overtype the zero that appears with the new data value.

◇ Now press ▶ to move to list L_2 and enter the free-eating rat data (ten values in all).

There is an alternative way to enter data into lists using commands entered on the Home screen. First, move to the Home screen by pressing 2nd [QUIT] and then press CLEAR. To enter the numbers 5, 6, 7, 8 into list L_6, use the following key sequence.

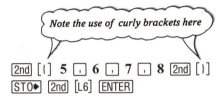

Note the use of curly brackets here

2nd [{] 5 [,] 6 [,] 7 [,] 8 2nd [}]
STO▸ 2nd [L6] ENTER

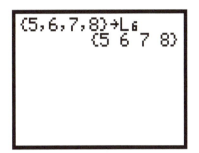

If the data to be entered are in a particular sequence they may be entered from the Home screen using the **seq** command. **seq** requires five arguments, separated by commas.

For example, to enter into L_6 the first 50 square numbers, 1, 4, 9, 16, 25, …, 2500, use the following key sequence:

2nd [LIST] ▶ 5 [X,T,Θ,n] [x²] [,] [X,T,Θ,n]
[,] 1 [,] 5 0 [,] 1 [)] STO▸ 2nd [L6]
ENTER

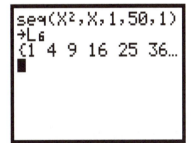

Sorting lists

Sorting lists into order is done using options 2 and 3 in the STAT EDIT menu. With both **SortA** (ascending order) and **SortD** (descending order) you must specify which list you wish to sort.

For example, to sort list L_1 into ascending order, press the following:

STAT **2** 2nd [L1] [)] ENTER

To check that the list has been sorted, press STAT **1** and run the cursor down list L_1. The values should be in ascending order.

Now sort list L_2 into descending order by pressing

STAT **3** 2nd [L2] [)] ENTER

Again, use STAT **1** to check that list L_2 has been sorted.

The method for sorting lists with paired data is dealt with in Section 5.5.

5.2 Summary statistics for single-variable data

1-Var Stats

Summary statistics for a batch of data are obtained using **1-Var Stats**, which is option 1 in the STAT CALC menu. You must specify which list you wish to summarize.

To obtain summary statistics for the data in L_1, press [STAT] [▶] **1** [2nd] [L1] [ENTER].

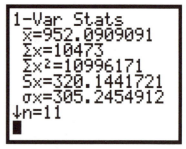

The first six summary values will be displayed on the screen.

Other summary statistics can be seen by scrolling downwards.

To obtain summary statistics for L_2, you could repeat the process, substituting L_2 for L_1.

Alternatively, you could edit the last instruction by pressing:

[2nd] [ENTRY] [◀] [2nd] [L2] [ENTER]

Brain stretcher   Deep thought!

In the book *The Hitchhiker's Guide to the Galaxy*, by Douglas Adams, the super-computer called Deep Thought came up with the answer to the ultimate question of life, the universe and everything.

It was 42.

Can you make your calculator come up with this answer as often as possible? For example, the **1-Var Stats** display produces 11 summary statistics. How many of those which have been covered so far in this book can you make equal to 42 at the same time?

Summary statistics using menus

Summary statistics are also available using option 5, **Statistics**, of the VARS menu. This option contains five submenus listing the statistics that are available. For example, Q_1 and Q_3 (the lower and upper quartiles) are available using the PTS submenu.

To see this submenu, press [VARS] **5** [◄].

Options 7 and 9 give the values of Q_1 and Q_3.

The values obtained using the [VARS] key refer to the last list that you used with **1-Var Stats**, which in this case is L_2.

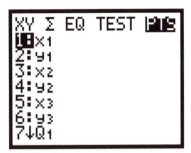

So, for example, to calculate the interquartile range for L_2, you would press

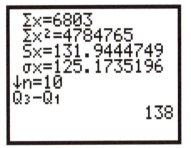

[VARS] 5 [◄] 9 [−] [VARS] 5 [◄] 7 [ENTER]

There are too many summary values in the VARS Statistics submenu to list here, but you may wish to explore them yourself. Note that not all the values listed are available after using **1-Var Stats**. Some are available only after using **2-Var Stats**, and others (contained in the EQ submenu) after using one of the regression options in the STAT CALC menu.

Finally, the LIST MATH submenu provides the range of useful summary statistics shown on the right. Note that here it is not necessary to have used **1-Var Stats** beforehand, but you do need to specify which list is to be used.

In particular, option 5, **sum**, is a very convenient way of producing the total of all the values in a list.

To use this menu, for example, to calculate the highest value in list L_1, press the following:

[2nd] [LIST] [►] [►] 2 [2nd] [L1] [)] [ENTER]

You should see the display on the right.

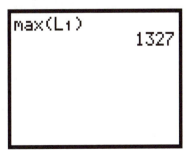

> **Brain stretcher**   *More deep thought*
>
> Can you produce this display?
>
> ```
> Q1
>                              42
> Σx
>                              42
> maxX
>                              42
> ```
>
> The entries on the left are all in the VARS Statistics submenus; what list could they be operating on?
>
> What if $n = 42$ as well?

5.3 Plots for single-variable data

Switching off all existing plots

Before setting up and displaying a plot, make a habit of switching off all existing plots. This is done with option 4 of the STAT PLOT menu.

◇ Press [2nd] [STAT PLOT] **4** [ENTER].

Confirm that all three plots (in options 1–3) are off, by pressing [2nd] [STAT PLOT].

◇ Note that you may also need to deselect any functions which are selected in the Y= list.

To do this, press [Y=]. If any of the = signs are highlighted, move the cursor over them and press [ENTER].

(An alternative way to deselect these functions is to use the On/Off option in the Y-VARS submenu within VARS.)

◇ It may also be necessary to clear any drawing done previously. To do this press [2nd] [DRAW] **1** [ENTER].

Boxplots

Here are the stages involved in displaying boxplots for the data in lists L_1 and L_2 on the Graphing screen.

◇ Select Plot 1 by pressing

[2nd] [STAT PLOT] **1**

Select the options shown on the right. To do this, move the cursor to each required option and press [ENTER] to confirm your selection. Also type in the required **Xlist** name and frequency.

The six icons alongside **Type** represent

⊡⋮	a scatterplot
⌐	a line graph
⊞	a frequency diagram
⊡⋯	a modified boxplot
⊡	a regular boxplot
⟋	a normal probability plot

(The TI-83 Guidebook refers to a frequency diagram as a *histogram*.)

◇ Press [2nd] [STAT PLOT] **2** to choose **Plot 2** and select the options shown here.

◇ Press [ZOOM] **9** to automatically set the screen boundaries, and draw the boxplots on the Graphing screen.

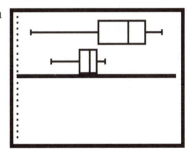

◇ If required, press [WINDOW] to adjust **Xmin** and **Xmax** and set **Ymin = 0** in order to prevent the horizontal axis from running through the middle of the plot. The settings of the remaining items in WINDOW can be ignored for boxplots. Finally, press [GRAPH] to see both boxplots displayed on the Graphing screen.

Modified boxplots

The TI-83 allows you to draw what are called modified boxplots, which are selected using the fourth **Type** icon ⊡⋯ when you are setting up the statistical plots.

The boxplots are similar to regular boxplots, except that points more than 1.5 times the interquartile range are plotted individually beyond the end marks of the boxplot. You can trace these points, which are known as outliers.

The display on the right shows a regular and modified boxplot for the free-eating rat data in L2.

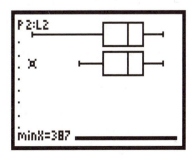

Brain stretcher   *Changing lists – changing boxplots*

Enter any 10 values into the list L3.

Draw a boxplot.

On the Home screen enter the following:

$$L_3 \times 2 \rightarrow L_4$$

You will meet this method of entering data again in Section 5.8. Check to see the values that have appeared in L4.

Can you predict what the boxplot for L4 will look like? Check your predictions.

What if you enter:

$L_3 \times 2 + 3 \rightarrow L_4$?

or

$L_3 \div 2 - 2 \rightarrow L_4$?

or …?

Using TRACE with boxplots

To obtain the five summary statistics needed to complete a sketch of a boxplot, use the [TRACE] key.

Press [TRACE] and then use ◄ and ► to read off the five summary statistics for **Plot 1**. Notice the **P1:L1** in the top left-hand corner of the screen, indicating which plot is being read and from which list the data are taken. The current cursor position is displayed at the bottom left corner.

Press ▼ and then ◄ and ► to obtain the five statistics for **Plot 2**.

Note that the **P1:L1** in the top left-hand corner has changed to **P2:L2**, indicating that **Plot 2** values, taken from list L2, are currently being displayed.

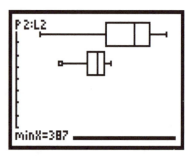

Frequency diagrams

The calculator provides another type of diagram for one-variable data, the frequency diagram. It is referred to in the calculator manual as a histogram. To see how to plot a frequency diagram for the data in list L1, proceed as follows.

◇ Turn off any existing plots by pressing

[2nd] [STAT PLOT] **4** [ENTER]

If necessary deselect any functions in the Y= menu and turn off any drawing using the DRAW menu.

◇ Select **Plot 1** by pressing [2nd] [STAT PLOT] **1** and choose the options shown here.

◇ Press WINDOW and adjust the settings to these.

```
WINDOW
 Xmin=0
 Xmax=1500
 Xscl=100
 Ymin=-5
 Ymax=5
 Yscl=1
 Xres=1
```

◇ Press TRACE ▶ ▶

◇ You should see the display on the right on the Graphing screen, indicating that the list L_1 has one item of data between 200 and 300. The height of each bar is equal to the frequency. **min** and **max** refer, respectively, to the minimum and maximum values in the particular interval where the cursor is currently positioned.

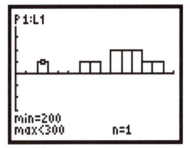

```
P1:L1




min=200
max<300      n=1
```

In this case, 200 is the smallest value in the group and all values from 200 up to, but not including, 300 are included in the group. The next interval would include 300 and go up to, but not include 400, and so on.

◇ By moving the cursor further to the right, you should see that there are two items of data between 900 and 1000, indicated by $n = 2$. Notice that the width of the bars is 100 units, the value of **Xscl** currently set in WINDOW.

◇ Return to the WINDOW menu and change **Xscl** to 250 (or some other value) and then press GRAPH.

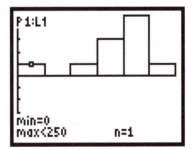

```
P1:L1




min=0
max<250      n=1
```

◇ This has the effect of regrouping the data. Once again, press TRACE and use the right cursor key to read off the new interval boundaries (as indicated by the values of **min** and **max**). By changing **Xscl** you can see the effect of grouping the data in different ways.

◇ Finally, press ZOOM 9 and see the effect of **ZoomStat** here. The diagram fits the screen well, but pressing WINDOW shows that the calculator has chosen to set **Xscl** to 279 – not a very useful interval. In general, when plotting frequency diagrams, it is better to adjust the window setting manually.

5.4 Frequency data

Entering frequency data

When some of the values in a batch of data occur more than once, it is often convenient to record the number of times that each different value appears, rather than to record all the individual numbers. Consider, for example, the following ordered batch:

$$1 \ 1 \ 1 \ 1 \ 1 \ 2 \ 2 \ 2 \ 2 \ 2 \ 2 \ 2 \ 3 \ 3 \ 3 \ 3 \ 4 \ 4$$

Rather than entering all 21 numbers into list L1, the values (1, 2, 3, 4) can be put in list L1 and the frequency of each value (6, 8, 5 and 2, respectively) in L2.

Note that although two lists are used to store the data, only one 'variable' is involved – the data actually consist of a single batch of 21 numbers. You must make sure there are the same number of data items in the two lists. However, do not confuse this with paired data, such as those given in Section 5.5.

◇   Clear lists L1 and L2.

◇   Enter 1, 2, 3, 4 in L1 and their corresponding frequencies 6, 8, 5, 2 in L2.

◇   Press [STAT] [▶] 1 [2nd] [L1] [,] [2nd] [L2] [ENTER].

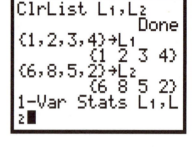

Notice that two list names are entered – the data values in the first list and the frequencies in the second.

You should see this screen of summary values.

Notice that $n = 21$, indicating that the original 21 items of data have been used in calculating these summary statistics.

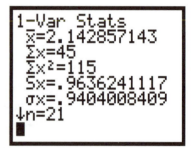

Graphing frequency data

There are two possible ways of plotting frequency data on the TI-83: using a boxplot and using a frequency diagram. The procedure is very similar to that used when the data are stored in a single list. The only detail that is different is that, when setting up the plots, you must enter the location of the frequencies. For example, to obtain a boxplot for the frequency data which you entered above, select the options shown below. (Do not forget to switch off existing plots first.)

Notice that the final line on the screen, marked **Freq:**, is set to L2, indicating that the frequencies are in L2, whereas, when the data are all in a single list, **Freq:** is set to 1.

◇   Press [WINDOW] and adjust the settings to those shown here.

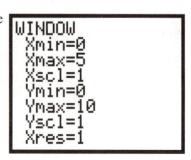

◇ Press [GRAPH]

Notice that, in this instance, the boxplot appears to have lost its left 'whisker'. This is explained by pressing [TRACE] [◀] [◀].

This reveals that, in this case, both **minX** and Q_1 have the same value, 1.

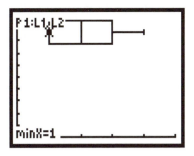

Plotting frequency data in the form of a frequency diagram is done in a similar way to that of a boxplot.

◇ Select Plot 1 by pressing [2nd] [STAT PLOT] **1** and select the display options as shown here.

The WINDOW settings selected for the boxplot are still suitable; there is no need to adjust them.

◇ Now press [GRAPH] followed by [TRACE] [▶].

Notice that the width of the bars is 1 unit, (the current value of **Xscl**). The flashing cursor is over the first bar, which is 6 units high because $n = 6$.

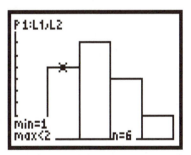

The display shows that for this bar **min=1**, **max<2** and **n=6** and yet there are six ones and eight twos. This indicates that the TI-83 is counting only the 1s. It counts all values from the minimum (**min=1**) up to, but not including, the maximum (**max<2**).

A less ambiguous frequency diagram can be obtained by changing the **Xmin** value in the WINDOW menu to 0.5. This ensures that the integer values correspond to the midpoints of each bar. Pressing [TRACE] then gives, for the first bar, **min=0.5**, **max<1.5** and **n=6** (the number of values).

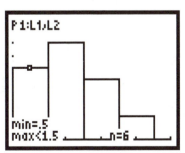

Brain stretcher **Stairs**

How were the following frequency diagrams produced?

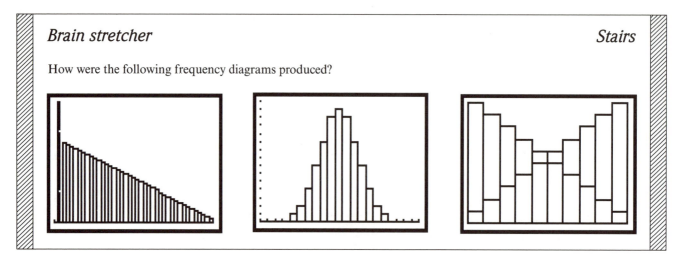

5.5 Summary statistics for paired data

The features described in Sections 5.5 and 5.6 are illustrated by the data in Table 5.2: the ages and percentage of body fat of 16 people.

Table 5.2 Human age (years) and percentage body fat

Age	50	27	27	58	54	60	53	39
Body fat (%)	31.1	17.8	7.8	33.0	29.1	41.1	34.7	31.4
Age	23	58	61	56	45	23	57	53
Body fat (%)	9.5	33.8	34.5	32.5	27.4	27.9	30.3	42.0

Source: A Handbook of small data sets (ed. D. J. Hand et al.), Chapman & Hall, 1994, p. 13

paired data Notice that these are **paired data**: the first values in each list, for example, are linked because they have been obtained from the same person: a fifty-year-old with 31.1% of body fat.

Enter the data, putting the 16 age values into L4 and the corresponding 16 body fat values into L5.

Since these are paired values, calculations can be done using **2-Var Stats** from the STAT CALC menu.

The two lists where the data are stored must be named, separated by a comma. Press

[STAT] [▶] 2 [2nd] [L4] [,] [2nd] [L5] [ENTER]

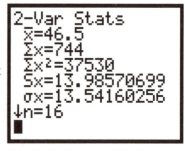

Two additional screens of information are displayed by scrolling downwards using the [▼] key.

These summary statistics may also be obtained using the VARS menu and choosing option 5, **Statistics**. Note, however, that although the statistics in the X/Y and $\sum$ submenus are available with **2-Var Stats**, the statistics in the PTS and TEST submenus and most of those in the EQ submenu are not. For example, the value of n is given as 16, because there are 16 pairs, but selecting Q_1 produces an error message because this option is available only with **1-Var Stats**.

It is possible to sort data in one of the paired lists into ascending or descending order while at the same time preserving the pairing. To do this, you must include in your Sort command both the list to be sorted and the list to which it has been paired. The first-named list is the one that is sorted.

For example, to sort list L4 in descending order, while at the same time preserving the pairing with list L5, press

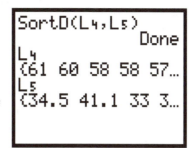

$$\boxed{\text{STAT}} \ \ 3 \ \ \boxed{\text{2nd}} \ \ \boxed{\text{L4}} \ \ \boxed{,} \ \ \boxed{\text{2nd}} \ \ \boxed{\text{L5}} \ \ \boxed{)} \ \ \boxed{\text{ENTER}}$$

Examine the lists either on the List screen or the Home screen, as shown here, and you will see that list L4 is now in descending order but the pairing has been preserved.

Try out the effect of reversing the order of L4 and L5 in this last key sequence.

5.6 Plots for paired data

Scatterplots

The stages involved in plotting a scatterplot with age (list L4) on the horizontal axis (x-axis) and body fat percentage (list L5) on the vertical axis (y-axis) are given below.

◇ Switch off existing plots. If necessary, deselect any functions in the Y= menu and turn off any drawing.

◇ Select Plot 1 from the STAT PLOT menu and choose the settings as shown.

Notice that, when a scatterplot is selected, there is a choice of marks which are used to indicate points on the screen.

◇ Press $\boxed{\text{WINDOW}}$ and alter the settings to suitable values like those shown here.

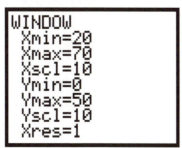

Alternatively, **ZoomStat** can be used.

◇ Press $\boxed{\text{GRAPH}}$ to display the scatterplot.

◇ Press $\boxed{\text{TRACE}}$ and then use $\boxed{◁}$ and $\boxed{▷}$ to see displayed, in turn, each of the sixteen pairs of values.

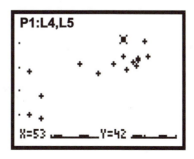

Line graphs

Another plot available for paired data is a line graph or *xy* line. When setting up the plot, choose the second option for TYPE, marked ⌐⌐. A line graph is like a scatterplot but the data points are connected by lines in the order in which they appear in lists L4 and L5.

Change the setting for **Plot 1** and obtain a line graph instead of a scatterplot to see what it looks like. A line graph is usually only useful if the *x*-values have been sorted into ascending order.

You will meet line graphs frequently in Chapters 6 and 7.

One further type of plot (for paired data) is available on the TI-83. This is a normal probability plot, represented by the sixth icon, ⌐. Details are on page 12–37 of the *TI-83 Guidebook*, but its use is beyond the scope of this book.

Brain stretcher   *Deep thought 3*

Enter the following data batches, being careful to maintain the order in which the values occur:

$\{2, 2, 0, 3, 4, 5, 3, 6\} \rightarrow$ L1

$\{1, 5, 3, 3, 5, 3, 1, 1\} \rightarrow$ L2

Set **Plot 1** so that it displays a line graph, with **Xlist** as L1 and **Ylist** as L2.

Use **ZoomStat** to draw the graph.

5.7 Combining lists

Lists of data can be combined and manipulated by making use of [STO▸] on the Home screen. Some examples are given below. In each case, you may wish to return to the List screen to check which values have been stored in the lists.

Adding the values in two lists together

Clear the existing data lists. Enter the values 1, 2, 3, 4 into L1 and the values 5, 6, 7, 8 into L2. Then on the Home screen enter the expressions below.

Press	See	Explanation
[2nd] [L1] [+] [2nd] [L2] [STO▸] [2nd] [L3]	L1+L2▸L3 　　　{6 8 10 12}	Add L1 and L2 and place the results in L3. Note that the results in L3 appear on the Home screen as {6 8 10 12}.

STAT 1

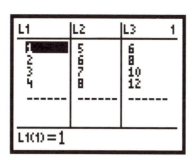

Check that L3 really does contain the values 6, 8, 10 and 12.

If L1 and L2 had contained lists of different lengths the calculator would have responded with the error message: ERR: DIM MISMATCH.

Finding the deviations from the mean

The following example calculates the mean of the values in L3 and stores the deviations from that mean in L4.

Press	See	Explanation
STAT ▶ 1 2nd [L3] ENTER	1-Var Stats x̄=9 Σx=36 Σx²=344 Sx=2.581988897 σx=2.236067977 ↓n=4	Calculate the mean of the values in L3. Note that the mean, $\bar{x}$, is 9.
2nd [L3] − VARS 5 2 STO▸ 2nd [L4] ENTER (5 selects the Statistics menu, then 2 selects $\bar{x}$, the most recently calculated mean.)	L3−x̄→L4 {-3 -1 1 3} ■	Find the deviations from the mean and store them in L4. The deviations have appeared on the Home screen: {‾3 ‾1 1 3}.

Finding the squares of values in a list

Press	See	Explanation
2nd [L4] x² STO▸ 2nd [L5] ENTER	L4²→L5 {9 1 1 9} ■	Enter the squares of the values of L4 into L5.

Finding the squares of the deviations from the mean

This example shows how to perform a more complicated set of instructions on a list of values. It involves performing the instructions in the last two subsections together in a single stage. In other words, it operates on list L3 and puts the squares of the deviations from the mean into L6.

Press	See	Explanation
[STAT] [▶] **1** [2nd] [L3] [ENTER]	1-Var Stats $\bar{x}=9$ $\Sigma x=36$ $\Sigma x^2=344$ $Sx=2.581988897$ $\sigma x=2.236067977$ ↓n=4	Calculate the mean of the values in L3.
[(] [2nd] [L3] [−] [VARS] **5 2** [)] [x²] [STO▶] [2nd] [L6] [ENTER]	$(L_3-\bar{x})^2 \rightarrow L_6$ {9 1 1 9}	Find the squared deviations by subtracting the mean from each value in L3 and squaring the deviations. The results are stored in L6.
[STAT] **1** [▶] [▶] [▶] [▶] [▶]	L4 L5 L6 6 ... L6(1)=9	Check that L6 really does contain the same values as L5. The values in L5 and L6 are identical.

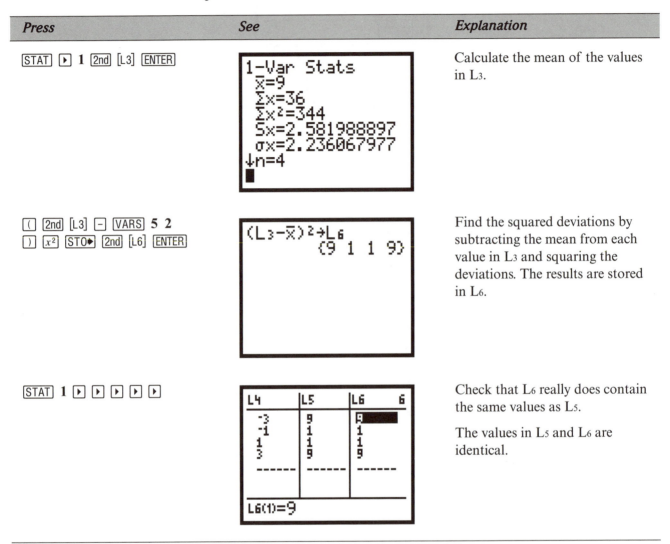

Joining and comparing lists

In this example the list of numbers in L2 is added on to the end of the list in L1. Start by clearing all lists (use option 4 in the MEM menu). Enter {1, 2, 3, 4} in L1 and {5, 6, 7, 8, 9} in L2.

In Chapter 4 you were shown two ways to concatenate or join two lists. the first method involved a series of steps as follows.

Since L1 contains 4 values and L2 contains 5, L3 will have 9 values. Return to the Home screen and follow these steps.

Press	See	Explanation
9 [STO▸] [2nd] [LIST] [▸] 3 [2nd] [L1] [ )] [ENTER] 9 [STO▸] [2nd] [LIST] [▸] 3 [2nd] [L2] [ )] [ENTER]	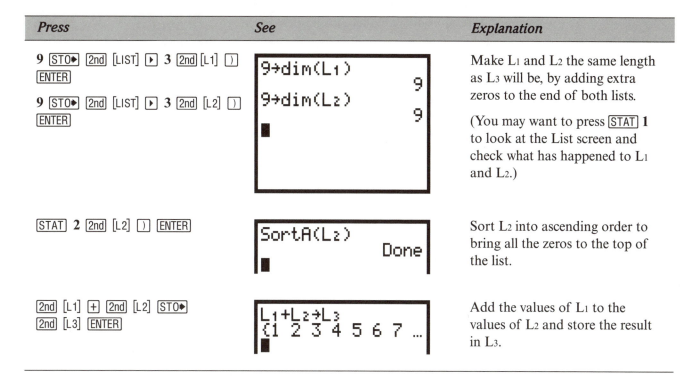	Make L_1 and L_2 the same length as L_3 will be, by adding extra zeros to the end of both lists. (You may want to press [STAT] 1 to look at the List screen and check what has happened to L_1 and L_2.)
[STAT] 2 [2nd] [L2] [ )] [ENTER]	SortA(L₂) Done	Sort L_2 into ascending order to bring all the zeros to the top of the list.
[2nd] [L1] [+] [2nd] [L2] [STO▸] [2nd] [L3] [ENTER]	L₁+L₂→L₃ {1 2 3 4 5 6 7 ...	Add the values of L_1 to the values of L_2 and store the result in L_3.

A second method uses **augment** (option 9 in the LIST OPS menu) to store a combined list. Use **augment** to store the combined list in L_4.

Now compare the lists in L_3 and L_4. Since they contain a small number of values, they can be compared easily on the list screen. If they were longer lists you could compare them easily as follows.

Enter on the Home screen $L_3 - L_4 \rightarrow L_5$.

Now work out the sum of the values in L_5 by using option 5 in the LIST MATH menu to enter **sum(L_5)**.

5.8 CATALOG

You have already met a large number of the TI-83 facilities, many of which are contained in menus. You may well be finding it difficult to remember which menu you need, especially if you have not used the particular facility for some time. Fortunately, the TI-83 has an alphabetical list of all the functions and instructions contained in a CATALOG, and this provides an alphabetical means of pasting the facility onto the Home screen (or other appropriate screens).

Starting from the Home screen press [2nd] [CATALOG].

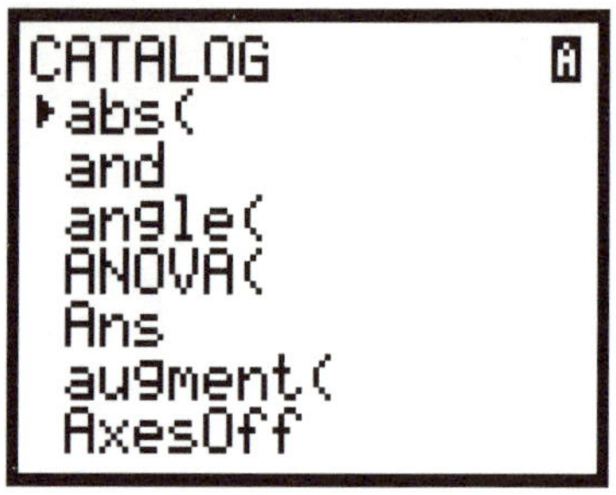

Move the cursor downwards to scroll through the functions and instructions. Most of these you have not used yet, but some you will recognize. Suppose you wished to paste **seq(** onto the Home screen. You could scroll down until you reached it, but this would take a very long time. Alternatively press **S** (that is the third function of the black key marked **LN**) and the cursor will jump to the entries beginning with S. When the cursor is beside **seq(**, press [ENTER] to paste it onto the Home screen.

```
CATALOG          A
▶abs(
 and
 angle(
 ANOVA(
 Ans
 augment(
 AxesOff
```

```
CATALOG          A
 Sci
 Select(
 Send(
▶seq(
 Seq
 Sequential
 SetUpEditor
```

If the problem is not where to find the function or facility but rather how to use it, you will need to refer to Appendix A of the *TI-83 Guidebook*. For example, **seq** is on p. A-31, and there you are reminded about how to use its five arguments.

Brain stretcher   *What does dim do?*

Option 3 in the LIST OPS Menu is labelled **dim**. See if you can find out what it does without using the *TI-83 Guidebook*.

Try entering

dim(L_1)
dim(L_2)
…

Or try

$3 \rightarrow$ dim(L_1)
$5 \rightarrow$ dim(L_1)
…

Can you predict what $0 \rightarrow$ dim(L_1) would do?

Brain stretcher   Statsnaps

Can you produce the following screen displays on your TI-83?

```
1-Var Stats
 x̄=3
 Σx=9
 Σx²=35
 Sx=2
 σx=1.632993162
↓n=3
■
```

```
2-Var Stats
↑n=3
 ȳ=3
 Σy=9
 Σy²=29
 Sy=1
↓σy=.8164965809
```

```
σx
                0
x̄
                6
Σx
               24
■
```

```
n
                3
x̄
               10
Med
                2
■
```

```
{Σx,Q₃,Σx²,n}
        {0 1 2 3}
```

```
{minX,n,maxX,Σx,
Σx²}
  {0 4 10 20 168}
■
```

Chapter 6 Line graphs and list arithmetic

In this chapter, you will use your calculator to display a line graph of a set of data, looking, in particular, at the effect different window settings can have on the shape of a graph. You will also learn how to use the calculator to carry out arithmetic on lists of numbers in order to simplify repetitive calculations.

6.1 Displaying and interpreting a line graph

In Chapter 4, you saw how to draw a scatterplot on your calculator. The values to be plotted on the horizontal axis were entered into one list in the calculator, and the corresponding values to be plotted on the vertical axis were entered in another list. You then used the STAT PLOTs menu to set up a scatterplot and displayed the points on the Graphing screen.

line graph

If you choose a different option in the STAT PLOTs menu, the calculator will draw a **line graph** from the set of data. The calculator plots the points in the order in which their coordinates occur in the lists, joining each point to the previous one with a line.

To demonstrate how to use the calculator to draw line graphs, this chapter uses data taken from a 1:25 000 Ordnance Survey map showing part of the Peak District in Derbyshire. A section of the map is reproduced in Figure 6.1. Locate Hollins Cross on the map where the two thick lines cross. It lies at the top of a ridge, roughly north-west of Castleton. Notice the broken line shown on the map, which runs roughly north-west to south-east through the ridge at Hollins Cross. Imagine that a vertical cut has been made down through the ridge along that line. What would the profile of the ridge look like? How does the slope of the hillside change as the ground rises from the Vale of Edale in the north-west up to Hollins Cross and then falls again towards Castleton in the south-east?

By entering height information given by the contour lines and distance information calculated from the map, you can display the profile of the ridge at Hollins Cross on your calculator. Table 6.1 gives heights in metres estimated from the contour lines and distances measured in millimetres directly from the map. Distances measured on the map north-west from Hollins Cross are shown as negative to distinguish them from distances measured along the line towards the south-east.

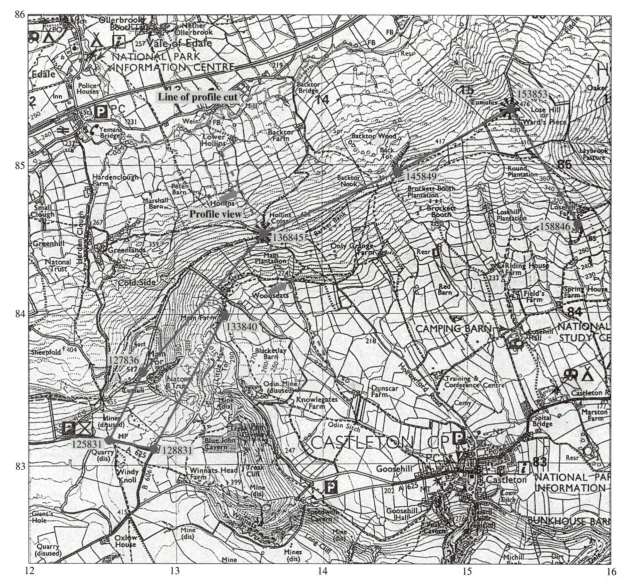

Figure 6.1   *Map of part of the Derbyshire Peak District. © Crown copyright (399582)*

Table 6.1   Map distances and estimated heights to the north-west and south-east of Hollins Cross

Map distances (millimetres)	Height (metres)	Map distances (millimetres)	Height (metres)
⁻31	230	2.5	370
⁻23	250	5	350
⁻17	270	7	330
⁻13	290	9.5	310
⁻10.5	310	11	300
⁻8.5	330	13	280
⁻6	350	17.5	260
⁻3.5	370	21	250
⁻2	380	25	240
⁻1	390	30	230
1	390		

Displaying a line graph

To display a profile of the ridge, you must enter these data into your calculator, then convert the map distances to metres using the map scale, and finally choose an appropriate window to display a line graph showing height in metres against distances in metres.

Here are the steps to follow.

◇ Clear the lists on your calculator and enter the map distances in list L_1 and the heights in list L_2. Note that there are 21 values in each list – a useful check that you have not omitted a value or entered one twice.

◇ Now you need to scale the data in list L_1, so that it represents distances in metres. The scale of the Ordnance Survey map is 1:25000. So 1 millimetre on the map represents a distance of 25000 millimetres on the ground or 25000/1000 = 25 metres.

So each entry in list L_1 must be multiplied by 25 to convert it to metres on the ground. All the data values in L_1 can easily be multiplied by 25 like this.

Press [2nd] [QUIT] to return to the Home screen.

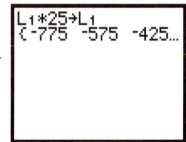

Press [2nd] [L1] [×] **2 5** [STO▸] [2nd] [L1] [ENTER].

You should see the display shown on the right. What you have done is told the calculator to multiply all the values in list L_1 by 25 and then to store the results back in L_1.

The first three new values in L_1, representing the first three distances in metres, have appeared on the screen. You can inspect the other values in L_1 either by scrolling to the right through the list on the Home screen or by pressing [STAT] **1** and checking the lists on the List screen.

◇ The next step is to set up the plot for a line graph of the heights in L_2 against the distances in L_1.

Press [2nd] [STAT PLOT] and select **Plot 1**.

The icon ⌐⌐⌐ represents a line graph.

Use the cursor keys and [ENTER] to select the options shown on the right. The **Xlist** and the **Ylist** values can be inserted by pressing [2nd] [L1] and [2nd] [L2] respectively.

Selecting L_1 for **Xlist** and L_2 for **Ylist** results in distances being plotted horizontally and heights being plotted vertically. This feature allows you to choose which list is to be plotted against which.

◇ Press ZOOM **9**.

You should get the display shown on the right.

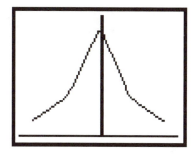

◇ Finally, press WINDOW to view the values which have been automatically set for **Xmin**, **Xmax**, **Ymin** and **Ymax**.

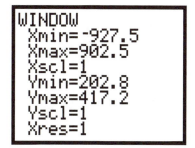

WINDOW
 Xmin=-927.5
 Xmax=902.5
 Xscl=1
 Ymin=202.8
 Ymax=417.2
 Yscl=1
 Xres=1

Exercise 6.1 *Hill profile*

Describe in words the shape of this profile.

How accurate a representation is this of the profile of the ridge?

Alternative window settings

The display reproduced above indicates a steeply sided peak. Hollins Cross is at the top. To the left of the peak is the profile of the ridge to the north-west and to the right is the profile of the slope to the south-east. The ground appears to slope away very steeply on both sides, getting less steep the further away from Hollins Cross you go.

The visual impression given by the display is that the gradient at the top of the ridge is very steep indeed. However, this is very misleading. The problem here is that the vertical scale has been exaggerated by the viewing window which has been set. A total horizontal distance of around 1800 metres and a vertical height change of around 200 metres are being represented over roughly the same screen distance. In other words, the viewing window exaggerates the vertical scale by about nine times relative to the horizontal scale. So the profile looks much more 'peaky' than it actually is.

Exercise 6.2   *Looking through different windows*

Here are two examples of the same Hollins Cross data, displayed with different window settings. You can see the effect on the profile. What window settings are needed to reproduce these? In both cases, the **Xscl** and **Yscl** settings are 100, so the tick marks along the axes give a clue to the other settings used.

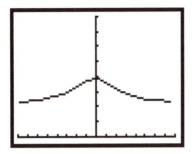
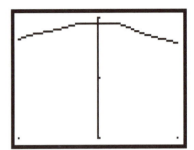

In the display on the left, the vertical axis runs from 0 to 800 metres. The slopes look less steep, although the height scale is still twice the distance scale.

In the display on the right, the height scale is from 200 to 400 metres, but the horizontal axis now goes from ⁻100 to 100 metres. Now the display shows only the profile of the ridge close to the top. Both axes cover the same distances, so this second display gives a visual impression which is closer to what the actual profile looks like. The height drops only by about 30 or 40 metres in 100 metres each side of Hollins Cross.

However, providing equal intervals on the horizontal and vertical axes still does not give a totally fair impression of the slope of the ridge. There is a further complication due to the fact that the display area of your calculator is not square, but fortunately the calculator has a built-in function to help overcome this problem.

First, press WINDOW and enter the window settings as shown here.

Now press ZOOM.

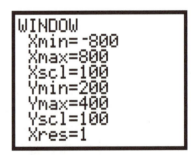

```
WINDOW
 Xmin=-800
 Xmax=800
 Xscl=100
 Ymin=200
 Ymax=400
 Yscl=100
 Xres=1
```

You should see the menu shown on the right. Like **ZoomStat**, all of these options allow you to adjust the viewing window quickly. The option required now is number 5: **ZSquare**. This will scale the viewing window so that distances on the horizontal and vertical axes are equal.

```
ZOOM MEMORY
1:ZBox
2:Zoom In
3:Zoom Out
4:ZDecimal
5:ZSquare
6:ZStandard
7↓ZTrig
```

Press **5** or, as usual when selecting from a menu, move the cursor down using ⬇ and then press ENTER.

The profile of the ridge, as shown on the calculator, should now look like this.

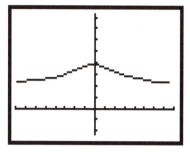

To see what has happened to the window settings, press WINDOW.

You should see that the settings have changed to those shown on the right.

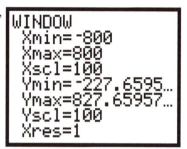

```
WINDOW
 Xmin=-800
 Xmax=800
 Xscl=100
 Ymin=-227.6595…
 Ymax=827.65957…
 Yscl=100
 Xres=1
```

The horizontal scale still ranges from ⁻800 to 800 metres, but now the vertical scale corresponds to a height change of over 1000 metres. Because the screen itself is slightly wider than it is high, it can display a longer distance horizontally than it can vertically. But using **ZSquare** means that equal screen distances correspond to equal distances in reality. The visual impression of the profile at Hollins Cross is now least distorted by the viewing window.

Brain stretcher   *Look through other windows*

Some of the following displays could not possibly represent the Hollins Cross data, no matter which window settings are used. Which ones?

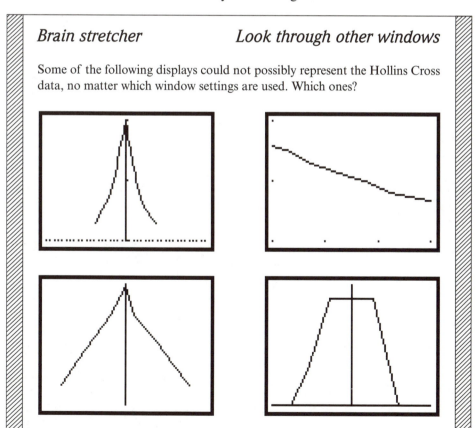

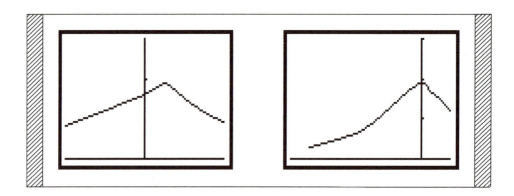

Using [TRACE] and calculating gradients

In Chapter 4, you used the trace facility on the calculator to move from point to point on a scatterplot and to display the corresponding values at the bottom of the screen. This facility can also be used with line graphs. Try pressing [TRACE] now. When you repeatedly press ▸, you can see the flashing cross move along the profile of the ridge with the corresponding distances and heights displayed **gradient** below. This enables you easily to find the **gradient** of the ridge between any two points.

The gradient is defined as:

$$\text{gradient} = \frac{\text{change of height}}{\text{horizontal distance}}$$

So using [TRACE], the two adjacent points on the extreme right of the profile would have the following values:

$$X = 625 \qquad Y = 240$$
$$X = 750 \qquad Y = 230$$

Thus:

$$\text{gradient} = \frac{240 - 230}{625 - 750} = \frac{10}{^-125} = {}^-0.08$$

So the gradient at the bottom of the south-east slope of the ridge is ⁻.08. This might well be stated as 1 in 12.5, or possibly as 8%. The negative sign indicates that it is a downward slope.

All this calculation could have been done on the Home screen of the calculator, perhaps noting down on paper the x- and y-values from lists L1 and L2, and then entering those numbers in an expression like the one shown on the right.

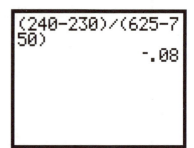

Note the importance of brackets in this calculation.

Alternatively, since 240 and 230 are the 20th and 21st values in L2, and 625 and 750 are the 20th and 21st values in L1, the calculation could have been entered like this.

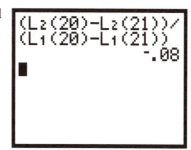

Here L2(20) is used to indicate the 20th value in list L2, and so on.

Exercise 6.3   *Finding the gradient using* TRACE

Using the trace facility on the calculator, and an appropriate viewing window, calculate the gradients near the top and the bottom of the north-west slope of the ridge.

Plotting a route

National **grid references** used on Ordnance Survey maps in the UK include six digits. The first three digits represent what are known as an **easting** and the last three digits make up the **northing**. The eastings and northings can be treated as coordinates and plotted on a graph, the eastings plotted along the horizontal axis and the northings plotted along the vertical axis.

grid references
easting
northing

The map is covered by grid lines spaced 1 kilometre apart and labelled with two-digit numbers which are the first two digits of an easting or a northing. Each kilometre square can be subdivided into smaller squares by imaginary lines 100 metres apart. These imaginary lines provide the third digit of an easting or a northing.

For example, Figure 6.2 shows that the grid reference of Hollins Cross is 136845. The easting is 136 since it lies about 6 tenths of the way across the squares to the east of grid line 13. The northing is 845, indicating a position 5 tenths of the way north of grid line 84.

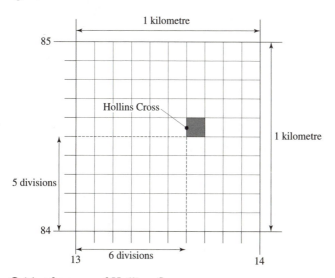

Figure 6.2   Grid reference of Hollins Cross.

In this section, you will be asked to enter on your calculator the eastings and northings of the grid references of places along the route of a walk. You will then be able to use the calculator to display a plot of the route. In the next section you will be able to use these grid references to calculate the straight-line distances between the points on the walk using Pythagoras' theorem. Doing this on the calculator quickly gives an estimate of the total distance of the walk, and avoids you having to make repeated calculations by hand.

Table 6.2 is a list of places and grid references for the walk which is marked on Figure 6.1. In the third and fourth columns of the table, the grid references have been split up into eastings and northings, or horizontal and vertical coordinates.

Table 6.2 Grid references for the walk

Location	Grid reference	Easting (horizontal)	Northing (vertical)
Mam Farm	133840	133	840
A625 road	128831	128	831
Footpath	125831	125	831
Mam Tor	127836	127	836
Hollins Cross	136845	136	845
Back Tor	145849	145	849
Lose Hill	153853	153	853
Losehill Farm	158846	158	846

The first task is to plot the data and display a line graph representing the route of the walk.

◇ Clear all the lists and enter the eastings into L_1 and the northings into L_2.

◇ Now select STAT PLOT and set the parameters of **Plot 1** (set **Plot 2** and **Plot 3** to **Off**). In order to get the eastings plotted horizontally and the northings vertically, make sure that **Xlist** is set to L_1 and **Ylist** is set to L_2. Check that your settings are like those shown on the right.

◇ Since the route of the walk is contained between eastings of 120 and 160, and between the northings of 830 and 860, the window settings shown here are appropriate. Press WINDOW and enter these settings on your calculator.

◇ Now press GRAPH and display the route of
the walk. Each location on the route is joined
to the next by a straight line.

The tick marks on the horizontal and vertical
axes correspond to the grid lines 12, 13, 14,
15 and 16 (eastings) and to 83, 84, 85 and 86
(northings) respectively.

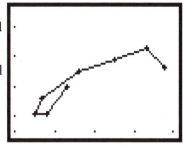

Grids – and moving around the Graphing screen

There is a feature of the calculator, **GridOn**, which enables you to make this
display look rather more like a map. This option is found within the FORMAT
menu. Find [FORMAT] now: it is the second function of the ZOOM key.

Press 2nd [FORMAT].

The FORMAT menu, shown on the right,
should appear. This is a similar to the MODE
menu as it has optional settings on each line.
The default settings are shown here.

Press ⏷ ⏷ ▶ ENTER to select GridOn.

Return to the Graphing screen by pressing
GRAPH.

The grid should have appeared, not marked
with lines as you may have expected, but
marked by dots where the grid lines would
cross. The spacing of these dots depends on the
Xscl and **Yscl** values which have been set in
WINDOW.

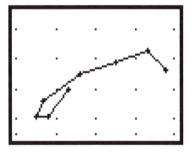

Of course, on the map the grid is square, whereas here the dots are at the corner
of rectangles, so the display can be improved still further by pressing ZOOM 5 to
select the **ZSquare** option.

Now press TRACE. You will see the usual flashing cursor appear at the first point
of the walk, 133840. At the bottom of the screen, you will see the coordinates of
this point's grid reference. Pressing ▶ moves the cursor to the next point on the
route. (Notice that on this occasion pressing the right cursor key actually moves
the cursor to the left!)

Continue pressing ▶ so that all of the points on the route, together with the
coordinates of their grid references, are displayed in turn.

One final feature of the TI-83 is worth mentioning in this subsection. You have
seen that using TRACE causes coordinates to be displayed at the bottom of the
screen, but only the coordinates corresponding to the data that have been
entered in the lists. Suppose you wanted to know the coordinates of one of the
other points on the screen – one of the tick marks on the axes or one of the grid
points, perhaps. This can be done by using the cursor keys *before* you use TRACE.

Press GRAPH to ensure that tracing is not selected and press any of the cursor keys. A non-flashing cross appears together with its coordinates. The cross can be moved around at will by holding down any of the cursor keys. Try it for yourself.

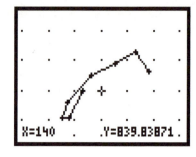

The display on the right shows the cross placed over one of the grid points with the corresponding coordinates given below.

Exercise 6.4 *From screen points to map points*

On the following screen display, six small boxes have been plotted representing particular points near the route of the walk.

For each of the six boxes:

(a) Move the non-flashing cursor on your calculator to the position marked by one of the small boxes and note down the coordinates that are displayed at the bottom of the screen (rounding them to the nearest integer).

(b) Use the map (Figure 6.1) to identify the points that have been marked.

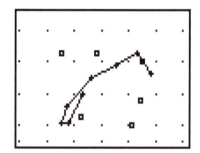

Before going any further, you may wish to remove the grid points from the Graphing screen by selecting **GridOff** from the FORMAT menu.

6.2 Arithmetic with lists

In this subsection, for every pair of points on the walk from Mam Farm to Losehill Farm, you will calculate the straight-line distances and also estimate the time taken. Fortunately, rather than doing all these calculations individually, there is a short cut which enables them all to be done at once.

Straight-line distances – Pythagoras' theorem

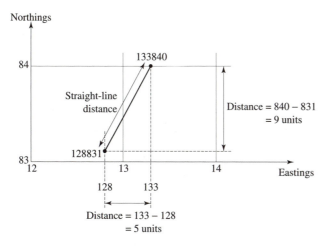

Figure 6.3   Using Pythagoras' theorem on an OS map.

Figure 6.3 shows the first two points on the walk connected by a straight line. This line forms the hypotenuse of a right-angled triangle. The eastings give the length of the horizontal side. You can see that it goes from 128 to 133. Remember that eastings and northings represent real distances in units of 100 metres or 0.1 km. So the length of the horizontal side is $133 - 128 = 5$ units.

Similarly, the northings give the length of the vertical side. It goes from 831 to 840, a distance of $840 - 831 = 9$ units.

By **Pythagoras' theorem**, the distance along the hypotenuse is

$$\sqrt{(133 - 128)^2 + (840 - 831)^2} = 10.3 \text{ (to one decimal place)}$$

Pythagoras' theorem

So the straight-line distance between the two points is 10.3 units (rounded to one decimal place). You could do a similar calculation for each stage of the walk. However, since the calculation is essentially the same for each stage of the walk, there is a quicker way which makes use of the names of lists, rather than the actual numerical data that they contain. In general, you need to work out the horizontal and vertical distances using the eastings and northings, and then use Pythagoras' theorem to work out the lengths of each hypotenuse.

Take the eastings first. Each easting needs to have subtracted from it the easting of the next location in the list. If you did this in a table, it would look like this.

Table 6.3   Calculating distances from eastings

Easting	Next easting	Distance between
133	128	$133 - 128$
128	125	$128 - 125$
125	127	$125 - 127$
127	136	$127 - 136$
136	145	$136 - 145$
145	153	$145 - 153$
153	158	$153 - 158$
158		

Do you see the pattern here? The first column is the original list of eastings, and the second column is that list moved up by one place. The third column is the second list subtracted from the first. Do not worry that some of the 'distances' are negative. All this means is that the easting of the next location is further to the east, and hence will be a larger number than the current easting. Since the differences are squared in Pythagoras' theorem, which makes them all positive, the negative sign has no effect on the calculations.

The northings are similar. You could set up another column for 'Next northings' and so work out the differences between the northings of consecutive locations.

You already have the original eastings and northings in lists L_1 and L_2 of your calculator. Now you need to produce lists containing the 'Next easting' and 'Next northing'. The method involves the following steps which are explained in detail below.

◇   Copy list L_1 to list L_3, and list L_2 to L_4.

◇   Remove the first data values in L_3 and L_4 to produce the required 'Next' columns.

◇   Remove the last data values in L_1 and L_2 which will no longer be of any use.

It would be possible to copy list L_1 to list L_3 by entering [2nd] [L1] [STO▸] [2nd] [L3] on the Home screen.

However, here is an alternative, more direct method.

Press [STAT] **1** [▸] [▸].

You should see the empty list L_3 as shown here.

Now rather than entering all the eastings again, press [▲] to select the whole of L_3. Notice that the highlighting is now right at the top of the screen and $L_3 =$ is displayed at the bottom.

Press [2nd] [L1] [ENTER].

The whole of L_1 will be copied to L_3.

Now remove the first data value (133) by simply pressing [DEL].

Your display should now look like the one on the right and L_3 is now the same as the 'Next easting' column in Table 6.3.

Now use a similar process to copy list L_2 into L_4 and remove the first data value. Check that the list L_4 contains seven values, the first of which is 831.

One final adjustment needs to be made to the lists before you can enter the formula for Pythagoras' theorem. Since you will not need the final elements, 158 and 846, from lists L_1 and L_2, respectively, you should delete them now. It is necessary to do this in order to make the lists all the same length – if you try to combine lists of different lengths the calculator will produce an error message. Check to make sure that you have exactly seven data values in each list L_1, L_2, L_3 and L_4.

Now for the big formula! Recall that the calculation carried out above to calculate the distance between the first and second data values was

$$\sqrt{(133 - 128)^2 + (840 - 831)^2} = 10.3 \qquad (1)$$

It seems appropriate to give all the distances correct to one decimal place, so change the Mode setting of your calculator so that it displays only one decimal place. If you have forgotten how to do this, look back to Chapter 1.

Each pair of eastings and northings must now be subtracted to find the horizontal and vertical distances between them. These differences must then be squared and added. Then the square root must be calculated to find the straight-line distance between consecutive locations by Pythagoras' theorem.

The calculation can be defined on the lists as a whole, with the answers stored in list L_5. Your calculator will then carry out the calculation for each of the elements in the list.

So the calculation to be carried out will be similar to the one in Equation (1) above, with particular numbers replaced by the lists:

$$\sqrt{(L_1 - L_3)^2 + (L_2 - L_4)^2} \text{ stored in } L_5$$

This is best entered on the Home screen.

Press

2nd [QUIT]
2nd [√] ([ ) 2nd [L1] – 2nd [L3] ( )) x^2
+ ([ ) 2nd [L2] – 2nd [L4] ( )) x^2 ( ))
STO▸ 2nd [L5]

Check that your display is as shown here and then press ENTER.

$\sqrt{((L_1-L_3)^2+(L_2-L_4)^2)} \to L_5$

Press STAT 1 and scroll across to have a look at the calculated distances for each stage of the walk. Notice that at the bottom of the screen the first data value of L_5 is given to at least eight decimal places, whereas in the list itself it is given to only one. This serves as a reminder that setting the number of decimal places using Mode causes the calculator only to change the way it *displays* numbers: it still calculates and stores them with its usual accuracy.

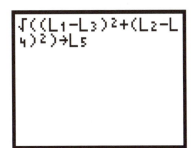

L3	L4	L5	5
128.0	831.0	10.3	
125.0	831.0	3.0	
127.0	836.0	5.4	
136.0	845.0	12.7	
145.0	849.0	9.8	
153.0	853.0	8.9	
158.0	846.0	8.6	

L5(1)=10.29563014…

Remember that the distances in L5 are given in units of 100 metres or 0.1 km. It would be useful to convert them to kilometres by dividing them all by 10. This can be done easily on the List screen by pressing

▲ [2nd] [L5] [÷] **1 0** [ENTER]

List L5 should now contain the straight-line distances in kilometres for each stage of the walk. You may be thinking that all this was quite difficult and that it might have been easier simply to apply Pythagoras' theorem to each set of data values in turn. However, the method you used here would work equally well if there were lots more stages to the walk. Even for only seven stages, the number of key presses needed was far less using this generalized method to operate on the lists.

You can easily add all the values in L5 to get an estimate of the total distance for the walk using any of the methods for finding the sum of data values in a list that were covered in previous chapters. The total distance should be 5.9 km.

Exercise 6.5 *As the crow flies*

Many species of birds migrate, covering vast distances every year. But not the crow. The longest recorded movement by an English Carrion Crow (*Corvus corone corone*) occurred in 1992–3. The bird was ringed as a nestling in Budby, Nottinghamshire (GR 462370) in May 1992 and found a year later in Freckenham, Suffolk (GR 566272). How far had this crow flown? The units of the eastings and northings given in the grid references here are 1 kilometre.

Walking time – Naismith's rule

In the previous subsection, you calculated the distances for each part of the walk from Mam Farm to Losehill Farm. Figure 6.4 shows the route card made out by a walker in planning that walk. It contains information about grid references, compass bearings, distances between points on the walk and the total ascent for each stage.

Date	11 April 1995				
From: Mam Farm		grid ref: 133840		starting time: 10 am	
To: Losehill Farm		grid ref: 158846		est. arrival time:	
Path to	Grid reference	Compass bearing (degrees)	Distance (kilometres)	Height climbed (metres)	Estimated time (minutes)
A625 road	128831	212	1.0	90	
Footpath	125831	287	0.3	20	
Mam Tor	127836	352	0.5	107	
Hollins Cross	136845	24	1.3	0	
Back Tor	145849	91	1.0	40	
Lose Hill	153853	35	0.9	76	
Losehill Farm	158846	156	0.9	0	
Total			5.9	333	

Figure 6.4 Route card for the walk.

There is a rule of thumb which is used by hill walkers to estimate the time taken to walk across open, hilly country. The formula, known as Naismith's rule, is as follows:

$$\text{Time in hours} = \frac{\text{horizontal distance in kilometres}}{5} + \frac{\text{total ascent in metres}}{600}$$

Exercise 6.6   Time for a walk

You should be able to enter a single formula on your calculator to work out the predicted time for each stage of the walk on the route card. You should also now be familiar with the techniques of working with lists, so what follows is just an outline of the procedure.

◇   You probably already have the horizontal distances in list L_5. Copy that list to L_1 and enter the heights climbed for each stage in list L_2. Clear all the other lists.

◇   Enter the Naismith formula on the Home screen using the data values in L_1 and L_2 to calculate the time for each stage of the walk. Store the results in list L_3.

◇ L_3 will contain the times in hours. Convert these to minutes using a list operation and store the result in L_4.

◇   Use the **sum** function in the LIST MATH menu to add up the elements of L_4 and so obtain an estimate for the total time of the walk in minutes.

◇   Enter the calculated times in the final column of the route card in Figure 6.4. Also enter the estimated arrival time.

Exercise 6.7   Modified Naismith

When preparing a route card, walkers often measure the straight-line distance on the map in millimetres.

How would you modify the formula for Naismith's rule, so that map measurements of the walk could be entered in your calculator directly in millimetres, without first converting to kilometres?

If your calculator is still set to display one decimal place, you may want to change it back to floating point mode now.

Brain stretcher   *Lost on the List screen?*

Try to predict what effect each of the following key sequences will produce on the List screen, and then try out your predictions.

Start by clearing all the lists and entering the data values {1, 2, 3, 4, 5} into list L1 on the List screen.

(a) [▶] [▲] [2nd] [L1] [x^2] [ENTER]

(b) [▲] **1 0** [−] [2nd] [√] [2nd] [L2] [ )] [ENTER]

(c) [▶] [2nd] [L1] [( ] **1** [ )] [+] [2nd] [L2] [( ] **1** [ )] [ENTER]

(d) [▲] [▲] [2nd] [L1] [+] [2nd] [L2] [ENTER]

(e) [▲] [CLEAR] [ENTER]

(f) [◀] [▲] [CLEAR] [ENTER]

(g) [◀] [▲] [CLEAR] [ENTER]

Chapter 7 Using Y= to draw graphs

In this chapter, you will extend your knowledge of the graph-plotting techniques that the TI-83 calculator provides. First, you will draw distance–time graphs and use them to calculate average speeds. This is followed by a section which explains how your calculator displays graphs in a different way – based on formulas, using the Y= key. You will learn how to enter simple formulas and explore the resulting graphs and tables of values.

Also in this chapter you will be encouraged to look more closely at the calculator's display. Why are some lines not as straight as they should be?

Finally, you will be shown how to write and store a short program on your calculator.

7.1   Distance–time graphs

In Chapter 6, you completed a route card for the walk from Mam Farm to Losehill Farm which showed the distance of each stage and the estimated time to walk the distance predicted by Naismith's rule. Look back at the route card now. You can use this information to display a distance–time plot of the walk on your calculator.

On your calculator, clear all six lists and then enter the data below. Enter the time for each stage of the walk in list L_1, and the corresponding distances in list L_2.

L_1 time (minutes)	L_2 distance (km)
0	0
21	1.0
6	0.3
17	0.5
15	1.3
16	1.0
18	0.9
10	0.9

Now you need the **cumulative** times and distances: that is, the total time and distance so far at each stage of the walk.

cumulative

The TI-83 provides a means of calculating cumulative sums of elements in a list using one of the commands listed in the LIST OPS menu. First, return to the home screen by pressing 2nd [QUIT].

Press

2nd [LIST] ▶ 6 2nd [L1]) STO▶ 2nd [L3] ENTER.

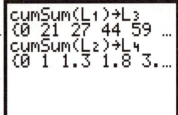

This has the effect of storing the cumulative sums of the L_1 values in list L_3. Check on the List screen to see that this list has been entered correctly.

Now store the cumulative sums of L_2 in L_4.

Using **ZoomStat**, display a distance–time plot of the cumulated data. You should choose a line graph from the STAT PLOT menu, plotting L_3 along the horizontal axis and L_4 along the vertical axis.

Your calculator should produce something looking like this.

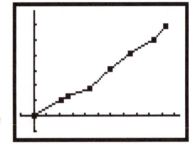

Notice that the graph is made up of a series of separate straight-line sections, each with a different slope. Each straight-line section corresponds to a section of the walk, and the gradient of each straight line corresponds to the average speed over the section, according to the time predicted by Naismith's rule.

Exercise 7.1 *Walking speed*

Describe in words how the predicted average walking speed varies from point to point along the walk. Bear in mind that steeper gradients on a distance–time graph represent faster speeds, whereas gentler gradients represent lower speeds.

In a distance–time graph the gradient of a straight-line section is equal to the change in distance divided by the time taken to travel that distance. The gradient gives the average speed for the section of the walk:

$$\text{average speed} = \frac{\text{distance}}{\text{time}}$$

So over the first section of the walk:

$$\text{average speed} = \frac{1.0}{21} = 0.048 \text{ km per minute}$$

In more familiar units of measurement, this is $0.048 \times 60 = 2.9$ km per hour.

The third stage of the walk, from the footpath up to the top of Mam Tor, is steeper (check with the route card) so you would expect a lower average speed.

$$\text{Average speed} = \frac{\text{distance}}{\text{time}} = \frac{0.5}{17}$$

$$= 0.029 \text{ km per minute, or about } 1.8 \text{ km per hour}$$

Now you could repeat this calculation for each section of the walk. This would give a list of average speeds which could be plotted to get a visual representation of how walking speed varies with time. But, as you saw in Chapter 6, you can easily set up the calculator to do this repetitive calculation.

On the calculator follow these steps.

◇ Press [STAT] **1** to display the lists of data.

◇ Move the cursor so that it is over L5 *above* the list as shown here.

◇ You want to divide each distance in L2 by the corresponding time in L1, and store the result of the calculation as a list in L5, so try pressing

[2nd] [L2] [÷] [2nd] [L1] [ENTER]

Why has an error occurred?

The reason is that the first element of list L1 is zero, and the calculator will not allow division by zero. To avoid getting this error message, you could replace 0 at the top of list L1 by a small number, say, 0.001. The first division would then be 0/0.001 which is acceptable to the calculator, and which would give an answer of zero as required.

Press **1** to quit from the entry which is causing the error, make the change to L1(1) and re-enter the division instruction for L5. You should see the results appear in list L5.

Because you have divided distances in kilometres by times in minutes, the numbers in L5 are average speeds expressed in kilometres per minute. To express these as kilometres per hour, you must multiply each element in L5 by 60. To do this:

◇ Place the cursor on L5 above the list.

◇ Press [2nd] [L5] [×] **6 0** [ENTER].

You should see the data values in L5 change to speeds in kilometres per hour.

By examining these values and relating them to the route card you should be able to pick out the sections where the highest and lowest speeds are reached on the walk.

The highest speed is 5.4 km per hour, reached on the last section between Lose Hill and Losehill Farm. The lowest speed is 1.8 km per hour, reached on the climb up to Mam Tor.

The next exercise provides an opportunity to practise producing a distance–time graph and calculating average speeds in another context – steam trains!

Exercise 7.2   Steam train, steam train...

Table 7.1 gives the distance between stops and part of the timetable for a Sunday service of the train BN1 of the Severn Valley steam railway.

(a) Use this information to display a distance–time graph of the journey of train BN1 on your calculator.

(b) Use the list operations on your calculator to produce a list of the average speeds during the journey.

Table 7.1   Extract from the Severn Valley Railway timetable

	Distance (km)	BN1
Bridgnorth	0	dep. 11.00
Hampton Loade	7.2	arr. 11.17 dep. 11.20
Highley	3.3	arr. 11.28 dep. 11.30
Arley	3.5	arr. 11.38 dep. 11.41
Bewdley	6.0	arr. 11.54 dep. 11.58
Kidderminster	4.5	arr. 12.09

7.2   Conversion graphs

Conversion graphs are used to convert from one system of units to another. For example, they can be used to show the relationship between metric and imperial measurements, between different currencies, or between different temperature scales. Many conversion graphs are straight lines which have a constant slope, or gradient. They describe a relationship between the scale along the horizontal axis of a graph and the scale along the vertical axis, and are often of the general form:

value on vertical axis = gradient × value on horizontal axis

So, for example, the formula to convert from miles to kilometres is:

distance in kilometres = 1.61 × distance in miles

If you enter this relationship appropriately, using [Y=], the key in the top left-hand corner of the keyboard, your calculator will display the corresponding conversion graph.

First, you must make sure that all STAT PLOTS are off. The quickest way of doing this is to select and confirm the **PlotsOff** option, by pressing [2nd] [STAT PLOT] **4** [ENTER].

Now press $\boxed{Y=}$ and you should see the display shown on the right. (There are in fact ten functions, from Y_1 through to Y_0, as you can see if you scroll downwards.)

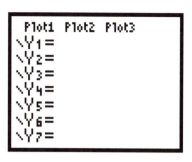

Notice the line at the top of the screen. If any of **Plot 1**, **Plot 2** or **Plot 3** were highlighted, it would mean that the corresponding plots were switched on. You can switch them on and off from this $Y=$ screen by selecting them with the cursor and pressing $\boxed{ENTER}$. Try switching one on and off now.

If there are any entries after the $=$ signs, position the cursor over the entry (anywhere after the $=$ sign will do) and press $\boxed{CLEAR}$.

In Chapter 4, when setting up a STAT PLOT on the calculator, you met the terms 'x-axis' and 'y-axis', which refer to the horizontal and vertical axes respectively. To plot a graph relating kilometres to miles, you can use Y_1 to represent the distance in kilometres and use X for the distance in miles. Then kilometres will be plotted along the vertical or y-axis and miles along the horizontal or x-axis.

The formula

$$\text{distance in kilometres} = 1.61 \times \text{distance in miles}$$

can be entered as

$$Y_1 = 1.61 \times X$$

The symbol $\times$ is the multiplication sign. The symbol X is provided on the calculator by the $\boxed{X,T,\Theta,n}$ key, to the left of the $\boxed{STAT}$ key. Locate it now. Using this key is a quicker and more convenient alternative to pressing $\boxed{ALPHA}$ **X**.

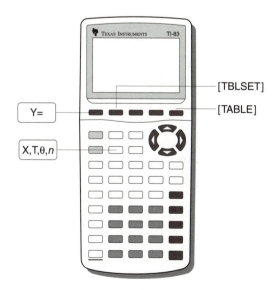

Position the cursor after $Y_1 =$ and press the following:

1 . 6 1 ⌧ X,T,Θ,*n*

The display should now look like this. Notice that the $=$ sign is highlighted to show that the formula is selected.

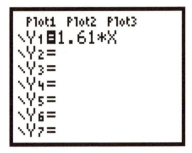

Now press WINDOW and set up the ranges on the *x*- and *y*-axes. For this example, the *x*-axis should represent 0 to 20 miles, and the *y*-axis should represent 0 to 35 km. Suitable window settings would be as shown here.

Press GRAPH and the calculator plots a graph of the formula.

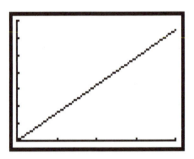

origin   The graph is a straight line (well, almost!) with a constant slope. The line passes through the **origin** of the graph, that is the point representing zero on both axes.

TABLE and TBLSET

Such a graph is a *diagrammatic* representation of the relationship between Y_1 and X, but there is another related feature of the calculator which provides a *numerical* representation of the relationship. Using [TABLE], the second function of the GRAPH key, will produce a table of values of X with corresponding values of Y_1.

However, before you try this out, press 2nd [TBLSET] using the second function of the WINDOW key. You should see something like the display shown here.

If your calculator shows any other value for **TblStart**, overtype it with a zero. If necessary, move the cursor to the right of Δ**Tbl**= and enter a 1 there. These values will ensure that a table is produced with X starting at 0 and going up in steps of 1 each time. (Δ is the Greek capital letter 'delta', corresponding to the letter D and is often used in mathematics to stand for a difference.)

Now press [2nd] [TABLE] and you should see a table of values like the one on the right.

Notice the values of Y1. Each is 1.61 times its corresponding value of X.

Press and hold down the ▼ key in order to see increasing values of X and Y1.

X	Y1	
0	0	
1	1.61	
2	3.22	
3	4.83	
4	6.44	
5	8.05	
6	9.66	

X=0

Now press [2nd] [TBLSET] again. You will probably find that **TblStart** has changed, indicating where you were in the table when you finished using the ▼ key. Try changing **TblStart** and **ΔTbl** to various different values and then press [2nd] [TABLE] to see the results.

Exercise 7.3 *Conversion tables*

Choose suitable settings for **TblStart** and **ΔTbl**, so that you can read off values from the table to complete the following.

Miles (X)	Kilometres (Y1)
30	
1.4	
10.86	
	6.44
	170
	5.0

Gradients

Now press [GRAPH] once again and think about the gradient of the line that is displayed. In Chapter 6, you saw that graphs could be made to look more steep or less steep by changing the window settings. Also in that chapter, a gradient was defined as:

$$\text{gradient} = \frac{\text{change of height}}{\text{horizontal distance}}$$

Here the graph does not represent heights and horizontal distances but distances in kilometres and distances in miles. A more general definition of the gradient of a graph is:

$$\text{gradient} = \frac{\text{change in } y\text{-values}}{\text{change in } x\text{-values}}$$

You have seen from the table that as the x-values are increased by 1, the y-values increase by 1.61. So the gradient of the line must be 1.61, and this is equal to the coefficient of X (that is, the number in front of the X) in the conversion formula.

Using TRACE

The trace facility behaves in a similar way for graphs drawn using the [Y=] key as for STAT PLOTS. It allows you to find the *x*- and *y*-values (also known as **coordinates** **coordinates**) of points on the graph.

Try pressing [TRACE] now.

The usual flashing cursor appears on the graph and at the bottom of the screen the *x*- and *y*-coordinates of the cursor position are displayed.

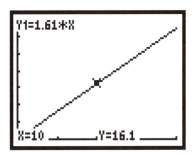

One difference is that at the top left-hand corner you will see Y1=1.61*X, indicating that this graph corresponds to the formula stored in Y1. (Recall that with STAT PLOTS there is **P1:L1** or **P2:L2,L3** and so on in the top left-hand corner, corresponding to **Plot 1** operating on L1, **Plot 2** operating on L2 and L3, and so on.)

As you have seen before, you can move the cursor along the line by using the [◄] and [►] keys. The coordinates at the bottom of the screen change as the cursor moves. Move the cursor and notice as you do so that the *x*-coordinate changes in equal fixed steps. These steps constrain the cursor position. You cannot move to just *any* position on the line. Try it for yourself and estimate the step size. Compare this process with the way that the table facility works. Notice that these step sizes are not the same as the current value of **ΔTbl**. So what does determine this step size?

Pixels

pixels The calculator screen is divided up into small squares, called **pixels** (standing for picture elements), and the cursor can only move from one pixel to the next. If you look very closely at the screen in good light, you may be able to see this grid of squares.

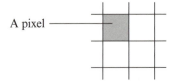

A pixel

Every shape that your calculator screen displays, whether it is a number, a mathematical symbol, a letter or a graph, must be made up from illuminated pixels. All the letters and digits on the Home screen, for example, are based on a 5 by 7 grid of pixels. Clear your calculator screen, enter a few digits and letters and look carefully at them. Each one is made by turning some of the 35 pixels in the grid on, and leaving the rest off. Figure 7.1 shows how the digit 3 is formed, for example.

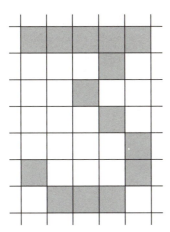

Figure 7.1 Pixels in a 5 by 7 grid making up the digit 3.

Many digital displays use similar ways of making up characters and symbols. Think for a moment where you might have seen one. Do they all use a 5 by 7 grid? Many displays use 3 by 5 grids. The information produced by trace on the Graphing screen is an example of this. Such displays have been specially designed – you might like to think about whether a 3 by 5 grid is the smallest grid that could be used to display all the digits, letters and symbols you might need. If a smaller grid were used, would it still achieve a legible display?

Brain stretcher   *Pixel designs*

How would you arrange pixels in a 3 by 5 grid to represent letters of the alphabet, symbols and digits?

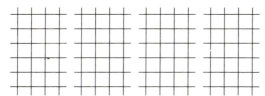

Some are harder than others. For example, how would you make an M, a Q or a W? And what about N?

The total screen area of the TI-83 calculator is 96 pixels wide and 64 high. The graph-drawing area is slightly smaller, however, at 95 pixels wide by 63 high. This means that there are 94 steps from pixel 1 to pixel 95 horizontally and 62 steps from pixel 1 to pixel 63 vertically. So, for any particular WINDOW setting, the x-range is divided up into (**Xmax** − **Xmin**)/94 discrete steps, and the y-range into (**Ymax** − **Ymin**)/62 discrete steps. In the display shown on p. 116, **Xmax** is 20 and **Xmin** is 0, so the size of each step in the x-direction (defined from the middle of one pixel to the middle of the adjacent one) should be (20 − 0)/94 = 0.21276... Starting at the left-hand edge of the screen the values of x represented by the centres of the pixels should be 0 (the first pixel), 0.21276..., 0.42553..., 0.63829..., and so on up to 20 (the 95th pixel).

Check this for yourself. Press $\boxed{\text{TRACE}}$ and move the cursor to X = 0, Y = 0. Then read off the values of X as you press $\boxed{\blacktriangleright}$ to move the cursor one step at a time along the graph.

The y-coordinate also changes as the cursor moves. The movement in the y-direction is also in a series of steps. If you look carefully, you will see that the graph itself is more like a staircase than a straight line, with some pixels next to each other in the horizontal direction. However, the value of the y-coordinate displayed at the bottom of the screen is not determined by the steps on the graph, but by the formula itself. So, for example, if you move the cursor so that X = 6.170, the y-coordinate will show 9.934 as you would expect, because $Y_1 = 1.61 \times X$. So here $Y_1 = 1.61 \times 6.170 = 9.934$. Now if you move the cursor one place to the right, the x-coordinate will change to 6.383 and the y-coordinate will be shown as 10.277 (because $Y_1 = 1.61 \times 6.383 = 10.277$).

If you look carefully, however, you will see that although the cursor has moved one position horizontally to the right along, the 'staircase' graph, the y-value has not changed sufficiently for a higher pixel to be turned on.

In summary, the calculator divides up the x-range into 94 steps. As the cursor moves along a given line, for each step in the x-direction it calculates the y-value from the formula.

Exercise 7.4   *Converting pounds to kilograms*

(a) Display a graph to convert from pounds to kilograms, using the information that 1 pound is equivalent to 454 grams. Choose the window so that masses up to 10 pounds can be represented. You will need to:

   ◇   write down the formula relating kilograms to pounds

   ◇   enter the formula in your calculator

   ◇   choose an appropriate window

(b) Use $\boxed{\text{TABLE}}$ to estimate:

   (i)   the equivalent mass in kilograms of 6 pounds

   (ii)   the equivalent mass in pounds of 2.5 kilograms

(c) Now repeat these estimates using the trace facility.

What is the step size used by the calculator in the x-direction?

7.3   Not-so-straight lines

You have already seen that a 'straight' line on the calculator display is not as straight as one you would draw yourself with a ruler on graph paper. The reason for this is that the calculator display is made up of a discrete rectangular grid of pixels each of which can only be either on (showing black) or off.

The plotting area on the calculator is 95 pixels wide by 63 high. The effect of 'discretizing' the plotting area by dividing it into small discrete squares is to introduce some distortion into the shape of a graph.

Look at Figure 7.2. This shows a straight-line graph drawn on squared paper. Now think of the squares as pixels on your calculator display. If the line passes through a pixel, the pixel is turned on. Figure 7.3 shows the effect: the line is now represented by a 'staircase' of pixels.

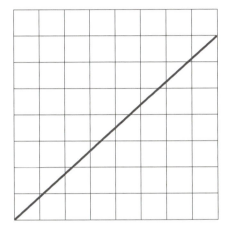

Figure 7.2   A straight line drawn on squared paper.

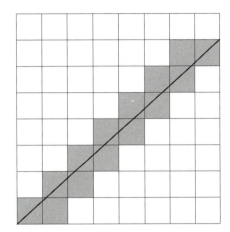

Figure 7.3   A straight line represented by pixels.

On a sheet of graph paper a line can be drawn anywhere. In principle, there are an infinite number of separate points on the paper that the line could pass through. On the calculator, however, there are only a finite number of pixels. This finite number places limits on what can be displayed without distortion. If you have access to a computer, you may have noticed this effect for yourself, where some 'straight' lines or edges are displayed on the screen as jagged 'staircases'. The more pixels, the greater the resolution of the display and the smoother the lines appear.

For straight lines on your calculator, the 'staircase' effect varies with the slope of the line. Figure 7.4 shows some examples. In (a), the line is horizontal and only a horizontal row of pixels is on. The line appears straight with no distortion. In (b), however, the line cuts across the corners of pixels – which must be on if the line passes through them – and you see a strong 'staircase' effect. In (c), the line cuts the pixels diagonally resulting in a single straight line. In (d), the steeper slope causes the line to pass through several pixels vertically for each one horizontally, and the 'straight-line' display is made up of a series of short, displaced vertical lines.

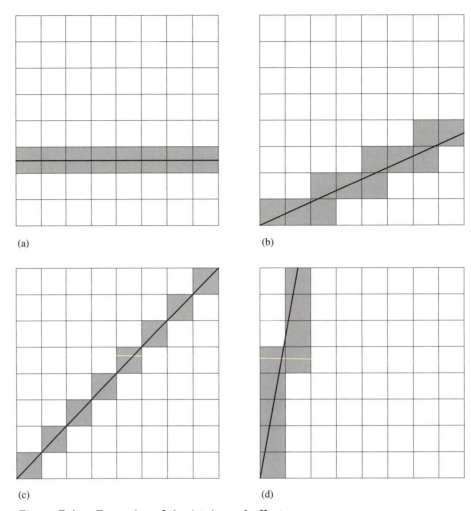

(a)

(b)

(c)

(d)

Figure 7.4   Examples of the 'staircase' effect.

Brain stretcher   *Maxpix*

What is the maximum number of pixels that can be on when a 'straight' line crosses a rectangular grid of pixels?

Think about an 8 by 8 grid like those above, or a 2 by 3 grid.

What about the 95 by 63 grid of the graph-drawing area of the TI-83?

On your calculator, you can display more than one graph at a time. Carry out each of the following steps to display three straight lines, each with a different slope. You will see the effect of the screen resolution on the appearance of the graph.

Press $\boxed{Y=}$ and clear any existing entries by positioning the cursor alongside the = sign and pressing $\boxed{CLEAR}$.

Position the cursor after Y$_1$ =. Press **0 . 5** ⊠ [X,T,Θ,*n*] [ENTER].

The cursor should now be at Y$_2$=. Press [X,T,Θ,*n*] [ENTER].

The cursor should now be at Y$_3$=. Press **8** ⊠ [X,T,Θ,*n*] [ENTER].

Leave Y$_4$, Y$_5$ ... and so on blank.

The screen should look like this.

You should recognize these as the formulas for three straight-line graphs, with slopes of 0.5, 1 and 8 respectively.
(Remember that the formula Y$_2$ = X is really Y$_2$ = 1 × X, hence a slope of 1.)

```
Plot1 Plot2 Plot3
\Y1∎0.5*X
\Y2∎X
\Y3∎8*X
\Y4=
\Y5=
\Y6=
\Y7=
```

Now press [WINDOW] and enter the settings shown here.

```
WINDOW
 Xmin=0
 Xmax=10
 Xscl=2
 Ymin=0
 Ymax=10
 Yscl=2
 Xres=1
```

Press [GRAPH] and the calculator will display the graphs together, plotting them one at a time. If you plotted the graphs on paper they would all be straight lines. On the calculator display (shown enlarged below), notice the different distortions caused by the finite resolution of the screen and the patterns formed by the pixels in the different 'staircases'.

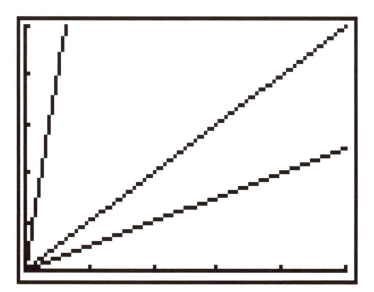

The window size sets both the *x*- and the *y*-axes to run from 0 to 10. This means that the range of 10 units will be spread over 95 pixels along the *x*-axis, but spread over only 63 pixels along the *y*-axis. The visual effect of squashing the vertical axis is to reduce the apparent slope of the graph. As you have seen in Chapter 6, you could correct this effect by pressing ZOOM and selecting 5: **ZSquare**. Do it now.

This recalculates the window size so that the step size is the same on both the *x*- and *y*-axes (that is, equal numbers of pixels represent equal quantities on both axes). The straight line with a slope of 1 should now run at 45 degrees to both axes.

Now press TRACE.

Notice that the flashing cursor is on the graph with the smallest slope, and that Y1=0.5*X has appeared in the top left-hand corner of the screen, indicating that you are tracing the graph plotted from this formula.

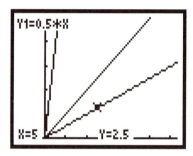

Pressing the cursor keys ⏶ or ⏷ will cause the cursor to jump to another graph and the formula in the top left-hand corner tells you which one. When you jump to graph 3, the cursor actually disappears from the screen. However, the coordinates at the bottom of the screen help you understand where the cursor has gone. Use the ⏴ key to bring the cursor back into the display area. For values of X above 1.129, the corresponding value of Y will be off the screen.

Exercise 7.5 *Trace or Table*

In this exercise, you are asked to carry out the same calculations using two different methods.

◇   Using TRACE position the cursor on graph 1 at X = 5. What is the corresponding value of Y?

By using the ⏶ or ⏷ keys to move between graphs (without changing the value of X), find the corresponding values of Y on graphs 2 and 3.

◇   Press 2nd [TBLSET] and set **TblStart** to 0 and Δ**Tbl** to 1.

Press 2nd [TABLE] and find the value of Y_1 corresponding to X = 5.

Use ⏵ to find the values of Y_2 and Y_3 corresponding to X = 5.

Finally in this section, practise your graphing skills with the next exercise, in which the straight line does not pass through the origin.

Exercise 7.6   Degree conversion

The formula to convert temperature from degrees Celsius to degrees Fahrenheit is

(Temperature in °F) = 1.8 × (Temperature in °C) + 32

◇ Press [Y=] and clear any entries.

◇ Enter the conversion formula using Y_1 to stand for temperature in °F and X to stand for temperature in °C.

◇ Display the conversion graph for the range ⁻50 °C to 50 °C, choosing suitable values for **Ymin** and **Ymax**.

◇ Using either the trace or the table facility, find the appropriate values of temperatures in °C and °F to complete the following table.

Temperature in °C	Temperature in °F
	100
20	
	32
⁻17.75	
	⁻40

◇ What happens to the graphing window if, when using [TRACE], you move the cursor outside the range ⁻50 °C to 50 °C?

7.4   Clearing the screen – at a stroke

By now, you will probably have realized that before you can start plotting anything on the Graphing screen you will usually need to clear away anything that has been plotted or drawn there before. There are in fact four different ways in which information can be displayed on this screen.

◇ Using [2nd] [STAT PLOT] allows you to draw scatterplots, *xy*-lines, frequency diagrams, modified boxplots, boxplots and normal probability plots.

◇ Using [Y=] allows you to draw the straight lines and curves associated with the functions specified in Y_1, Y_2, Y_3,...,Y_0.

◇ Using [2nd] [DRAW] allows you to draw on the screen in a variety of different ways – lines, points, circles, shading and so on.

◇ Selecting **GridOn** from the FORMAT menu displays a grid of points on the Graphing screen.

Associated with each of these four ways of putting things *on* the Graphing screen is a way of getting that information *off* the screen.

◇ **PlotsOff** (option 4 in the STAT PLOT menu) removes any statistical plots.

◇ Deselecting each of the functions Y_1, Y_2, Y_3,...,Y_0 will ensure that they are not plotted. To do this, it is necessary to press [Y=] and then, after moving the flashing cursor over any of the '=' signs which are highlighted, press ENTER to deselect that function. If you try this, you will see that the = sign is no longer highlighted. An alternative way is to use the VARS Y-VARS menu – option 4 of the Y-VARS submenu is **On/Off**. Selecting **FnOff** from this menu will deselect all the functions.

◇ **ClrDraw** (option 1 in the DRAW menu) removes any drawing.

◇ **GridOff** (within the FORMAT menu) removes the grid of points from the Graphing screen.

So, unlike the Home screen, which can be cleared with a single stroke of the CLEAR key, clearing the Graphing screen can sometimes be a lengthy business. However, with a little extra effort now, you can set the calculator up so that in future you will be able to clear the Graphing screen at a stroke (or at three strokes of the keys to be precise!). This involves giving the calculator a series of instructions to carry out and then saving this procedure in its memory. The **program** series of instructions is also known as a **program**.

The calculator has enough memory space for lots of these programs, and you will write several others as you work through this book. Each program needs to be assigned a name consisting of up to eight letters. The program to clear the Graphing screen could well be called, say, CLEARGS. Once a program has been written and stored, all you need to do to make the calculator carry out, or **execute**, the list of commands is to press PRGM, select the program from the list **edit** of names that appears and press ENTER. It is possible to **edit** a program at any stage, which means changing the list of commands.

To execute, edit or create a new program you need to press the PRGM key.

Carry out the following steps to write and store the CLEARGS program, which will clear the Graphing screen and reset the window to the standard settings.

Start by pressing PRGM.

Select NEW by pressing ◄.

Confirm this selection by pressing **1** or ENTER.

```
EXEC EDIT NEW
1▪Create New
```

You are prompted to enter a program name, which can have up to eight letters. The alpha lock comes on automatically, so you just need to use the appropriate third functions of the keys.

For example, **C** is the third function of the PRGM key, and **L** is the third function of the) key.

Enter the program name **C L E A R G S** to produce the display shown on the right.

```
PROGRAM
Name=CLEARGS
```

Press [ENTER].

You are now looking at the **program edit screen.** The colon at the beginning of the line indicates that this is the beginning of a new command.

program edit screen

You are now ready to enter the sequence of commands. This is done by selecting appropriate options from various menus and pasting them to the program edit screen.

The first command in the program will be an instruction to turn off the statistical plots.

Select option 4 from the STAT PLOT menu by pressing [2nd] [STAT PLOT] **4**.

PlotsOff is pasted on to the program edit screen.

You may have noticed that the STAT PLOT menu looked rather different from usual. This is the case for several of the menus when you are writing or editing a program.

Press [ENTER] to move to the next programming line. Notice that a colon is automatically inserted for the next command.

Press [VARS] [▶] **4 2**.

This selects **FnOff** from the **On/Off** submenu in VARS Y-VARS and pastes it on to the program edit screen.

Press [ENTER].

To select **ClrDraw** from the DRAW menu and add it to the program, press [2nd] [DRAW] **1** [ENTER].

Finally, add the command **GridOff** by pressing [2nd] [FORMAT] [▼] [▼] [ENTER].

The program is now complete.

To leave the program edit screen and return to the Home screen it is necessary to press [2nd] [QUIT]. (This is one of the occasions when [CLEAR] will not do!) Do it now.

The program is now ready to be executed.

Press the [PRGM] key.

You should see the screen on the right. Notice that the name of the program you have stored is now displayed as part of the menu.

EXEC is highlighted on the top line so pressing **1** will select CLEARGS.

Pressing ENTER will cause the program to be executed and a comforting message appears, to indicate that it has been completed.

If you now press GRAPH you should see a clear Graphing screen.

You may want to try displaying a STAT PLOT or other drawings and using CLEARGS to switch them off.

Any time from now on, if you want to clear the Graphing screen, all you have to do is to press PRGM 1 ENTER.

Brain stretcher   *Programmed conversion*

Here is a very short program to convert temperatures in °C to temperatures in °F. You could easily adapt it to carry out other conversions, such as pounds to kilograms or pesetas to pounds.

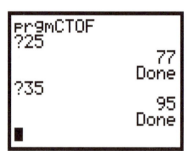

To enter the program you will need to press the following keys.

PRGM ◄ ENTER	Select **NEW** from the PRGM menu.
C T O F ENTER	Enter a name for the program.
PRGM ► **1**	Select **Input** from the PRGM I/O menu and paste to the program edit screen.
ALPHA **C** ENTER	Enter a memory location to hold the temperature in °C.
PRGM ► **3**	Select **Disp** (standing for Display) from the PRGM I/O menu and paste to the program edit screen.
3 2 ⊞ **1.8** ⊠ ALPHA **C** ENTER	Enter the formula to calculate the temperature in °F.
2nd [QUIT]	Return to the Home screen.

To run the program, press PRGM and select **CTOF** from the EXEC menu.

Press ENTER and a question mark appears, asking you to enter a number which will be stored in memory C. Enter a number, press ENTER and the corresponding temperature in °F is displayed. To run the program again, simply press ENTER.

Chapter 8 Formulas and functions

In Chapter 7, you saw how to store a simple formula in order to draw up a table of values and to plot its graph. All the graphs that you have produced so far are straight lines.

In this chapter, you will use some much more complicated formulas. Once you have entered the algebraic expressions on the Y= screen, you will be able to evaluate them for particular values of X. You can then construct tables of values to see how the values of the expressions change for regularly increasing values of X. Also, of course, you will be able to draw the graphs – which, for some of the formulas in this chapter, are anything but straight!

8.1 Storing algebraic formulas

This section deals with storing expressions and formulas, but first there are some things from earlier parts of this book which are worth recalling.

Formulas and mathematical functions

In Chapter 1, you saw how particular numerical values could be stored in the calculator's memory. For example, you stored the current VAT rate in memory V. In Chapter 7, you did something rather different: you stored *formulas* in the calculator's memory. For example, you stored the formula to convert from miles to kilometres.

In Chapter 1, a mathematical function was likened to a processor, which takes input numbers, processes them according to some rule, and produces output numbers. For example, a processor might take any input number, multiply it by 3, add 2 and square the result.

A formula which can be represented algebraically works in the same way: it takes an input and processes it to produce an output according to the rule encoded in the formula. For example, for the formula $B = (3A + 2)^2$ the input number is represented by A and the output number by B. Since A and B can stand for a whole variety of numbers they are known as **variables.**

variables

So a formula like $B = (3A + 2)^2$ specifies a mathematical function.

When you do algebra independently of the calculator, you have complete freedom in the choice of which letters to use for variables. However, the calculator imposes some restrictions on the symbols that can be used: x is used for the input variable and y for the output variable. This fits in with other uses of x and y in mathematics, such as their uses as names of coordinates and of axes when graphing.

With this choice of letters, formulas stored on the calculator always take the form

$y = $ expression involving x

In the example above, the formula has to take the form $y = (3x + 2)^2$.

dependent variable

independent variable

The variable y is called the **dependent variable**, because it depends on x (indeed, the formula shows exactly how it depends on x); x is called the **independent variable**.

As you have already seen, when doing algebra on the calculator there is no distinction between capitals and lower-case letters, though it is often important to keep them separate in other circumstances, where they may refer to *different* variables. In this book, key sequences involving the algebraic variable will always be written as X, but we shall consistently refer to the *x*-coordinate.

Storing a function

In Chapter 7, you saw how to enter a formula in your calculator using the Y= screen. Press the Y= key now.

$Y_1=$, $Y_2=$, $Y_3=$.... $Y_0=$ indicate that you can enter and store up to 10 functions at the same time. The numbers 1, 2, 3,...,0 serve only to distinguish the functions that have been stored; they have no algebraic significance. In particular, Y_2 (for instance) does not mean $Y \times 2$; it simply means the *y*-value for the second function. There may be expressions to the right of the equals sign in some lines of the display. Remove these existing functions using CLEAR.

Algebraic expressions are entered more or less as they are written, but the following points are worth noting.

◇   The X,T,Θ,*n* key can be used to produce an X in the display. (There are T, θ and n symbols on the key as well as the X because the same key is used in other situations, not dealt with in this chapter, in which the independent variable is taken to be T, θ or n.)

◇   Numbers are entered using the grey number keys in the usual way. It is particularly important to use the correct key for minus signs. If you have to enter a negative number (if your expression begins with a negative sign, for example) then you must use the grey (-) key, not the blue − one.

◇   The operations $+$, $-$ (when it denotes the numerical difference between two terms), $\times$ and $\div$ can be entered using the corresponding blue keys.

◇   It is not necessary to use the $\times$ key for multiplication: the convention that multiplication signs may be omitted works here, just as in written algebra. It is not wrong to use it, however, and of course it must be used when multiplying one number by another.

◇   Brackets should be used where there is any risk of ambiguity.

◇ x^2 can be entered by pressing X,T,Θ,*n* x^2, and other powers, square roots and so on (including those in the MATH menu) can be entered in the usual way.

◇   Fractions are entered using the $\div$ key. It is especially important to ensure that sufficient brackets are used to make it clear where the top and bottom of the fraction begin and end.

Here is an example to illustrate how to enter a complicated formula:

$$P = -\frac{2Q-1}{\sqrt{Q^2+1}}$$

The first step is to convert the function into the required form, which is

$$y = -\frac{2x-1}{\sqrt{x^2+1}}$$

Consider how to enter this expression. It includes an **algebraic fraction** with a numerator, $2x - 1$, and a denominator, $\sqrt{(x^2 + 1)}$, which must be carefully distinguished by brackets. When entering the denominator you must ensure that it is clear that the square root of the whole expression $x^2 + 1$ is taken. Another thing to note is that the right-hand side of the formula begins with a minus sign, which must be entered using the grey $\boxed{\text{(-)}}$ key.

algebraic fraction

On the Y= screen, place the cursor on the right of $Y_1=$ and press

$\boxed{\text{(-)}}$ $\boxed{(}$ **2** $\boxed{\text{X,T,}\Theta,n}$ $\boxed{-}$ **1** $\boxed{)}$

This completes the numerator. Note the use of brackets and the minus sign at the beginning.

```
Plot1  Plot2  Plot3
\Y1◘-(2X-1)
\Y2=
\Y3=
\Y4=
\Y5=
\Y6=
\Y7=
```

Now press

$\boxed{\div}$ $\boxed{\text{2nd}}$ $\boxed{\sqrt{}}$ $\boxed{\text{X,T,}\Theta,n}$ $\boxed{x^2}$ $\boxed{+}$ **1** $\boxed{)}$

Notice the square root and again the use of brackets in the denominator.

Also notice that when the expression became too long to fit on one line, it automatically ran over into the next one.

```
Plot1  Plot2  Plot3
\Y1◘-(2X-1)/√(X²
+1)
\Y2=
\Y3=
\Y4=
\Y5=
\Y6=
```

If you make an error when entering a function, it can be edited in the usual way by overtyping or by using the $\boxed{\text{DEL}}$ or $\boxed{\text{INS}}$ keys. However, if you make a syntax error of which you are not aware, the calculator will not indicate the error until it tries to evaluate the function. For example, if you used the wrong minus sign in the example above, it would not be until you tried to plot the graph or draw up the table of values, that the calculator would be able to identify the error.

The next exercise will give you more practice at entering algebraic functions.

Exercise 8.1   *Entering formulas*

(a) The surface area A of a sphere of radius r is given by the formula $A = 4\pi r^2$.

   Convert this to a suitable form using x and y and enter it as Y_2 on the Y= screen.

(b) Enter as Y_3 the formula for converting from °Celsius to °Fahrenheit:

$$f = \frac{9}{5}c + 32$$

(c) Enter as Y_4 the function $y = 0.5(x - 1.9)^2 - 5$.

You now have four functions stored in the Y= screen. You will need these functions in the rest of the chapter, so do not clear them from the Y= screen. However, it is safe to switch the calculator off if you want to take a break, as they will still be there when you switch on again.

The next three sections deal with three different ways of finding the values of y which correspond to particular values of x for the formulas in Y_1, Y_2, Y_3,...,Y_0.

8.2   Finding values from the Home screen

In this section, you will see how to work out the value of y for particular values of x using any formula which has been stored on the $Y=$ screen.

Suppose, for example, you wish to know the value of y corresponding to $x = 3.4$ when $y = 0.5(x - 1.9)^2 - 5$, the formula which is stored in Y_4.

Return to the Home screen, if necessary, and store 3.4 in X by pressing

3 . 4 [STO▸] [X,T,Θ,n] [ENTER]

The value of Y_4 can be evaluated using the VARS Y-VARS submenu.

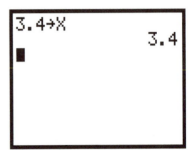

Press [VARS] [▶].

Notice that VARS Y-VARS has four submenus – you need the first of these at the moment.

Press **1** or [ENTER] to see the FUNCTION submenu.

Select Y_4 and paste it to the Home screen by pressing **4**.

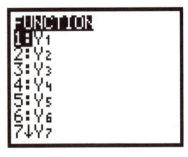

Press [ENTER] to evaluate y.

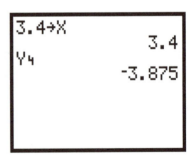

Now suppose you wish to use this formula to evaluate y for several values of x. You could repeat the procedure above, perhaps using [2nd] [ENTRY]; try this for $x = 9.2$.

Press

9 . 2 [STO▸] [X,T,Θ,n] [ENTER]
[2nd] [ENTRY] [2nd] [ENTRY] [ENTER]

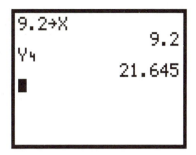

A slightly shorter (but perhaps less obvious) way of evaluating a function on the Home screen involves entering the name of the function followed by the value of x enclosed in brackets. For example, to evaluate Y_4 for $x = 9.2$ you can enter $Y_4(9.2)$. This can be read as 'Y_4 of 9.2'.

The two calculations done above can then be carried out like this.

Press

[VARS] [▸] **1 4** [(] **3 . 4** [)] [ENTER]
[2nd] [ENTRY] [◂] [◂] [◂] [◂] **9 . 2** [)] [ENTER]

```
Y4(3.4)
              -3.875
Y4(9.2)
              21.645
```

If you have to evaluate the function for several values of x, it is sometimes worth entering them into a list first. For example, suppose you needed to evaluate the function stored in Y_2 for the values 0.3, 1.5, 2.6, 3.9 and 4.5. First, enter these values into list L_1 in the usual way.

Then return to the Home screen and press

[VARS] [▸] **1 2** [(] [2nd] [L1] [)] [ENTER]

The values of Y_2 appear in a list as shown here. By scrolling to the right, using [▸] repeatedly, the remaining values can be seen.

```
Y2(L1)
{1.130973355 28…
```

Alternatively, the calculated values could themselves be stored in a list by entering $Y_2(L_1) \rightarrow L_2$.

Exercise 8.2   *Evaluating functions on the Home screen*

(a) Evaluate the function stored as Y_1 for $x = 5$.

(b) Using the formula stored in Y_3, find the Fahrenheit equivalents of 15°C, 18°C, and 30°C.

(c) The radii of the planets of the solar system, in thousands of miles, are given in the table below. Assuming that they are spherical (not quite accurate, but near enough), use the formula stored in Y_2 to find the surface area of each of the planets. You will probably find it best to store the radii in a list.

Planet	Radius
Mercury	1.52
Venus	3.76
Earth	3.96
Mars	2.10
Jupiter	42.90
Saturn	35.5
Uranus	16.0
Neptune	15.8
Pluto	1.09

8.3 More about tables of values

If you want to evaluate a formula for large numbers of values of x, then, as you saw in Chapter 7, it is often quicker to set up a table to display the values.

You should still have the functions that you entered in Section 8.1 stored in the Y= screen. If you have changed any of them, you should re-enter the formulas now.

```
Plot1 Plot2 Plot3
\Y1目-(2X-1)/√(X²
+1)
\Y2目4πX²
\Y3目1.8X+32
\Y4目.5(X-1.9)²-5

\Y5=
```

Start by considering the formula in Y1:

$$y = -\frac{2x-1}{\sqrt{x^2+1}}$$

Press [2nd] [TBLSET] and if necessary reset **TblStart** to 0 and **ΔTbl** to 1.

Now press [2nd] [TABLE].

The table shows the values of the functions Y1 and Y2 with each corresponding x-value. For the moment, ignore the values of Y2. Notice that when $x = 0$, Y1 = 1, when $x = 1$ Y1 = $^-$0.7071, and so on.

```
 X   | Y1     | Y2
 0   | 1      | 0
 1   | -.7071 | 12.566
 2   | -1.342 | 50.265
 3   | -1.581 | 113.1
 4   | -1.698 | 201.06
 5   | -1.765 | 314.16
 6   | -1.808 | 452.39
X=0
```

Move the cursor up and down the x-column to discover other values of x and Y1. For example, the value of the function Y1 when $x = ^-10$ is 2.0896. Notice that if you press ▶ the values of Y1 are displayed at the bottom of the screen with greater accuracy than in the table. For example, the value of Y1 when $x = ^-10$ is 2.08957809944.

If you just hold your finger on the ▼ key, the values of the function for increasing values of x flash by at a good pace. Watch carefully the values of Y1. You will find that they keep growing slowly and steadily in magnitude (though they remain negative), so that at $x = 40$, for example, the y-value is $^-1.974$. You may be consumed with curiosity to find out whether the y-value reaches $^-2$ and if so when. Has the y-value passed $^-2$ when x has increased to 100? To find out, keep pressing the cursor key until x gets to 100 … or until you get bored.

Of course, there is a quicker way. Press 2nd [TBLSET] and set **TblStart** to 0 and **ΔTbl** to 10.

Now return to the Table screen and watch the values of x increase by 10 at a time. If you now use the down cursor you will quickly see that when $x = 100$ the value of y has still not reached $^-2$.

One of the less fortunate effects of making **ΔTbl** large is that you lose the details about how the values of the function change between one x-value and the next. With this complicated function, for some values of x, the y-values change quite dramatically, but this cannot be appreciated with a large value of **ΔTbl**. The values of Y_1 stay quite close to $^-2$ for values of x above 10, and they also stay quite close to 2 for x below $^-10$. Check it and see. But more interesting things happen for x between $^-10$ and 10, which it might be worth exploring in some detail. To do so you need to choose a smaller value for **ΔTbl**.

First, change **ΔTbl** back to 1, and look at the table for x between $^-3$ and 3. There are at least two features worth noting.

The first is that the value of Y_1 changes sign between $x = 0$ and $x = 1$ (it is positive when $x = 0$ but negative when $x = 1$).

The second is that the value of Y_1 at $x = ^-2$ is larger than the values on either side, and indeed larger than any other value on display.

X	Y₁	Y₂
-3	2.2136	113.1
-2	2.2361	50.265
-1	2.1213	12.566
0	1	0
1	-.7071	12.566
2	-1.342	50.265
3	-1.581	113.1

X=-3

It would be interesting to look more closely at Y_1 near to these values of x, that is, between 0 and 1, and around $^-2$. Change **ΔTbl** to 0.1, set **TblStart** to 0, and look at the table again.

You should see that the value of the function Y_1 is actually 0 when $x = 0.5$. This confirms something that you should have suspected: if the function takes a positive value for $x = 0$, and a negative one for $x = 1$, it is likely to be zero somewhere in between.

Now look at the table near $x = ^-2$. You will see that the value of the function when $x = ^-2$ is still larger than its value on either side. It looks as though the function takes its largest, or maximum, value when $x = ^-2$.

More than one table

Press 2nd [TABLE] ▶ ▶.

This highlights the column of values for Y_2. Further presses of ▶ will reveal values of Y_3 and Y_4. Sometimes it is useful to be able to compare the tables of values of two functions and where they do not appear on the same screen, it is possible to compare them using ▶ and ◀.

However, in one of the exercises that follows, you will need to use only the table for Y_4, and those for Y_1, Y_2 and Y_3 will be rather in the way. There is a means of temporarily getting rid of them, by deselecting their formulas on the Y= screen.

Return to the Y= screen by pressing [Y=].

Notice that each of the four = signs is highlighted. Use the cursor keys to position the flashing cursor over one of the = signs and press [ENTER].

You should see the highlighting disappear, indicating that the function has been deselected. Pressing [ENTER] again will select the function once more.

Using this method deselect Y_1, Y_2 and Y_3. Now press [2nd] [TABLE] and you should see the table of values for Y_4 immediately, without having to scroll past Y_1, Y_2 and Y_3. Functions which have been deselected are not lost, but remain dormant until they have been selected again.

Functions can easily be selected or deselected on the Y= screen, or alternatively, if you wish to select or deselect *all* the functions, you can use one of the VARS Y-VARS submenus.

Press [VARS] [▶] **4** to display the menu shown here.

Choosing options 1 or 2 followed by [ENTER] will cause all the functions on the Y= screen to be selected or deselected respectively.

You used option 2, **FnOff**, as one of the instructions in the CLEARGS program.

Now practise using tables of values on the calculator by trying these exercises.

Exercise 8.3   *Investigating Y4 with a table*

Make a table of values of the function which is stored as Y_4:

$$y = 0.5(x - 1.9)^2 - 5.$$

Investigate whether there are any values of x for which the corresponding value of y is 0.

Is there is a maximum and/or a minimum value of y?

Exercise 8.4   *Alternative temperature conversions*

Some people use their own rule of thumb for converting temperatures from Celsius to Fahrenheit. They simply double the degrees Celsius and add 30.

Just how good an approximation is this?

You should already have the accurate conversion formula stored as Y_3. In Y_5 enter the formula which will be appropriate for the approximation described above.

Compare the tables of values for the two functions. For which value of x does the value of Y_5 equal the value of Y_3? For what range of temperatures is the approximation reasonable?

8.4 *Drawing a graph of a function*

Using the calculator to produce a table of values is useful, but it is often even better to use the calculator to draw a graph of a function. You have already seen how this is done for simple conversion graphs in Chapter 7. In this section you will produce the graphs for some of the more complicated functions which you have already stored. There are several steps involved in producing the graph of a function, and these are detailed below.

◇ Clear the Graphing screen.

The simplest way to do this is to use the program, CLEARGS, that you created in Chapter 7. Press PRGM, select CLEARGS and press ENTER.

◇ Enter or select the appropriate functions.

Suppose you require the graph of $y = 4\pi x^2$, the formula for the surface area of a sphere whose radius is x. The calculator can draw the graphs of up to 10 functions on the same screen, but to begin with it is best to concentrate on one function at a time. It will only draw graphs of functions which have been selected on the Y= screen. Using the program CLEARGS will have deselected all the functions. Go to the Y= screen and reselect Y2.

◇ Choose an appropriate viewing window.

As you will know from previous experience, you press WINDOW to select which part of the graph you will see. When you are going to view a graph for the first time, and you have no idea what to expect, the best choice for the viewing window is probably one with settings shown here.

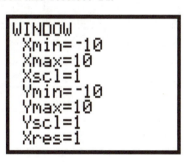

Because this window setting is very frequently needed there is a way of doing it automatically.

Press ZOOM to see the ZOOM menu shown here. Option 6, **ZStandard** will produce the required 'standard' window settings.

Press **6** now.

◇ Draw the graph.

Because in this case you used **ZStandard** (instead of setting the WINDOW manually), there was no need to press GRAPH.

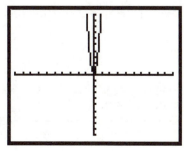

Your screen should show this display, which is really rather disappointing!

The problem is that the graph is compressed into rather too small a section of the screen. Evidently the standard window settings were not very suitable for this particular graph and you will need to alter them. Even though the present picture is not much good for representing the graph, it does show you what needs to be done to improve things. Firstly, there is nothing in the bottom half of the screen. So you could change **Ymin** from ⁻10 to 0. Secondly, the graph disappears off the top of screen at about $x = 1$ and $x = ⁻1$. You can tell this from the tick marks on the axes which are 1 unit apart. This happened because you set **Xscl** and **Yscl** both to 1. So you could reset **Xmin** to ⁻1 and **Xmax** to 1.

Press WINDOW and make these changes to the settings. Press GRAPH again and you should get this more satisfactory graph.

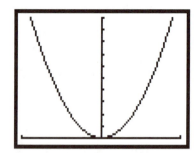

This is a nice smooth curve – well, almost! Although the 'staircase' effect is still present, you can see that, unlike the graphs you produced in the last chapter, this one is not a straight line but is genuinely curvy. This is a consequence of the fact that the function contains an x^2. The functions you graphed in Chapter 7 never involved anything more complicated than x.

Brain stetcher   *ZoomFit*

Investigate what happens to the viewing window when you use **ZStandard** followed by **ZoomFit** (Option 0 in the ZOOM menu).

Exercise 8.5   *Graphing areas of spheres*

The graph you have just drawn includes negative values of x. However, since x represents the radius of a sphere, so far as the practical use of the formula to calculate areas is concerned these negative values of x are of no interest. Redraw the graph so that x runs from 0 to 5. By trial and error, or by more systematic means if you can think of one, fix **Ymax** so that all of the screen is used.

Exercise 8.6   *The graph of Y_1*

Draw the graph of the function which is stored as Y_1:

$$y = -\frac{2x-1}{\sqrt{x^2+1}}$$

Concentrate on the region in which it has a maximum value and in which the value of y is 0.

Exercise 8.7   *Investigating ZOOM, option 4*

Option 4 in the ZOOM menu is **ZDecimal**. It is rather similar to **ZStandard**, because it provides some predetermined window settings.

Investigate **ZDecimal** for yourself. Why have these particular window settings been chosen? Using TRACE or the free cursor on the Graphing screen provides a clue.

8.5   Exploring graphs and solving equations

In this section, you will use more of the options from the ZOOM menu. You have already seen how options 4, 5, 6, 9 and 0 can be used to set the viewing window automatically, and in Chapter 9 you will see that **ZTrig** has a similar function.

The first three options in the menu are also extremely useful for exploring graphs, particularly when used in conjunction with the trace facility.

These three ZOOM facilities act like a zoom lens for a camera, or like a telescope. By using options 1 or 2, you can magnify a section of the graphing window so as to focus on a portion of the graph in greater detail. Alternatively, by using option 3, **Zoom Out,** you can draw back from the graph and see much more of it, in less detail.

You are going to investigate the graph of function Y4:

$$y = 0.5(x - 1.9)^2 - 5$$

Select it on the Y= screen, deselect any other graph currently selected and set the viewing window using **ZStandard**. Your graph should look like this.

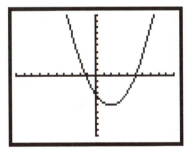

As you can see, this graph is somewhat similar in shape to the graph of $y = 4\pi x^2$, which you drew in the last section. However, this graph crosses the x-axis at two points. Since the y coordinate of both of these points is 0, it means that the function has the value 0 for the corresponding values of x. That is to say, at each of the two points where the graph crosses the x-axis, the value of x at the point is such that

$$0.5(x - 1.9)^2 - 5 = 0$$

In other words, the values of x at the points where the graph crosses the x-axis are **solutions** of the equation. You can therefore solve this equation by finding the x-coordinates of these points on the graph, and the trace and zoom facilities enable you to do so efficiently and accurately.

solutions

You have already tackled this problem using the Table facility in Exercise 8.3. The method which you are about to use now is a graphical counterpart to the numerical approach you used there.

You can see straight away that the equation has two solutions. Using the tick marks on the x-axis, it looks as if the solutions lie round about $x = {}^-1$ and $x = 5$. To start with, concentrate on the solution near $x = 5$.

Press $\boxed{\text{TRACE}}$. The flashing cursor appears on the screen, located on the graph at the point whose coordinates, given at the bottom of the screen, are $x = 0$ and $y = {}^-3.195$. Notice also that Y4 = .5(X − 1.9)² − 5 appears in the top left-hand corner of the screen, reminding you that the graph on which the cursor is located is the graph of function Y4.

Press the $\boxed{\blacktriangleright}$ key to move the flashing cursor along the graph towards the right. It sticks to the graph as if it were on rails. At each press, it moves one pixel horizontally and the values of x and y at the bottom of the screen change accordingly. The x-value is determined by the pixel in which the cursor is located, while the y-value is the corresponding value of the function for this value of x, calculated from the formula.

Move the cursor along the graph until it is as close as possible to the point where the graph crosses the x-axis. You would know that you had positioned it *exactly* on this point if the y-value were to become 0. However, you will find that this does not happen. The best you can do is to find where the y-value changes sign as you move from one position of the cursor to the next. This occurs between $x = 4.893617$ and $x = 5.106383$. The solution of the equation must lie somewhere between these two values. This gives some idea of the solution, but not a very accurate one. To improve on it, you can use $\boxed{\text{ZOOM}}$.

Zooming in

Move to $x = 5.106383$, press $\boxed{\text{ZOOM}}$ and select option 2 from the menu, **Zoom In**.

This returns you to the graph as it was before. In order to activate the zoom, you need to press $\boxed{\text{ENTER}}$.

You should find that the graph is redrawn like this.

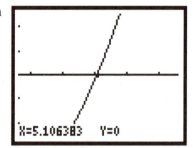

If your display is different from this, it may be that the magnification factors have been set differently on your calculator. If this is the case, you will need to carry out the three steps below; otherwise you can safely ignore them.

(a) To check the magnification factors, press:

$\boxed{\text{ZOOM}}$ $\boxed{\blacktriangleright}$ **4**

You should see the display shown here, the default settings.

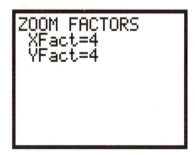

(b) If these factors are different from 4, reset them by overtyping.

This is the procedure to follow if you ever want to change either magnification factor.

(c) If you have had to reset the magnification factors, you will need to go back to the beginning: select **ZStandard** and follow the same procedure until you get the magnified graph as shown above.

The display above is a close-up of a small section of the original screen. It shows the section of the x-axis between $x = 2.6$ and $x = 7.6$ (approximately). The y-axis has disappeared from view (although its tick marks are still visible). The portion of the graph in the picture has become almost straight, and it slopes steeply up across the centre of the screen.

The picture has been magnified by a factor of four in both directions. The enlargement was centred on the last position of the cursor and that point is still in the middle of the screen marked by a flashing cursor.

Press ⌗TRACE⌗. Remember that you can tell when it is on by the appearance of the equation in the top left corner of the screen. Now repeat the procedure: locate the points where y changes sign and press ⌗ZOOM⌗ **2** ⌗ENTER⌗ to magnify the graph by another factor of four. Go through the same routine a few more times. You will soon find that the y-values on either side of the point where the graph crosses the x-axis are very small indeed and the corresponding values of x are something like 5.0615 and 5.0623. The solution of the equation must lie between these values, and is therefore 5.062, correct to three decimal places.

If you press ⌗WINDOW⌗ at any stage in this process, you will find that the settings have changed. The calculator has reset them automatically to the values appropriate to the current viewing window. This can be useful, because it tells you exactly which region of the graph you are looking at.

Exercise 8.8   *Another solution*

Select the **ZStandard** option again. You have just found the value of the solution corresponding to the right-hand point where the curve crosses the x-axis.

Now find the value of the other solution to the equation, to three decimal places.

Zooming with a box

There is another way of seeing a close-up of a small section of the Graphing screen. This involves defining a 'zoom box' by selecting for yourself exactly which region of the screen is to be magnified. Work through each of the following steps using the function which is stored in Y_1:

$$y = -\frac{2x-1}{\sqrt{x^2+1}}$$

◇ Ensure that only Y₁ is selected on the Y= screen and choose **ZStandard**.

◇ Press ZOOM and select option 1, **ZBox**. This produces the display shown here.

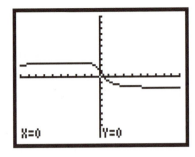

Notice that there is a flashing cursor on the screen, and that its coordinates are given at the bottom. This is not the trace cursor. It is a different shape and it is not constrained to move only on the graph. Try using the cursor keys to test this. The purpose of this cursor is to pick out the corners of the box which is to be magnified.

◇ Move the cursor to the right and down until it is near the point $x = 2$, $y = {}^-2$. Now press ENTER; this registers that point as a corner of the zoom box.

◇ Start moving the cursor again with the arrow keys. Now you will find that it leaves a line showing where it has been, and, if you move it both up and to the left, this line widens out to form a box. Move the cursor to a position similar to the one shown here.

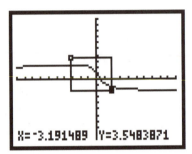

◇ Press ENTER again. This instructs the calculator to redraw the graph so that your chosen box exactly fills the screen. It is, of course, magnified in the process, using whatever scale factors are necessary for the box you selected.

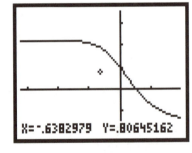

Notice that the **ZBox** cursor is still on the screen ready to be used again.

Using **ZBox** gives you considerable control over the area that is being enlarged and, of course, if you define a very small box, you can zoom in very quickly.

More than one graph

Finally, it is worth considering what happens when you have two graphs displayed at once.

Go back to the Y= screen and turn on Y₄ as well as Y₁. Choose the **ZStandard** option. You should see, plotted one after another on the screen, the graphs of both of the functions

$$y = -\frac{2x-1}{\sqrt{x^2+1}}$$

and

$$y = 0.5(x - 1.9)^2 - 5$$

These two graphs cross each other at two points. The y-coordinates at these points must equal *both* $-(2x-1)/\sqrt{(x^2+1)}$ (because the points lie on Y_1) *and* $0.5(x-1.9)^2-5$ (because the points lie on Y_4). Since the y-coordinate is equal to both of the expressions simultaneously, these expressions must be equal to each other. This means that the x coordinate of each of these two points is a solution of the awful-looking equation

$$0.5(x-1.9)^2 - 5 = -\frac{2x-1}{\sqrt{x^2+1}}$$

However, to solve this equation, all you have to do is to find the x-coordinates of the two crossing points – using TRACE and ZOOM, this is quite straightforward.

Exercise 8.9 *Solving simultaneous equations*

Choose one of the two points where the graphs of Y_1 and Y_4 cross each other.

Use **ZBox** or **Zoom In** and find the x-coordinate of the point. Repeat the process until you are sure that your answer is correct to three decimal places.

This will be one of the two possible solutions to the awkward looking equation above.

8.6   Calculations on the Graphing screen

The TI-83 has several powerful facilities within the CALC menu which allow you to solve equations very easily. Begin by ensuring that only the equations in Y_1 and Y_4 are selected and that the standard window settings have been chosen.

Now press 2nd [CALC] and you should see the menu shown here.

Each of these options allows you to obtain values from the graphs currently drawn on the Graphing screen.

For example, press **1** to obtain the **value** option.

You will see the screen shown on the right, which invites you to enter the x-coordinate of any point on the screen. Try it now and you will see the corresponding value of Y_1. Pressing ▲ or ▼ produces the value of Y_4.

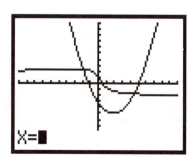

Option 2, **zero**, in the CALC menu allows you to calculate the zero values of functions. That is, for example, the value of X where Y_1 is zero. This is the equivalent of solving the equation $Y_1 = 0$ or

$$-\frac{2x-1}{\sqrt{x^2+1}} = 0$$

When you use this option the calculator asks you to specify a left bound and a right bound between which it will search for a zero value.

Press [2nd] [[CALC] **2**.

Move the cursor to a point on the graph of Y_1 with x-coordinate roughly $^-1$. Press [ENTER] to confirm that this value will be the left bound. Notice the black triangle which appears on the screen.

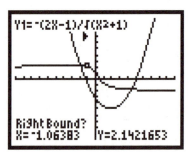

Now move to about X = 2 and select a right bound by pressing [ENTER].

Finally, you are asked to guess where you think the zero value will be. Move the cursor to the point (roughly) where the graph crosses the x-axis as shown here.

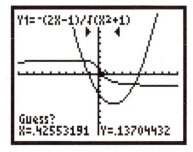

Press [ENTER] and the zero value is calculated.

Option 5, **intersect**, of the CALC menu allows you to find the points of intersection of two curves. Here you are asked to specify the two curves by, if neccessary, moving the cursor to another curve by pressing [▲] or [▼]. As with option 2, **zero**, you are asked to provide a guess before the accurate calculation is carried out.

You will use these and other options from the CALC menu in later chapters.

Exercise 8.10   *Solving equations with CALC*

Use options from the CALC menu to calculate the following correct to three decimal places:

(a) the values of Y_1 and Y_4 where X = 0

(b) the solutions of $0.5(x - 1.9)^2 - 5 = 0$

(c) the solutions of

$$0.5(x - 1.9)^2 - 5 = -\frac{2x-1}{\sqrt{x^2+1}}$$

Brain stretcher   *Transforming graphs*

Enter the formulas shown here on the
Y= screen.

Y4 is the same complicated formula that
you used earlier in this chapter, and Y1,
Y2 and Y3 gradually build up to Y4 in
complexity.

```
Plot1  Plot2  Plot3
\Y1=X²
\Y2=(X-1.9)²
\Y3=.5(X-1.9)²
\Y4=.5(X-1.9)²-5

\Y5=
\Y6=
```

(a) Select only Y1 and Y2. The formulas are the same except that X in Y1
    has changed to X−1.9 in Y2. Draw and compare their graphs. Where are
    their minimum values? What effect did the −1.9 in Y2 have? What
    happens if you change the 1.9 to something else?

(b) Now select just Y2 and Y3. The only difference in their formulas is the .5
    in Y3. What effect does this have on the graph? Try other numbers
    instead of .5.

(c) Finally select just Y3 and Y4. Compare their formulas and their graphs.

(d) Does what you have done enable you to make any predictions about
    how, for example, the graph of $y = x/3$ might be related to the graph of

$$y = .5\left(\frac{x-1.9}{3}\right) - 5?$$

Can you make any general statements about the shapes of such graphs?

Chapter 9 Repeating patterns

In this chapter, you will use the trigonometric function keys of the calculator and will explore the shape of their graphs. This will involve using one of the remaining options in the ZOOM menu, **ZTrig**, and also the **Radian** and **Degree** options on the Mode screen.

You will also carry out an extended mathematical investigation, using your calculator to draw a series of graphs from which you will extract data to use in the investigation.

The third section of the chapter introduces some new programming instructions within the context of musical scales. Finally, there is a summary of all the TI-83 graphing facilities you have met so far and a series of optional activities which use many of them.

9.1   Trigonometric functions

In the centre of the TI-83's keyboard are three keys labelled SIN, COS and TAN. Locate them now.

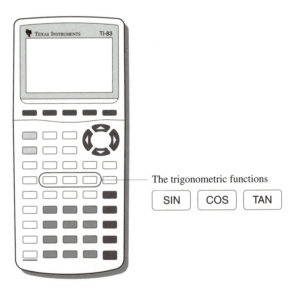

The trigonometric functions

trigonometric functions

You may have met these abbreviations before: sin is short for sine, cos for cosine and tan for tangent. They are known as **trigonometric functions** (or trig. functions for short) and are frequently used for calculating lengths and angles in triangles. (Since a pentagon is a five-sided shape, a 'trigon' might be three-sided: hence, the word trigonometric – to do with measuring triangles.)

In Exercise 9.1, there are some examples of calculations which involve these functions, but first you will need to check that your calculator is operating with the correct MODE settings.

Press MODE and look at the third line of the menu.

There are two commonly used units for measuring angles: *degrees* and *radians*. For the next exercise, you will need to use the more familiar unit, degrees, so select and confirm this option before returning to the Home screen.

To calculate the sine, cosine or tangent of an angle you need to press the appropriate trig. function key, followed by the size of the angle in degrees.

For example, to calculate the sine of 20°, simply press

   SIN **2 0**) ENTER

The second functions of these keys, marked [SIN⁻¹] [COS⁻¹] [TAN⁻¹] provide their inverse functions: they allow you to calculate the angle if you already know the value of the trig. function. For example, to calculate the angle which has a cosine of 0.7 press

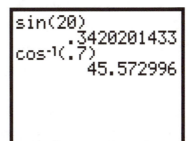

   2nd [COS⁻¹] **. 7**) ENTER

Notice that the calculator forces you to use brackets when you specify angles within trigonometric functions. This removes any possible ambiguity. In mathematics you may write sin 20° or sin *x* or sin 2*x* but on the calculator these must be entered as sin(20), sin(X) and sin(2X).

Exercise 9.1   *Calculations with sin, cos and tan*

(a) Use your calculator to calculate the following, giving your answers to three decimal places. You may wish to use MODE to set the calculator to show three decimal places.

   (i)   The tangent of 64°

   (ii)   The sine of 1°

   (iii) The angle whose sine is 0.4

   (iv) The angle whose cosine is 0.4

(b) Set up the Y= screen as shown here.

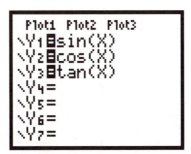

   Use TABLE with appropriate values of ΔTbl and TblStart to complete the following table.

Angle in degrees	Sine	Cosine	Tangent
0			
30			
45			
60			
90			—
180			
270			—
360			

You may have noticed a certain symmetry in the values of sine and cosine between 0° and 90°. In general, the sine of an angle is equal to the cosine of (90° minus the angle). Or using symbols:

$$\sin x° = \cos (90 - x)°$$

You may also have been surprised that there are values of sine, cosine and tangent for angles greater than 90°. Although the trig. functions are most frequently used for calculations in right-angled triangles (where the angles are no greater than 90°), sines and cosines exist for *all* angles, positive and negative, large and small. However, there are some exceptions for the tangent function, as you will have found when you tried to work out the tangent of 90° or 270° on the calculator.

A more effective way of understanding how the values of the trigonometric functions vary is to look at their graphs.

First clear the Graphing screen by executing the program CLEARGS.

Press Y= and select the formula Y₁ = sin(X). Check that Y₂ and Y₃ are deselected.

Next you need a suitable viewing window. The standard window, provided by option 6 in the ZOOM menu, is not appropriate here – try it if you like – but there is another pre-programmed window setting which is ideal.

This can be obtained from option 7, **ZTrig**, in the ZOOM menu. Choose it now by pressing ZOOM 7.

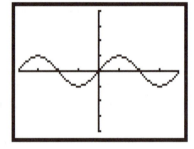

You should obtain the graph of sin x as shown here. The values of x (the angles in degrees) run from ⁻352.5 to 352.5, and each tick mark on the x-axis represents 90°.

Press TRACE and by moving the cursor to the right you can check all the values of sin x that you obtained in Exercise 9.1.

Exercise 9.2   *Describing y = sin x*

Imagine you are describing the graph of $y = \sin x$ to someone who cannot see the screen. Describe any visual features that strike you and make a note of them.

This graph is quite different from those you have seen so far: it repeats regularly, over and over, forming a series of peaks and troughs. Its y-values are all between 1 (the peaks) and ⁻1 (the troughs). The curve passes through alternate tick marks on the x-axis, where x is ⁻360, ⁻180, 0, 180, 360 and so on.

This sine curve has a basic element called a **cycle** which is repeated over and over again.

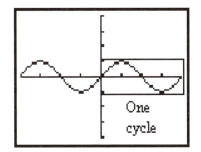

cycle

To get a better look at this basic element of the graph, press WINDOW and change the settings to those shown here. This will produce one complete cycle as large as possible on the screen.

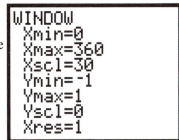

Press GRAPH; notice that the cycle is divided into four rather similar sections. The first section (from $x = 0$ to $x = 90$) is followed by its own mirror image (in a vertical line) to form the section from $x = 90$ to $x = 180$. The rest is another reflection (this time in the x-axis) of these two pieces moved along a bit.

Exercise 9.3 *Exploring cosine and tangent*

On the Y= screen, deselect $Y_1 = \sin(X)$ and select instead $Y_2 = \cos(X)$. Draw its graph, first using the existing window settings and then using **ZTrig**. What differences and similarities do you notice with the graph of $y = \sin x$?

Now deselect $Y_2 = \cos(X)$, select $Y_3 = \tan(X)$ and draw its graph. What differences and similarities do you notice now?

What are radians?

Earlier in this section, you selected **Degree** from the MODE menu, and in all the work you have done since then the values of x have represented degrees. For example, you have seen, both by direct calculation and by looking at the graph, that the sine of 180° is 0, and when you chose a window setting using the **ZTrig** option, the calculator set **Xscl** to 90°.

However, there is another unit which is sometimes used to measure angles: the radian. But what is a radian and how big is it compared with a degree? You, no doubt, have a feel for the size of one degree: it is pretty small, as you need 90 to make up a right angle and 360 to make a complete turn.

Press MODE; select and confirm **Radian** from the third line of the menu. Also ensure that **Float** is selected on the second line.

Select only $Y_1 = \sin(X)$ once more and, by selecting **ZTrig** from the ZOOM menu, draw its graph. This graph looks very similar to the sine graph you produced before, as indeed it should, because all you have done is to change the units that the angles are measured in.

Press [TRACE] followed by [▶].

When you did this in Degree mode, the x-values increased in steps of 7.5°. However, in Radian mode the x-values appear to increase by 0.1309. The reason for such a number appearing is far from obvious!

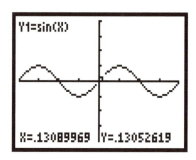

Exercise 9.4 *The equivalent of 180°*

(a) Continue moving the cursor to the right until it is half-way through the first cycle of the graph, that is until it is as close as possible to where the graph crosses the x-axis. By zooming in on this point, find as accurately as possible the value of x there. In Degree mode, this point corresponded to 180°.

(b) Using the [TBLSET] and [TABLE] keys, find the value of x just above 3 for which $\sin x$ is zero. By repeatedly decreasing the value of Δ**Tbl**, try to get as accurate a value of x as possible. This should confirm the value that you found in part (a).

Is this number familiar?

It turns out that 180° is the equivalent of π radians, and this means that

$$1 \text{ radian} = \left(\frac{180°}{\pi}\right) = 57.3° \text{ (correct to one decimal place)}$$

There are 2π radians, or 360°, in a whole turn.

Brain stretcher   *Trigonometric relationships*

Make sure that you still have $\sin(X)$, $\cos(X)$ and $\tan(X)$ stored in Y_1, Y_2 and Y_3 respectively, but deselect them all. Select Degree mode.

(a) Move the cursor alongside $Y_4 =$ and enter Y_1/Y_2 by pressing

[VARS] [▶] **1** **1** [÷] [VARS] [▶] **1** **2**

Select **ZTrig** and draw the graph. You have seen this graph before. What does this tell you about $\sin x/\cos x$?

(b) Now make $Y_4 = Y_1 + Y_2$ and draw its graph.

What does this tell you about $(\sin x)^2 + (\cos x)^2$?

<hr>

Brain stretcher   *Xres*

Plot a simple graph, say $y = 2x^2$ and display it using **ZStandard**.

Now try plotting the same graph with different values for **Xres**, which is in
Window. Try to work out what **Xres** does and why you might want to use
different settings of **Xres**.

<hr>

9.2 Some trigonometric patterns

In the following investigations, you will be asked to concentrate on the shapes of
the graphs that are produced and to compare one with another. It would not
really matter which of the two units, radians or degrees, you used, except for the
x-values used for the window settings. In what follows, where window settings
are suggested, the assumption is that you are using Radian mode.

Exercise 9.5   *Exploring y = sin 2x*

(a) On the Y= screen, enter $Y_1 = \sin(X)$ and
$Y_2 = \sin(2X)$. Press WINDOW and enter the
settings shown here.

Watch carefully what happens when you
press GRAPH.

The graph of $y = \sin x$ is drawn first
followed by the graph of $y = \sin 2x$.

```
WINDOW
 Xmin=0
 Xmax=6.4
 Xscl=0
 Ymin=-1
 Ymax=1
 Yscl=0
 Xres=1
```

(b) How does $y = \sin 2x$ compare with $y = \sin x$? What do they have in
common and what is different about them?

<hr>

Exercise 9.6   *Sine predictions*

Before you plot them on your calculator, write down what you think the graphs
of $y = \sin 3x$ and $y = \sin 5x$ will look like. How will they compare with the
graph of $y = \sin x$?

Test out your predictions using the calculator.

How accurate were your predictions? Can you generalize your predictions to the
graphs of the sines of other multiples of *x*, such as $y = \sin 7x$ or $y = \sin 8x$?

<hr>

Brain stretcher   ***Times of the sines***

(a) How do the graphs of $y = \sin{}^-x$, $y = \sin{}^-2x$ and $y = \sin{}^-5x$, compare with those of $y = \sin x$, $y = \sin 2x$ and $y = \sin 5x$?

What generalizations can you make here?

(b) How do the graphs of $y = 2\sin x$, $y = 3\sin x$ and $y = 5\sin x$ compare with the graph of $y = \sin x$?

What generalizations can be made here?

(c) Can you produce the following screen displays?

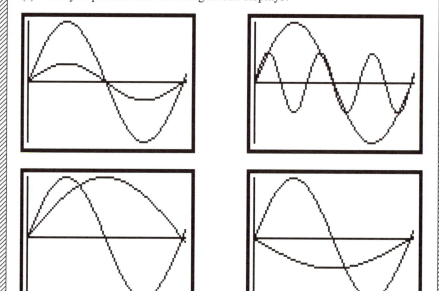

Periodic behaviour

In this section, you have looked at lots of curves which are very similar in shape and behaviour. They all belong to what is called the 'family' of sine curves. One particular feature of all the graphs in the family of sine curves is exact repetition, over and over again. You can imagine the shapes repeating endlessly off-screen, both to left and right.

period The mathematical word used to describe this property of some graphs is 'periodic'. In mathematics, the **period** of a function is a measure of how much x must change before the function begins to repeat itself exactly. The period is a length on the graph, the distance along the horizontal axis between two identical points of adjacent cycles.

Here once again is the graph of $y = \sin x$ drawn using the **ZTrig** window with the calculator set in Radian mode.

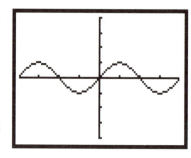

You can see that after four tick marks on the x-axis, the curve has completed one full cycle and starts again, repeating exactly what it did before. So for $y = \sin x$, the period is the length marked off between the origin and the fourth tick mark on the X axis.

But what do these tick marks represent? WINDOW helpfully tells you that the x-scale is in units of length 1.5707963... and this is actually a very close approximation to $\pi/2$. So the period of $y = \sin x$ is therefore $4 \times \pi/2 = 2\pi$.

What about the periods of $y = \sin 2x$, $y = \sin 3x$...?

You saw in Exercises 9.5 and 9.6 that in the graphs of $y = \sin 2x$ and $y = \sin 3x$ there were two and three cycles taking up as much space on the x-axis as one cycle of $y = \sin x$. Therefore, their periods must be half and one-third of the period of $y = \sin x$, or $2\pi/2$ and $2\pi/3$ respectively.

And, in general, the period of $y = \sin nx$ is $2\pi/n$.

Adding two sine curves

In this subsection, you will be asked to identify what happens when you add two members of the family of sine curves together.

The easiest case to consider is $y = \sin x + \sin x$. Will this produce the same graph as $y = 2\sin x$ or $y = \sin 2x$ or something different?

The first of these, $y = 2\sin x$ should seem more likely: after all, when you add two of the same numbers together you get 2 times that number (for example, $10^3 + 10^3 = 2 \times 10^3$ and not $10^{2 \times 3}$.)

If you are not convinced that $\sin x + \sin x = 2\sin x$, you could enter $Y_1 = \sin(X) + \sin(X)$ and $Y_2 = 2\sin(X)$ and draw the two graphs. They should turn out to be exactly the same. Now try drawing the graph of $y = \sin 2x$ and you will get something very different.

The next easiest case to explore might well be $\sin x + \sin 2x$. It might have been tempting to think that $\sin x + \sin 2x = \sin 3x$, but perhaps what you have just seen about $\sin x + \sin x$ not being equal to $\sin 2x$ makes that seem unlikely.

Exercise 9.7 $\quad$ sin(X) + sin(2X) versus sin(3X)

Set $Y_1 = \sin(X) + \sin(2X)$ and $Y_2 = \sin(3X)$. Graph them both on one screen. Are they exactly the same or do they differ? If they differ, how do they differ?

Clear the graph of $y = \sin 3x$ and draw just $y = \sin x + \sin 2x$ It seems that the result of adding two sine curves together is not (in this case at least) another sine curve. But it is a periodic curve nonetheless. How does the period of $\sin x + \sin 2x$ relate to the separate periods of $\sin x$ and $\sin 2x$? And in general, if you add two sines together, how does the period of the sum relate to the coefficients of x in the two contributing functions?

To begin with, you want to be able to compare the graph of $\sin x + \sin 2x$ with those of its two components. But you may soon want to look at $y = \sin 2x + \sin 3x$, and $y = \sin 3x + \sin 4x$, and so on.

There is a convenient way to ask the calculator to draw the graph of the sum of any two expressions. Follow through the following steps.

Press Y= and enter the formulas shown here.

Move the cursor over each of the first two =
signs and press ENTER so that the two formulas
are deselected.

Then position the cursor alongside Y3 as shown.

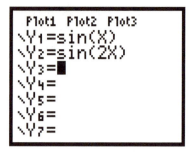

Press VARS ▶ 1 to display the Y-VARS
FUNCTION menu.

Press 1 to select Y1 and paste it on to the Y=
screen.

Press + VARS ▶ 1 2 to complete the formula
shown here.

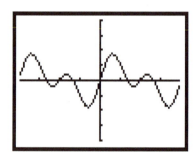

Now press ZOOM 7 to select **ZTrig** and obtain
the graph.

The combined curve is more complex than either of its two components, but it is
periodic nevertheless. Its period is four tick marks on the *x*-axis, so it has the
same period as $y = \sin x$, namely 2π.

The aim of the current investigation is to be able to predict the period of the
graph resulting from adding any two sine curves together. For example, what
would be the periods of $y = \sin 3x + \sin 6x$, or $y = \sin 7x + \sin 13x$, or even
$y = \sin 127x + \sin 9456x$?

Exercise 9.8   *The period of* $y = \sin 3x + \sin 6x$

Draw the graph of $y = \sin 3x + \sin 6x$. (Having set up Y3 as the sum of Y1 and
Y2, you can simply edit Y1 and Y2 to read sin(3X) and sin(6X), making sure that
you then remember to deselect their highlighted = signs.)

What do you notice about this graph? What is the period of the curve? In
particular, how does its period relate to 2π, the period of $y = \sin x$?

It may be easier to see how the period relates to 2π if you change the viewing
window so that the *x*-axis extends from 0 to 2π:

◇   Press WINDOW and change **Xmin** to 0.

◇   Alongside **Xmax**, enter 2π by pressing 2 2nd [π] ENTER; you will see the
numerical value 6.2831853 appear.

◇   Change **Xscl** to 0.

Do you now feel that you can predict the period of the sum of *any* two sine curves? You might have various conjectures at the moment, but remember that you have only looked at three cases and there are many more possibilities.

In the next exercise, you are asked to continue with the investigation. You will probably need to generate a range of data and record them carefully. The exercise suggests some systematic ways of doing this. In particular, you will need to record the two coefficients of x and the period of the sum of the two sine functions.

After each stage, it is best to make a note of any patterns that you spot or conjectures that you have. Keep in mind what you are trying to discover – a general rule which will tell you the period of the sum of any two sine curves.

Exercise 9.9   Continuing with the investigation

(a) Complete the following table, collecting the necessary data by entering appropriate functions in Y_1 and Y_2, drawing the graphs and looking carefully at the periods of the combined functions. You may need to use either the window settings of Exercise 9.8 or those provided by **ZTrig**.

Coefficients					
of x	1	1	1	1	1
	1	2	3	4	5
Period	2π	2π			

Write some notes about any patterns you notice.

(b) Complete the following table. You already know from Exercise 9.8 that the period of $y = \sin 3x + \sin 6x$ is $2\pi/3$ and you have just looked at $y = \sin x + \sin 3x$. This means you can enter the first and last periods straight away.

Coefficients						
of x	3	3	3	3	3	3
	1	2	3	4	5	6
Period						

Write some notes about any patterns you notice here and try to make some predictions.

(c) Create other similar tables and use them to check or extend any predictions you have made.

(d) Can you predict the period for each of the following?

$$y = \sin 5x + \sin 15x$$
$$y = \sin 6x + \sin 11x$$
$$y = \sin 6x + \sin 9x$$

In each case, make a prediction and check it by drawing a graph. If necessary, go back to part (c) and collect some more data to refine your predictions.

(e) Write down, as clearly and concisely as possible, a rule for predicting the period of the sum of any two sines.

9.3 Patterns in musical scales

twelve-note scale

All music is based on some sort of musical scale. In the Western musical tradition, the most common scale has 12 distinct notes, hence the name the **twelve-note scale**. The black and white notes on a piano keyboard provide a helpful representation of this scale

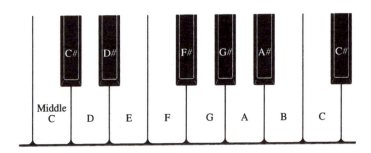

octave

A fundamental idea in musical scales is that of the **octave**. An octave describes the most basic musical interval, where the two notes in question sound essentially the same, but one is 12 semitones higher than the other. Thus, the note marked C at the right of the diagram above is exactly one octave, or 12 semitones, above the note marked C on the left. In this section, you will use your calculator to explore two ways of defining this twelve-note scale. One approach is called the method of equal temperament while the other, based on a method of ratios popularly attributed to Pythagoras, is termed Pythagorean.

In the calculator work that follows, the pitch of a note is linked to the length of string that would be required to make it. A starting point is the discovery, again attributed to Pythagoras, that the note produced by a half-length string is exactly one octave higher in pitch than that produced by the original string. For convenience, these two lengths will be called 1 unit and $\frac{1}{2}$ unit. The question you will investigate here is 'How long must the 11 intervening strings be if they are to produce the familiar twelve-note scale?'.

The equally tempered twelve-note scale

Modern pianos are tuned using the so-called 'equal temperament' method of tuning. This is based on a fixed relationship between successive semitone intervals.

But what exactly is this fixed relationship? In terms of the lengths of strings, the problem can be restated as follows. How can you reduce a length of 1 to a length of $\frac{1}{2}$ in twelve identical steps of equal proportion. If you let each step be the proportion r, the lengths of the strings can be written as follows:

String number	1	2	3	4	...	12	13
String length	1	r	r^2	r^3	...	r^{11}	r^{12}

Since you know that the thirteenth string is of length $\frac{1}{2}$, you can write:

$$r^{12} = \tfrac{1}{2}$$

In other words

$$r = \sqrt[12]{\frac{1}{2}}$$

Option 5 in the MATH menu of your calculator enables you to enter higher roots like this one.

To calculate r and store it in memory location R in your calculator, press the following:

1 2 [MATH] 5 . 5 [STO▸] [ALPHA] **R** [ENTER]

You can now calculate the length of each string in the twelve-note scale by working out successive powers of r. For example, the first note corresponds to a length of 1, the second note to a length of 0.9438743127 (or r), the third note to 0.8908987181 (or r^2), and so on.

Press the following to calculate the first six string lengths for this scale:

1 [ENTER]

[×] [ALPHA] **R** [ENTER]

[ENTER] [ENTER] [ENTER] [ENTER]

It would be useful to be able to store these values in a list, because you will later need to compare them with string lengths produced using a Pythagorean method.

One way of calculating the 13 string lengths and storing them in a list is to use the short program shown here.

```
PROGRAM:SCALE
:1→L
:For(C,1,13)
:L→L₁(C)
:L*R→L
:End
:
```

The program uses two instructions that you have not met before, **For** and **End**. These instructions set up a **loop** causing the two instructions between them to be carried out over and over again. This is explained in more detail below.   **loop**

Instruction	Explanation
: 1 → L	Store the first string length, with value 1, in location L.
: For (C, 1, 13)	This command sets up a loop which starts here and goes as far as the **End** command. The calculator will go through the loop repeatedly using each integer value of C from 1 to 13 inclusive. So the variable C is used to count the number of times the loop is executed.
: L → L₁(C)	Store the current value of L in the Cth position of list L₁. So, on the first time round the loop, L is stored in L₁(1), on the second time in L₁(2), and so on.
: L × R → L	Multiply L, the string length, by the value stored in R and store the result in location L. This means that the string length is changed each time through the loop.
: End	The end of the loop.

Press the following to enter the program now. You should be able to check each instruction that you enter against the complete program shown above.

$\boxed{\text{PRGM}}$ $\boxed{\blacktriangleleft}$ $\boxed{\text{ENTER}}$ **S C A L E** $\boxed{\text{ENTER}}$

1 $\boxed{\text{STO▶}}$ $\boxed{\text{ALPHA}}$ **L** $\boxed{\text{ENTER}}$

$\boxed{\text{PRGM}}$ **4** $\boxed{\text{ALPHA}}$ **C** $\boxed{,}$ **1** $\boxed{,}$ **1 3** $\boxed{)}$ $\boxed{\text{ENTER}}$

$\boxed{\text{ALPHA}}$ **L** $\boxed{\text{STO▶}}$ $\boxed{\text{2nd}}$ $\boxed{\text{[L1]}}$ $\boxed{(}$ $\boxed{\text{ALPHA}}$ **C** $\boxed{)}$ $\boxed{\text{ENTER}}$

$\boxed{\text{ALPHA}}$ **L** $\boxed{\times}$ $\boxed{\text{ALPHA}}$ **R** $\boxed{\text{STO▶}}$ $\boxed{\text{ALPHA}}$ **L** $\boxed{\text{ENTER}}$

$\boxed{\text{PRGM}}$ **7**

Check to make sure that your entire program is exactly the same as the one in the screen display reproduced above. If necessary use the cursor keys to return to any line that needs to be edited.

Finally leave the program edit screen by pressing $\boxed{\text{2nd}}$ $\boxed{\text{QUIT}}$.

Now clear list L₁, press $\boxed{\text{PRGM}}$ and execute the program. When it is completed, check the contents of L₁ and see the 13 string lengths recorded there. Check that the first and last of these lengths are what you know to be the correct lengths for these strings, 1 and $\frac{1}{2}$ respectively,

A Pythagorean twelve-note scale

You are now asked to carry out a similar procedure to the one above, but this time using a different approach to generate a twelve-note scale. The method is based on the Pythagorean principle that certain simple ratios of string lengths produce particularly harmonious intervals. A twelve-note, harmonious-sounding scale can be created by producing a sequence of rising notes, by means of repeatedly taking two-thirds of successive string lengths. However, because the intention is to fit the notes into one octave, there is a complication: using this method will quickly produce strings of lengths less than $\frac{1}{2}$, and such high notes will lie *outside* the octave (as represented within the range of lengths 1 to $\frac{1}{2}$). So, when a string length of less than 0.5 is created, the simplest solution is to bring that note down by one octave by doubling its string length. This has the effect of bringing it back into the single octave range from 1 to 0.5. Here is an example.

String number	String length
1	1
2	$1 \times \frac{2}{3} = \frac{2}{3}$
3	$\frac{2}{3} \times \frac{2}{3} = \frac{4}{9}$

This third string has a length of less than $\frac{1}{2}$, so its note falls outside the octave. We therefore move the note down one octave by doubling its string length (giving $\frac{8}{9}$), which now does lie in the range 0 to $\frac{1}{2}$, and continue as before, taking $\frac{2}{3}$ of this new value falling within the octave.

String number	String length
1	1
2	$\frac{2}{3}$
3	$\frac{4}{9} \times 2 = \frac{8}{9}$
4	$\frac{8}{9} \times \frac{2}{3} = \frac{16}{27}$
5	$\frac{16}{27} \times \frac{2}{3} = \frac{32}{81}$, then double to get $\frac{64}{81}$

Again, the fifth note produces a string length of less than 0.5, so its length is also doubled, giving $\frac{64}{81}$, and so on.

When you feel confident that you understand the method of generating notes described above, study the short program shown below. In this program, doubling of the string length takes place when R is less than 0.49, rather than 0.5. The reason for this will become clear later.

```
PROGRAM:SCALE
:1→L
:For(C,1,13)
:L→L₂(C)
:2/3*L→L
:If L<.49
:2L→L
:End
```

Notice that this program is very similar to the previous one you used in this section. It uses **For** and **End** to set up a loop, but also includes another new programming instruction, **If**. This has the effect of testing to see whether a condition (in this case L<.49) is true or false. If the condition is true, the next program instruction is carried out. Otherwise the next instruction is ignored.

Rather than entering an entirely new program, you could edit the one that you used previously. Follow through each of the following steps, checking each instruction that you edit against the complete program shown above.

◇ Press PRGM ▶ and select SCALE. The previous program should be displayed on the program edit screen.

◇ To change L_1 to L_2 on the third line, use the cursor keys to highlight L_1 and press 2nd [L2].

◇ Change the fourth line by moving the cursor to that line, pressing CLEAR and then pressing

   2 ÷ **3** × ALPHA **L** STO▸ ALPHA **L**

◇ Two extra lines are needed before **End**. To create space for these lines, highlight **End** and press

   2nd [INS] ENTER ENTER

◇ Position the cursor on the first blank line and press

   PRGM **1** ALPHA **L** 2nd [TEST] **5 . 4 9** ENTER
   2 ALPHA **L** STO▸ ALPHA **L**

Your program should now look exactly the same as the one displayed above.

Leave the program edit screen by pressing 2nd [QUIT].

First clear L_2 and then execute the program. When it is completed, have a look at the contents of list L_2. There you should see string lengths corresponding to the 13 notes of the scale produced using the Pythagorean principle.

Exercise 9.10   *Comparing the lists of string lengths*

You should now have the string lengths corresponding to the equally tempered twelve-note scale and a Pythagorean twelve-note scale in lists L_1 and L_2. Compare the corresponding numbers in the two lists. You might have expected some closer degree of similarity between these numbers. Can you explain why they look so different?

One reason that the numbers in the two lists do not match up is that the values in L_2 are not in sequence. If you run the cursor down list L_2, you will see that they are certainly not in descending order. This is easily remedied, by returning to the Home screen and using the **SortD** command (option 2 in the LIST OPS menu) to sort the L_2 values into descending order. Now compare the values in L_1 and L_2.

They certainly look *similar*, but they are not identical. The reason for the disparity is that these two scales have been formed in different ways; the values in L_1 are based on a twelve-note 'equal temperament' scale, whereas the lengths in L_2 are based on 'Pythagorean' intervals.

By the way, have a look at the last value in the L_2 list. The value .49327 is really very close to 0.5, but is actually *less* than 0.5. This is why 0.49 rather than 0.5 was used in line 5 of the program.

You have now produced the twelve-note scale by two different methods. It should be noted, however, that the second of these, which was based on the ratio $\frac{2}{3}$, should not be described as *the* Pythagorean scale, but rather as *a* Pythagorean scale. What characterizes any Pythagorean scale is that the intervals are based on string lengths which can be expressed as simple ratios. While the ratio $\frac{2}{3}$ certainly is a fundamental one, there are alternative possibilities as well. For example, it would be possible for a Pythagorean scale to include string lengths based on other simple ratios, such as $\frac{3}{4}$ and powers of $\frac{3}{4}$.

Finally, having produced twelve-note scales by the two different methods described here, you may be interested to compare and contrast the results in L_1 and L_2. The next two Brain stretchers provide some possible avenues for you to pursue.

Brain stretcher — Scattered string lengths

Plot L_1 against L_2 using a scatterplot.

Superimpose the line $y = x$ (using the Y= menu). If the values in the two lists were equal the points would lie on this line.

Does this provide any insight regarding how corresponding values in the two lists compare?

Brain stretcher — Differences and errors

Try entering one or more of the following on the Home screen. In each case, ask yourself what the values produced in the lists represent.

$L_1 - L_2 \rightarrow L_3$

$abs(L_1 - L_2) \rightarrow L_4$ (**abs** is in the MATH NUM menu)

$abs(L_1 - L_2)/L_1 \times 100 \rightarrow L_5$

The last of these provides a measure of the percentage 'error' of the Pythagorean string lengths compared with the string lengths based on 'equal temperament'.

9.4 Summary of the graphing facilities of the calculator

In Chapters 6–9, you were introduced to the following graphing facilities of the calculator.

◇ Entering functions on the Y= screen was discussed in Sections 7.2 and 8.1.

◇ The use of tables was introduced in Section 7.2 and developed further in Section 8.3.

◇ You have seen that window settings may be set either manually using WINDOW or automatically using one of the options from the ZOOM menu. **ZBox, Zoom In** and **Zoom Out** were introduced in Section 8.5, **ZDecimal** and **ZStandard** in Section 8.4, **ZSquare** in Section 6.1 and **ZTrig** in Section 9.1.

◇ You have used options from the VARS Y-VARS menu to enter Y1, Y2, etc. on the Home screen and to produce **FnOn** and **FnOff**, a quick way of selecting and deselecting functions on the Y= screen.

◇ In Section 6.1, you used two options from the FORMAT menu, **GridOn** and **GridOff**.

◇ In Chapter 6, you used line graphs to display data which had been previously stored in lists and this provided a link with the statistical plotting facilities that you met in Chapters 2–5.

All these graphing features are described fully in the *TI-83 Guidebook* (particularly Chapters 3 and 7).

Finally, here are some optional brain stretchers which you might like to try. They draw upon many of the graphical features introduced in Chapters 6–9.

Brain stretcher   *Graphical screensnaps*

Can you produce the following Graphing screens? The window settings have been set using **ZStandard**.

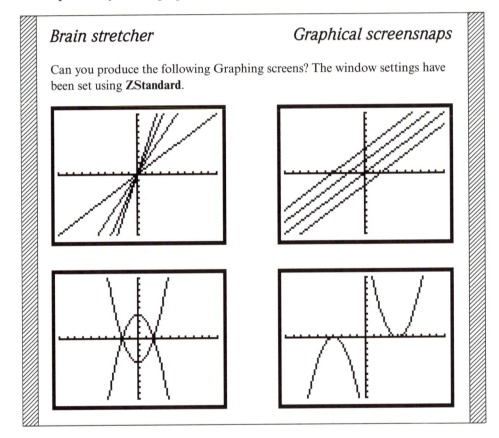

Brain stretcher   *Simple (?) straight lines*

Can you produce straight lines that:

(a) pass through the origin, at 45° to the axes

(b) are parallel to the horizontal axis

(c) are parallel to the vertical axis?

Brain stretcher — Round and about

Enter the functions shown below for Y1 and Y2. Then choose **ZDecimal** to produce the circle shown.

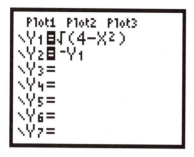
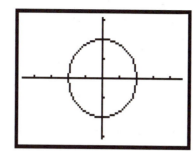

Why are two functions necessary?

Try changing Y1 in various ways. For example, what happens if you:

◇ change the 4

◇ insert a number before the square root sign

◇ insert a number before the X²?

Brain stretcher — Circling around

Can you produce the following graphing screens? **ZDecimal** has been used for the window settings.

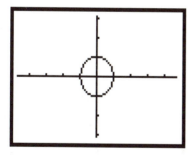
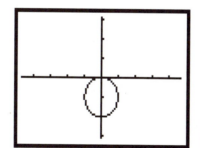
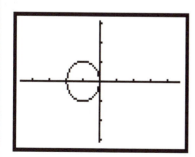
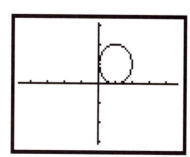

Brain stretcher   *Tabular screensnaps*

Can you produce these tables on your TI-83?

X	Y₁	Y₂
0	4	-16
1	1	-9
2	0	-4
3	1	-1
4	4	0
5	9	-1
6	16	-4

X=0

X	Y₁	Y₂
-10	144	20734
-5	49	2399
0	4	14
5	9	79
10	64	4094
15	169	28559
20	324	104974

X=-10

Brain stretcher   *MATH Graphs*

Each of the following graphs have been produced from simple functions which use options from the MATH menu. Which ones?

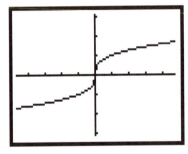

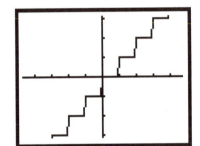

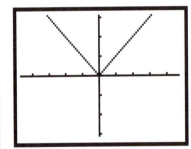

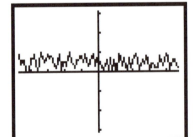

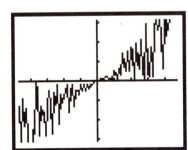

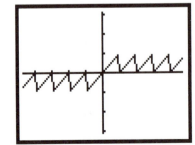

Brain stretcher *Lists and trigonometric relationships*

Press MODE and check that your calculator is in Degree mode and set to show 2 decimal places.

Produce ten random integers between 0 and 360 by entering **randInt(0,360,10)** and store them in list L1.

(a) Store $90 - $ L1 in L2.

Store cos(L1) in L3.

Store sin(L2) in L4.

Inspect the values in L2 and L4. What does this tell you?

(b) Store $180 + $ L1 in L2.

Store cos(L1) in L2.

Store cos(L2) in L4.

Inspect the values in L2 and L4. What does this tell you?

(c) Store $(\sin(L1))^2 + (\cos(L1))^2$ in L2.

Inspect the values in L2. What does this tell you?

Chapter 10 More about straight lines

One of the problems that arises frequently in many branches of both science and social science is to find a 'rule' to describe paired experimental data. This will be a theme in the next four chapters of this book. You will meet batches of paired data where the two data sets appear to be connected in some way. The challenge will be to find a mathematical relationship that best seems to connect the two variables representing the data sets, and then to make predictions based on that relationship.

A first step in describing the mathematical relationship is often to produce a scatterplot of the paired data to see whether there appears to be any pattern or trend. For example, look at the scatterplots below. Does there seem to be a pattern in each of the sets of points?

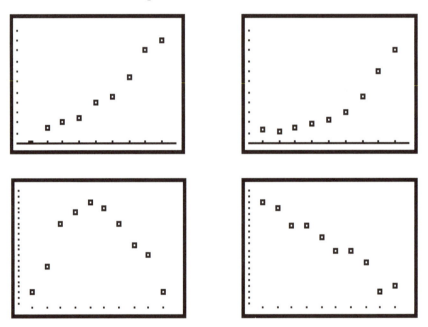

If there does seem to be a pattern, the next step is to decide what sort of curve or line will best fit the points. Is it a straight line or does some curve provide a better fit? Once this decision is made, you are well on the way to being able to produce a formula linking the two variables.

In the first section of this chapter you will consider situations where a straight line provides a good fit, and in Chapters 11–13 you will see how to fit various types of curve to paired data in a similar way. To do this you will be using the **statistical regression** features of your calculator.

statistical regression

The second section of this chapter introduces the shading facilities of the calculator. Just as lines on the graphing screen represent equations linking x and y, so shaded areas represent **inequalities** linking x and y.

inequalities

10.1 Fitting a linear model to data points

Table 10.1 shows the percentage of school-leavers who had no GCSE or equivalent qualifications over the period 1977 to 1992, given at three-year intervals. These data will be used to illustrate how to use your calculator to fit a linear model.

Table 10.1 School-leavers with no GCSE or equivalent qualifications

Year	1977	1980	1983	1986	1989	1992
%	17	14	12	12	8	7

Source: Social Trends 25 (1995), p. 53

Enter these paired data into your calculator. Enter the years (as 77, 80 and so on) into list L1 and the percentages into list L2.

Clear the Graphing screen, perhaps using the program CLEARGS which you met in Chapter 7 and which should still be in your calculator's memory. Next set up a scatterplot by pressing [2nd] [STAT PLOT] **1** and setting the options shown here.

Press [ZOOM] **9** to set the axes automatically and display the scatterplot.

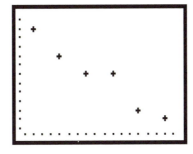

It should be clear that there is a fairly regular reduction in the percentages over time and it is easy to imagine that a straight line could be drawn which roughly represents the overall trend of the points. However, where exactly should this line be drawn? Where is the best possible position for such a line?

Any straight line can be described by an equation of the form $y = ax + b$. You can use the calculator's regression features to calculate the equation of the line which provides the best fit. It will calculate the values of a (the gradient of the line) and b (the intercept, where the line cuts the y-axis): a and b are known as the **regression coefficients**. It is then possible to enter the required equation on the Y= screen and so draw the regression line. The steps of the process are as follows.

regression coefficients

◇ Calculate the regression coefficients using the STAT CALC menu.

◇ Enter the regression equation on the Y= screen.

◇ Draw the graph of the line of best fit.

You will see in later chapters that this same procedure can be used to fit other curves as well as to fit the straight line needed in this case.

Carry out each of the following steps on your calculator.

Press STAT ▶ to see the STAT CALC menu shown here.

You require *linear* regression. (Linear means to do with straight lines.) Option 4 is the form that is required here as it will give the values of *a* and *b* in an equation of the form $y = ax + b$.

Notice that option 8 would give the coefficients of an equation of the form $y = a + bx$. Either option would do as long as you remember which way round the coefficients are given. In this chapter you will always use option 4.

Press **4** to paste **LinReg(ax+b)** on to the Home screen.

Now press

2nd [L1] , 2nd [L2]

to specify which two lists contain the data. The first list will contain the *x*-coordinates and the second the *y*-coordinates.

Press ENTER and the calculation is carried out.

The values of *a* and *b* are given to 10 significant figures.

The next step is to enter the equation on the Y= screen. It would be possible to enter Y₁ = ‾.6476190476X + 66.39047619 manually, but, fortunately, there is an easier way. Because the calculator has stored the values of *a* and *b,* it is possible to enter the complete regression equation from one of the VARS submenus as follows.

Press Y= and if necessary clear the expression alongside Y₁.

Press VARS **5** ▶ ▶ to display the submenu shown here.

Press **1** or [ENTER] to paste the regression equation on to the Y= screen.

Press [GRAPH] and the linear regression line is superimposed on the scatterplot.

Is this where you imagined the line of best fit would lie?

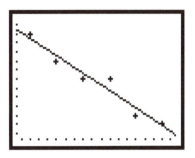

Once the equation of the regression line has been calculated and entered as Y_1, it is easy to use it to estimate or predict other data values. Suppose, for example, that you needed to estimate the percentage of unqualified school-leavers in 1982. You could simply enter $Y_1(82)$ on the Home screen. In the same way you could estimate what the percentage might have been back in 1960 or predict what it might become in the future – but only if you assume that the rate of decrease is constant over an extended period of time, or in other words that the straight line can be extended in both directions. Such an assumption is, of course, highly dubious!

Exercise 10.1 *Estimating and predicting*

(a) Estimate the percentage of unqualified school-leavers in 1985 and 1990.

(b) Assume that the rate of decrease was constant in the period before 1977 and use [TBLSET] and [TABLE] to estimate the likely percentage of unqualified school-leavers in 1970. In which year did the percentage fall below 20%?

(c) If present trends were to continue, when would all school-leavers have some qualifications?

The correlation coefficient r

Earlier you used the VARS STATISTICS EQ submenu to paste the regression equation on to the Y= screen. You may have noticed that the two regression coefficients, a and b, were also available on that screen. c, d and e are similar coefficients which are calculated when you use other types of regression.

Another important coefficient, r, is contained in option 7. It is known as the **correlation coefficient** and its value is an indication of how well the regression line fits the data points.

correlation coefficient

167

Press $\boxed{\text{VARS}}$ **5** $\boxed{\blacktriangleright}$ $\boxed{\blacktriangleright}$ **7** to paste *r* onto the Home screen. Press $\boxed{\text{ENTER}}$ and you should see its value, ¯.976087728 which is ¯.98 to two decimal places. Recall that in this last example the line of fit did not pass exactly through each point but did pass quite close to all of them.

Now suppose there were only two data points: the line of best fit would have to pass exactly through them both. So an easy way of exploring how *r* varies is to use just two pairs of values, representing the *x*- and *y*-coordinates of two points. This will involve changing the data in L1 and L2 and drawing a new line of best fit. There is a short-cut for doing this more easily than the method outlined above. If you enter **LinReg(ax+b) L1,L2,Y1** the values of *a* and *b* will be calculated and the new regression equation pasted automatically alongside Y1.

You will still require a scatterplot showing L2 against L1, so there is no need to change the STAT PLOT settings. For the next exercise it is best to reset the viewing window so that both axes run from 0 to 10.

Exercise 10.2   *Fitting a straight line to two data points*

(a) Enter the coordinates of the points (8, 5) and (4, 3) as paired data into the lists L1 and L2. (Note that L1 must contain the two *x*-coordinates, 8 and 4, and L2 the two *y*-coordinates, 5 and 3.)

Calculate the linear regression coefficients using **LinReg(ax+b) L1,L2,Y1**.

Then press $\boxed{\text{VARS}}$ **5** $\boxed{\blacktriangleright}$ $\boxed{\blacktriangleright}$ **7** $\boxed{\text{ENTER}}$.

Write down the values of *a, b* and *r*.

Now press $\boxed{\text{GRAPH}}$ and compare the features of the regression line with the values of *a* and *b*.

(b) Enter your answers from part (a) into the table below and repeat the process with each of the other pairs of points to complete the table. Do you have any theories about the way the value of *r* is related to *a* and *b*? If necessary, try other pairs of points to check or develop your theory.

Points	*a*	*b*	*r*
(8, 5) (4, 3)			
(2, 6) (4, 3)			
(2, 6) (8, 3)			
(2, 6) (8, 9)			

You have seen that with just two data points, the line of best fit always passes through them both and that the correlation coefficient is either 1 or ¯1 depending on whether the line slopes upwards or downwards to the right. With the school-leavers data in Table 10.1, the correlation coefficient, *r,* was equal to ¯.98 (to two decimal places) and the regression line sloped downwards to the right, passing quite close to, but not actually through, each of the points.

In general *r*, the correlation coefficient, is an indication of how closely the points lie to the regression line. It is a numerical measure of the strength of this relationship, and its value always lies somewhere in the range $^-1$ to $+1$. The diagram below summarizes how the correlation coefficient is interpreted.

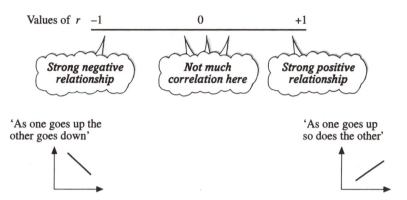

Some examples of scatterplots and their linear regression lines are given below, together with their corresponding correlation coefficients.

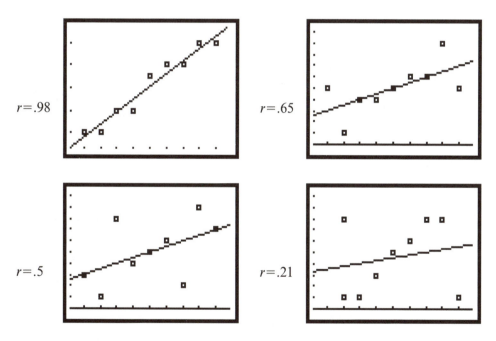

Notice the way that the value of *r* reduces towards zero as the points move further away from a straight line.

Brain stretcher   *No correlation*

What sort of scatterplot would have a correlation coefficient of zero?

Could you arrange four points so that *r* = 0? Enter the coordinates in L1 and L2 and check your conjecture.

What if you had three points, or five, or 10 or 100?

Two linear regression lines

Finally in this section, here is an example drawn from classical economic theory which uses linear regression within the context of supply and demand. It is worth pointing out that the situation is an artificial one and the data are simplified in order not to obscure the underlying process.

Suppose that you are trying to decide on the best selling price of a new variety of yoghurt. The higher the selling price, the more producers would be likely to manufacture the new yoghurt, but the fewer people would be likely to buy it. You have the results of two surveys, summarized in Table 10.2. One, from consumers, suggests the number of yoghurts likely to be sold over a range of different prices – likely amount demanded reduces as the price rises. The other, from possible producers, indicates the total quantity which would be likely to be supplied by them at different selling prices – likely amount supplied increases as the price rises.

You could find the regression equations both for the likely demand at different prices and for the quantities likely to be supplied at different prices. If these regression lines are plotted and the point of intersection located, the coordinates of that point would indicate where the quantity demanded is balanced by the quantity supplied. This is called the equilibrium price, as it is where the price is likely to stabilize.

Table 10.2 Results of surveys into supply and demand for new yoghurt

Possible selling price (pence)	Likely amount demanded by customers (millions per week)	Likely amount supplied by manufacturers (millions per week)
15	30	11
20	26	15
25	23	20
30	19	25
35	16	30
40	12	34

Input the data from Table 10.2 into L_1, L_2 and L_3 and clear the Graphing screen using the program CLEARGS.

Exercise 10.3 *Supply and demand*

(a) *The demand model*

Set up a STAT PLOT giving a scatterplot of L_1 against L_2, choose an appropriate viewing window and confirm that the points lie close to a straight line.

On the Home screen enter **LinReg(ax+b) L_1,L_2,Y_1** to evaluate *a* and *b*.

Press Y= to confirm that the regression equation is displayed and then check that the graph appears to be a good fit.

(b) *The supply model*

Set up a second STAT PLOT to give a scatterplot of L1 against L3. Choose a different mark to represent the points on the plot from the symbol you used for Plot 1.

Evaluate the linear regression coefficients and enter this second regression equation as Y2.

(c) *Simultaneous models*

Press GRAPH; notice that you have four things on the Graphing screen now: two scatterplots and two regression lines.

Press TRACE and **P1:L1,L2** will appear in the top left-hand corner of the screen, indicating that you are tracing Plot 1. Press ▾ ▾ and the top left-hand corner changes to Y1, indicating that you are now tracing the Y1 line.

(d) *Setting the price and production level*

Zoom in, if necessary, to find the x-coordinate of where the two regression lines intersect. Since this represents the equilibrium price of the yoghurt in pence, this price should be stated as a whole number of pence.

Use the table facility to find the corresponding number of yoghurts produced and sold, to an appropriate level of accuracy.

10.2   *Inequalities and linear programming*

In earlier chapters you have used the Y= screen to enter an equation and then you have drawn a line representing that equation. The line is made up of all the points whose x- and y-coordinates satisfy the equation. For example, the line whose equation is $y = x + 5$ is made up of points such as (0, 5), (10, 15), (11.3, 16.3) and so on.

Instead of an equation, with an equals sign, consider what is called an **inequality**, with a less than ($<$) or greater than ($>$) sign. For example, suppose you had the inequality $y < x + 5$. How would this be represented in graphical form? There are certainly a lot of points where the y-coordinate is less than the x-coordinate plus 5. In fact all the points which lie below the line $y = x + 5$ satisfy this inequality, so the way to represent the inequality graphically is to shade that particular part of the graph. There is a way of doing this on the calculator using a setting on the Y= screen.

inequality

First clear the Graphing screen using the program CLEARGS. Next choose the standard window setting using option 6 in the ZOOM menu.

Press Y= and clear any functions in Y1 or Y2.

Press X,T,Θ,*n* ＋ **5**.

Do not press ENTER.

Now press ◄ ◄ ◄ ◄ ◄ to move the cursor to the left of Y1.

The graph style icon is now highlighted. The TI-83 provides seven different style icons for graph drawing, with the line (`) being the default setting.

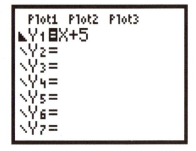

Press ENTER until the required style is displayed, as shown on the right. This is the ▙ icon, which produces shading below the graph.

Press GRAPH and you should see the region below the line $y = x + 5$ shaded with vertical lines.

Now shade all the points that satisfy another inequality, $y > 3 - x$ by pressing

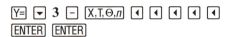

Y= ▼ 3 — X,T,Θ,*n* ◄ ◄ ◄ ◄ ◄
ENTER ENTER

Press GRAPH and the resulting display is shown on the right. The Graphing screen has now been divided into four regions.

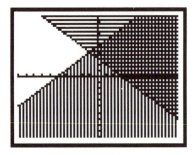

Exercise 10.4 *The four regions*

Spend a few moments classifying what each region represents, in relation to the four inequalities $y > x + 5$, $y < x + 5$, $y > 3 - x$ and $y < 3 - x$.

Brain stretcher   *Another shading option*

Option 7 of the DRAW menu also allows you to shade the screen. It requires 2, 3, 4 or 6 arguments. (Remember that arguments are the numbers or expressions that must appear in brackets separated by commas.)

Find out how this calculator feature works by trying the following entries and others of your own choice. You will probably want to clear the screen between each shading.

Shade(X−10,X+10)

Shade(X−10,X+10,4)

Shade(X−10,X+10,⁻4,4)

Shade(X−10,X+10,⁻4,4,3,5)

Rearranging inequalities

Equations and inequalities come in lots of different forms and are not always in the form that the calculator expects. You have seen that an equation such as $x + y = 30$ has to be rearranged into the form $y = 30 - x$ in order to enter it onto the Y= screen.

In the same way, an inequality such as $x + y > 30$ has to be entered on the calculator in the form $y > 30 - x$.

There are a number of algebraic rules for rearranging equations and similar ones for rearranging inequalities. However, there are one or two differences in the rules and these provide potential pitfalls – so proceed with caution!

First, here are the rules for rearranging equations and some examples of how to use them.

If two expressions are equal, then the equality will be maintained if you:

◇   add or subtract the same number to or from both sides

◇   multiply or divide both sides by the same number

Start with	Do this	End up with
$x + y = 30$	Subtract x from both sides	$y = 30 - x$
$y - x = 40$	Add x to both sides	$y = 40 + x$
$x + 0.5y = 20$	Subtract x from both sides and	$0.5y = 20 - x$
	multiply both sides by 2	$y = 40 - 2x$
$x - 0.5y = 30$	Subtract x from both sides and	$-0.5y = 30 - x$
	multiply both sides by $^-2$,	$y = {}^-60 + 2x$
	which is equivalent to	$y = 2x - 60$

Now here are the corresponding rules for inequalities.

If one expression is less than another, then the inequality will be maintained if you:

◇   add or subtract the same number to or from both sides

◇   multiply or divide both sides by a *positive* number.

But if you multiply or divide both sides by a *negative* number, the sign of the inequality is reversed.

This final rule is the awkward one. In practice, it is best simply to avoid multiplying or dividing by a negative number. In almost all situations you can do a bit more manipulation to avoid doing this. Here is an example.

Start with	Do this	End up with
$20 - y > x$	Add y to both sides and	$20 > x + y$
	subtract x from both sides,	$20 - x > y$
	which is equivalent to	$y < 20 - x$

Rearrange the following inequalities into one of the forms '$y <$ something' or '$y >$ something':

(a) $x + y > 30$

(b) $x + 0.5y > 20$

(c) $y - x < 30$

(d) $x - y < 30$

(e) $x - 0.5y < 20$

Once you have rearranged an inequality into the appropriate form, you are ready to represent it on the calculator by drawing the appropriate shaded area.

Shading unwanted regions

When you are solving a problem which involves two or more inequalities, it may sometimes be easier to shade the region which is *not* represented by the inequality, leaving the region in which you are interested unshaded.

linear programming   This is often the case in what are known as **linear programming** problems. Note that this rather misleading term does not have any direct connection with the programming of the calculator that you have been doing so far. Rather it is a historical term, used to describe a method of solving certain types of problems which involve inequalities. In these problems you normally have a number of constraints, all of which must be satisfied. It is often easier to shade the region which is ruled out by each constraint, leaving an unshaded part of the graph,
feasible region   known as the final **feasible region**, which contains the possible solutions of the problem.

The following is an example of a problem which can be solved using linear programming techniques.

Suppose two particular products are to be kept in stock by a shop. There are certain constraints upon the number of each that can be stocked and the shopkeeper has to take account of these constraints in deciding how many of each product to buy.

Suppose that there will be x of one product and y of the other. Notice that both x and y must be positive whole numbers, you cannot stock $^-2$ or 3.46 items of either product. However, sales of the items dictate that $x + y$ should not exceed 30. The symbol $\leq$ means 'less than or equal' so, in symbols:

$$x + y \leq 30$$

This can be rearranged to

$$y \leq 30 - x \qquad (1)$$

Suppose also that storage space dictates that $x + 0.5y \leq 20$.

This can be rearranged to

$$y \leq 40 - 2x \qquad (2)$$

Make certain that *you* understand how inequalities (1) and (2) have been formed from their respective original constraints.

The next stage is to display the feasible region that satisfies both inequalities on the calculator's Graphing screen.

Exercise 10.6   *Unshaded feasible region*

(a) Set a suitable viewing window for the Graphing screen. Remember that neither x nor y can be negative, nor can either of them exceed 30 since $x + y \leq 30$.

(b) On the Y= screen enter $Y_1 = 30 - X$ and $Y_2 = 40 - 2X$.

Since inequality (1) is $y \leq 30 - x$, shade the unwanted region by selecting the 'shade above' icon ($\blacktriangledown$) in the Y= screen. Repeat this process for inequality (2).

The unshaded area represents the feasible quantities of the two products which could be stocked by the shop.

In the last exercise you shaded the unwanted areas ruled out by inequalities (1) and (2). This left a large number of possible pairs of whole-number values of x and y in the feasible region. Which of these many pairs of values should be chosen? In such situations there are usually other factors which are likely to determine the quantity stocked. For example, the potential profit attached to each product is likely to be an important consideration.

Suppose, for example, that in this case the profit on each of the two products is 3 units and 2 units, respectively. (Do not worry about what these units represent for the moment – each unit could be ten pence, one pound, ten pounds, or whatever.) Since the shop will be stocking x items, each producing a profit of 3 and y items, each producing a profit of 2, the total profit will be $3x + 2y$. Of course, the shopkeeper is likely to want the total profit to be as large as possible. So it would be useful to know which of the points in the feasible region produces the largest value for $3x + 2y$. One way of working this out is to draw a series of lines representing different total profits, say 20, 30, and so on, and use a trial and error approach to find the maximum possible profit within the feasible region.

Start with a profit of 20 units. This would be represented by the equation $3x + 2y = 20$, which can be rearranged to

$$y = (20 - 3x) \div 2$$

Draw this line on the same graph as the feasible region, by setting $Y_3 = (20 - 3X)/2$ in the Y= menu and pressing GRAPH.

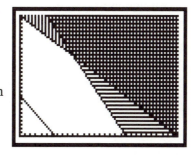

This new line joins the points which represent a profit of 20, and there are several of these within the feasible region.

Now draw the line which represents a profit of 30, by entering Y4 = (30 − 3X)/2 and pressing GRAPH.

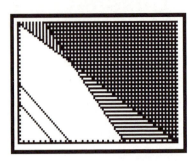

Notice that the profit lines $y = (20 − 3x)/2$ and $y = (30 − 3x)/2$ are parallel, and any other profit lines will also be parallel to these two. You can see that it is possible to fit lines representing a much bigger profit than 30 into the feasible region.

Change Y3 to (50 − 3X)/2 and Y4 to (60 − 3X)/2.

Press GRAPH.

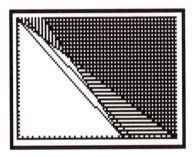

It appears that the maximum profit will be more than 60, but perhaps not as much as 70 since that line will probably all lie outside the feasible region. Whatever the maximum profit is, it will occur near the top right-hand corner of the feasible region.

Try making Y3 = (65 − 3X)/2.

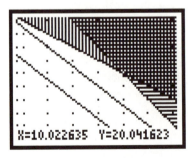

It looks as though the maximum profit will be just above 65 units and it would be useful to see the area of the feasible region just above the line Y3 = (65 − 3X)/2 more clearly. To do this you could use one of the zoom facilities. Try using either **ZBox** or **Zoom In** for yourself.

A further possible step is to superimpose a grid of points on the display to represent each of the possible whole-number values of x and y. To do this you need to use the FORMAT menu and select **GridOn** as you did in Chapter 6. However, check that the window settings are **Xscl** = 1 and **Yscl** = 1, so that each pair of values of x and y has its own grid point.

Finally, use the cursor keys to find the coordinates of the point that represents the maximum profit. As shown here, this is the point where $x = 10$ and $y = 20$.

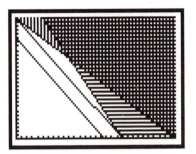

This means that it would be best for the shopkeeper to buy 10 of the first product and 20 of the second in order to maximize profits.

In general, the point which represents the maximum profit is always likely to be at one corner of the feasible region.

Chapter 11 Quadratic functions

The theme throughout this chapter is quadratic functions: that is, functions which include terms involving x^2 but no higher powers. Such functions have curved graphs which are known as **parabolas**, and you will explore the properties of these graphs in Section 11.1. Section 11.2 introduces the feature in the MATH menu which calculates the gradients of graphs, and you will use this to study the way in which the gradient of a parabola changes.

parabola

In Section 11.3 you will use another of the regression facilities of the calculator: this time to fit a quadratic function to a set of data points.

The chapter concludes with another addition to your calculator's collection of programs – one which will be useful when you need to solve a quadratic equation.

11.1 Graphs of quadratic functions: parabolas

The curve shown on the right is an example of a parabola. It has been produced by drawing the graph of a function of the form

$$y = ax^2 + bx + c$$

with particular numbers instead of a, b and c.

Every parabola is symmetrical about its axis and has a maximum or minimum point which is known as its vertex.

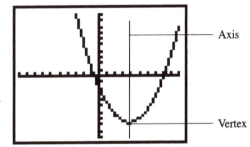

Axis

Vertex

Exercise 11.1   *The effect of a*

(a) Set up your Y= screen as shown here. (Notice that all the minus signs have been entered using the blue ⊟ key.)

Draw the four parabolas by selecting **ZDecimal** from the ZOOM menu. What effect do you think increasing the value of a like this has?

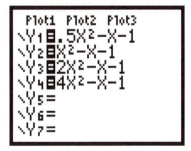

(b) Now change each of the values of a, making them all negative. To do this, position the flashing cursor to the right of the equals sign and press 2nd [INS] (-). (Notice that you have to use the grey (-) key here.)

Draw the four new parabolas. What is the effect of making the value of a negative?

Exercise 11.2   The effect of c

Set up your Y= screen as shown here.

Draw the four parabolas. What effect does changing the value of c like this have? Where does each parabola cut the vertical axis?

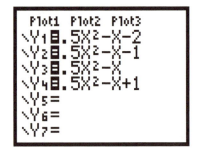

```
Plot1 Plot2 Plot3
\Y1∎.5X²-X-2
\Y2∎.5X²-X-1
\Y3∎.5X²-X
\Y4∎.5X²-X+1
\Y5=
\Y6=
\Y7=
```

Locating the vertex

It is often necessary to find the coordinates of the vertex, and you saw in Chapter 8 two ways in which this can be achieved. You can either use the Graphing screen and repeatedly zoom in on the vertex or you can use the Table screen with repeatedly smaller values of **ΔTbl**. The next two exercises ask you to find the vertex of the graph of the function $y = 2x^2 + x/2 - 3$ using these two methods.

Start by clearing all previous graphs and drawings by executing the program CLEARGS. Then, on the Y= screen enter $Y_1 = 2X^2 + X/2 - 3$. Choose **ZStandard** and display the graph.

Exercise 11.3   Zooming in on the vertex

Repeatedly use TRACE and **Zoom In** to get as close a view as possible of the vertex of the parabola. Using just these two facilities, produce as good an estimate as possible of the values of x and y at the vertex.

Exercise 11.4   Locating the vertex using TABLE

(a) Press [2nd] [TBLSET] and set **TblStart** to 0 and **ΔTbl** to 0.1.

Press [2nd] [TABLE].

By moving up or down, find the minimum value of Y_1. This is the value which corresponds most closely to the vertex. What is the corresponding value of X?

(b) Reset **TblStart** to the value of X you obtained in part (a) and set **ΔTbl** to .01.

Again find the extreme value of Y_1. Several of the values of Y_1 which are displayed will appear to be the same because they have been rounded to three decimal places. However, if you position the cursor over any one of these values, you will see its more accurate value at the bottom of the screen. Again, make a note of the corresponding value of X.

(c) Repeat this procedure until you are convinced that you have the best possible values for the coordinates of the vertex.

In the last two exercises you will have found that it is quite an awkward process to find accurate figures for the coordinates of the vertex of the graph of the function $y = 2x^2 + x/2 - 3$. However, there is an option in the CALC menu which can help. Return to the standard Graphing screen by pressing ZOOM **6** and then press 2nd [CALC] to see the CALC menu. Option 3 in that menu, **minimum**, will enable you to calculate the coordinates of the vertex. It uses a method similar to those for other options in the CALC menu that you met in Chapter 8. You are first asked to specify a left and a right bound within which the minimum value falls and then to provide a guess.

Try using this option now and you should find that the coordinates of the minimum point are calculated automatically, confirming the values from Exercise 11.4.

In a similar way, option 4 in the CALC menu allows you to calculate a maximum value, for example the vertex of an inverted parabola.

Given the x-value, find y

It is relatively straightforward to find the value of y for a particular value of x using a quadratic function, or indeed any function defined on the Y= screen.

Suppose, for example, you wished to find the value of y when $x = 3$ for the quadratic function you used before, $y = 2x^2 + x/2 - 3$.

The ZOOM or TABLE techniques could be used. For example, you could find the value of y when $x = 3$ by zooming in on that point or by setting **TblStart** to 3 and looking at the table. Other efficient methods are to enter $Y_1(3)$ on the Home screen or to press TRACE **3** ENTER.

If you require the values of y corresponding to several different values of x, TABLE often becomes a more attractive method, especially using an additional facility available on the TABLE SETUP screen.

Press 2nd [TBLSET] and use the cursor and ENTER to highlight the option **Ask** in the row labelled **Indpnt** (referring to the 'independent' variable). The top two settings **TblStart** and **ΔTbl** will now be ignored, so do not worry about the numbered values displayed there.

Press 2nd [TABLE] and you will see the empty columns below X (the independent variable) and Y_1 (the dependent variable).

Suppose you wanted to find y for each of the four values of x: .5, ⁻1, .125, $\frac{1}{3}$. Simply enter these values in the independent column and the corresponding values appear beside them.

Given the y-value, find x

There is a direct but fairly complicated method of finding the value of x for a given value of y. However, first try using the ZOOM or TABLE facilities, or perhaps a combination of the two.

Work through the following example where the problem is to find the x-value when $y = 3$ for the function $y = 2x^2 + x/2 - 3$.

First look at the overall shape of the curve using the standard viewing window.

Press ZOOM **6**.

Use the tick marks on the y-axis to locate $Y = 3$. It is immediately clear that there are *two* corresponding values of x.

For the moment, concentrate on the positive value of x, on the right of the graph.

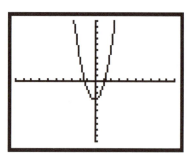

Press TRACE and move the cursor to the right. Using the coordinates displayed at the bottom of the screen, select the point which gives a y-value as close as possible to $Y = 3$.

Make a note of the corresponding x-value, rounded to one decimal place: 1.7.

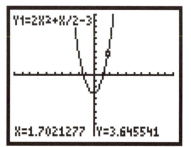

Press 2nd [TBLSET] and set **TblStart** to 1.7 and **ΔTbl** to .1. Make sure that **Indpnt** is set to **Auto**.

Press 2nd [TABLE] ▲.

The value of Y_1 passes through 3 between $X = 1.6$ and 1.7.

X	Y₁
1.6	2.92
1.7	3.63
1.8	4.38
1.9	5.17
2	6
2.1	6.87
2.2	7.78

X=1.6

Press 2nd [TBLSET] and set **TblStart** to 1.6 and **ΔTbl** to .01.

Press 2nd [TABLE].

The value of Y_1 passes through 3 between $X = 1.61$ and 1.62.

You now know that the required value of x is 1.6 (correct to one decimal place).

X	Y₁
1.6	2.92
1.61	2.9892
1.62	3.0588
1.63	3.1288
1.64	3.1992
1.65	3.27
1.66	3.3412

X=1.6

Press 2nd [TBLSET] and set **TblStart** to 1.61 and **ΔTbl** to .001.

Press 2nd [TABLE].

The value of Y_1 passes through 3 between $X = 1.611$ and 1.612.

X	Y₁
1.61	2.9892
1.611	2.9961
1.612	3.0031
1.613	3.01
1.614	3.017
1.615	3.024
1.616	3.0309

X=1.61

If it were necessary to know the value of x to even greater accuracy, it would be possible to continue further with this procedure. Try it, if you like.

You may be thinking that repeatedly using ZOOM, rather than TABLE, is an easier way of finding the required value of x. ZOOM can work well sometimes, but it is very easy to get lost on the Graphing screen and it is also more difficult to be sure about the level of accuracy of the x-value that you have found. You might want to convince yourself of this by trying the above example using ZOOM, rather than TABLE, repeatedly.

An alternative way of finding the values of x for a particular value of y makes use of an option in the CALC menu. If you require to know the values of x when $y = 3$ where $y = 2x^2 + x/2 - 3$ it is equivalent to solving the two simultaneous equations:

$$y = 2x^2 + x/2 - 3 \quad \text{and} \quad y = 3$$

As you saw in Chapter 8 two such equations can be solved by plotting their two graphs and using option 5, **intersect,** from the CALC menu. You are asked to solve these two equations in the next exercise.

Exercise 11.5   *Solving for a particular value of y*

Ensure that $Y_1 = 2X^2 + X/2 - 3$ and enter $Y_2 = 3$. Draw their two graphs and use the CALC menu option 5, **intersect**, to find the values of x when $y = 3$ and $y = 2x^2 + x/2 - 3$.

11.2   *The gradient of a parabola*

There is a function on your calculator which will find the approximate gradient of a curve. It is option 8 of the MATH menu and is labelled **nDeriv**. This stands for **numerical derivative** (the derivative of a function is another word for its gradient.) The gradient of a curve (as opposed to a straight line) is different at every point along its length. The calculator works out the value of **nDeriv** by finding the average gradient over a very tiny section of the curve. Because the gradient of a curve indicates how it is changing, **nDeriv** is a powerful facility for finding rates of change.

numerical derivative

nDeriv requires three arguments: that is, it must be followed by a pair of brackets containing three items separated by commas. You need to specify:

◇   the equation of the curve, either directly (for example, $2x + 3$) or using one of the functions in the Y= menu (for example, Y1)

◇   the variable (usually x)

◇   the x-coordinate of the particular point at which you require the gradient

Investigate how the **nDeriv** function works by doing the following exercises.

Exercise 11.6   *The gradient of a straight line*

(a) Enter each of the following on the Home screen (suggested key presses are given). At each stage, before you press ENTER try to guess what will be displayed.

Home screen entry	Press
nDeriv(2X + 3, X, 2)	MATH **8 2** X,T,Θ,*n* + **3** , X,T,Θ,*n* , **2**)
nDeriv(2X + 3, X, 3)	2nd [ENTRY] ◄ ◄ **3**
nDeriv(2X + 3, X, ⁻5)	2nd [ENTRY] ◄ ◄ (-) **5**)
nDeriv(2X + 3, X, 10)	2nd [ENTRY] ◄ ◄ ◄ **1 0**
nDeriv(7X + 3, X, 2)	MATH **8 7** X,T,Θ,*n* + **3** , X,T,Θ,*n* , **2**)
nDeriv(7X + 3, X, 10)	2nd [ENTRY] ◄ ◄ **1 0**)
nDeriv(7X + 3, X, 100)	2nd [ENTRY] ◄ **0**)

(b) Write down what the results of part (a) tell you about the gradients of a straight line.

Exercise 11.7   *The gradient of the parabola y = x²*

(a) Enter the following on your calculator and record the gradient of the curve at the points where $x = {}^-2, {}^-1, 0, 1, 2$.

Home screen entry	Gradient
nDeriv(X^2, X, $^-2$)	
nDeriv(X^2, X, $^-1$)	
nDeriv(X^2, X, 0)	
nDeriv(X^2, X, 1)	
nDeriv(X^2, X, 2)	

(b) How does the gradient of the curve at any point relate to the *x*-coordinate of the point? Calculate the gradient at other points to check your conjecture.

Using nDeriv on the Y= screen

One way of checking the result of the last exercise involves entering nDeriv on the Y= screen.

Press Y= and set Y₁ and Y₂ as shown on the right.

Notice that Y₂ has been set up to be the function which is the gradient of Y₁ at *all* values of *x*. (Hence the need for the third argument to be X.)

```
 Plot1 Plot2 Plot3
\Y1◼X²
\Y2◼nDeriv(Y1,X,
X)
\Y3=
\Y4=
\Y5=
\Y6=
```

Now press [2nd] [TBLSET] and set **TblStart** to ⁻10 and **ΔTbl** to 1.

Press [2nd] [TABLE].

The Y_1 column shows the values of x^2 and the Y_2 column shows the gradients of $y = x^2$ at particular values of x. Notice that all the Y_2 values are double the corresponding x-values, confirming the result you found in Exercise 11.7. Use the cursor keys to move up and down the table to check that this is always the case.

You could alter the values of **TblStart** and **ΔTbl** to any values and then check the Y_2 column again. Do this until you are convinced that the gradient of $y = x^2$ is always twice the value of x.

Now suppose you were to plot the graph of Y_2, what do you think you would get? You know that the value of Y_2 is always twice the value of x, or in symbols, $Y_2 = 2X$, and you should recognize this as the equation of a straight line.

Press [GRAPH] now and see what you get.

You should see the graph of $y = x^2$ and the graph of its gradient function, $Y_2 = \text{nDeriv}(Y_1, X, X)$, which is the straight line $y = 2x$.

If you are not convinced that it is the line $y = 2x$, trace the points on Y_2 to check that every y-value is twice the corresponding x-value. Alternatively you could input the function $Y_3 = 2X$ and plot its graph on the same screen. It should overwrite the graph of Y_2 exactly.

So the gradient function of the parabola $y = x^2$ is a straight line. But what about the gradients or derivatives of other quadratic functions? Will they also give straight lines, and if so which ones? That is the focus of Exercises 11.8 and 11.9.

Exercise 11.8   The gradient of $y = 2x^2 + 3$

On the Y= screen set $Y_1 = 2X^2 + 3$ and leave $Y_2 = \text{nDeriv}(Y_1, X, X)$.

Look at the table of Y_2 and plot the graphs of Y_1 and Y_2. What is the equation of the straight line produced by Y_2?

Exercise 11.9   The gradients of other quadratics

Use a similar procedure to find the equation of the gradient for each of the following quadratic functions.

(a) $y = 4x^2 + 3$

(b) $y = x^2 + 3x$

(c) $y = 2x^2 + 3x$

(d) $y = 4x^2 + 5x$

(e) $y = x^2 + 3x - 1$

Do you notice any patterns in your results? In particular, how do the coefficients in the equations of the straight line relate to the coefficients in the equations of the parabolas?

Do your results allow you to make a general statement about the gradient of any quadratic function of the form $y = ax^2 + bx + c$?

The gradient of other functions

So far you have shown that:

◇   the gradient of a straight line is a constant

◇   the gradient of a quadratic function is a straight line

How about other functions? There is a branch of mathematics, called calculus, which obtains these gradient or derivative functions theoretically, but with your calculator you can investigate them practically. However, be warned: these investigations are truly brain stretching!

Brain stretcher   *The gradients of cubic functions*

Using the basic technique of Exercise 11.8, try to predict the gradient function of each of the following. The shape of the graph of the gradient function should provide some clue to get you started.

$y = x^3$

$y = x^3 + 3$

$y = 2x^3 + 3x$

$y = 4x^3 + 3x^2$

$y = x^3 + x^2 + 3x - 1$

In each case, you will be able to check your guess by entering it as Y3 and comparing its graph with Y2.

Maximum and minimum points

As you saw in Section 11.1, it is difficult to locate the vertex of a parabola graphically. As you zoom in on the graph, it looks more and more like a straight horizontal line, so it is difficult to decide just where the maximum or minimum point lies. However, the fact that the gradient of the curve there is zero can be used to overcome this problem. Rather than zooming in on the vertex itself, you can zoom in on where its gradient function equals zero.

Here is an example of how you might use this technique to find the coordinates of the vertex of the parabola representing $y = 7x^2 + 20x + 8$. Follow through each of the steps outlined below.

Set up your Y= screen as shown on the right.

Draw the graph of the parabola and its gradient function using **ZStandard**.

Now, suppose you wish to find the coordinates of the vertex. Using TRACE, the best you can do at the moment is probably $X = {}^-1.489$ and $Y = {}^-6.260$.

```
Plot1 Plot2 Plot3
\Y1◼7X²+20X+8
\Y2◼nDeriv(Y1,X,
X)
\Y3=
\Y4=
\Y5=
\Y6=
```

Rather than zooming in on that point, concentrate instead on the corresponding point immediately above it, where the straight line which represents Y2 = nDeriv(Y1, X, X) cuts the horizontal axis; that is, where the gradient function equals zero. Using **ZBox**, outline a small box around this point as shown here.

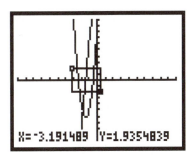

Press ENTER and use **ZBox** twice more.

Press TRACE ▾ in order to move onto the graph of Y2. Move left or right until the cursor is as close as possible to where the graph cuts the horizontal axis. You should get something similar to the display shown on the right, but the actual values will depend on your choice of the corners of the box.

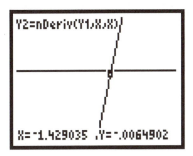

Now press ▴ to move to the graph of Y1. Because of the zooming you have done, the graph itself will be well off the screen now, but the coordinates representing the vertex will still appear at the bottom of the screen. You should get something like $X = {}^-1.429$ and $Y = {}^-6.286$.

If you require more accurate values, return to the Home screen and display the current value of X and of Y1(X).

```
X
            -1.429035015
Y1(X)
            -6.285712781
```

The method used here to find the vertex of a parabola can equally well be used to find the maximum and minimum points on other graphs.

Exercise 11.10   *Finding the vertex*

Find the vertex of the parabola $y = 7x^2 - 18x + 10$ using **nDeriv**.

Brain stretcher   *Turning points for cubics*

Investigate the maximum and minimum points of some cubic functions such as

$$y = \frac{x^3}{10} - 3x$$

Finally in this section, consider option 6 in the CALC menu which is labelled **dy/dx**. This symbol is used very frequently in calculus and is normally read as '*dy by dx*'. It stands for the rate at which *y* changes with respect to *x*, or in other words the gradient of the function. It is closely related to the **nDeriv** function described earlier.

To calculate directly the gradient at a point of any function on the Graphing screen such as the one shown here, simply press 2nd [CALC] **6**, move the cursor to the required point and press ENTER.

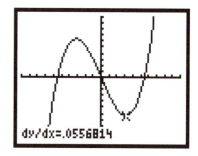

11.3   *Fitting a quadratic model to data points*

In Chapter 10, you used the linear regression facilities of the calculator to fit a straight line to a set of data points. In some cases where a linear model is inappropriate, a quadratic one may be better. The STAT CALC menu also **quadratic regression** includes a **quadratic regression** facility which will give you the 'best fit' quadratic curve for a given set of data points. It operates in a very similar way to the linear regression of Section 10.1 and you need to carry out the following steps.

◇   Enter data as coordinates into two lists.

◇   On a suitable viewing window, draw a scatterplot to represent the data points.

◇   Calculate the quadratic regression coefficients using the STAT CALC menu, pasting the regression equation onto the Y= screen.

◇   Draw the graph of the line of best fit.

An example of quadratic regression

Work through the following stages in order to fit the best quadratic curve to the four data points given below:

$$(^-1, ^-2) \quad (^-2, 3) \quad (1, ^-4) \quad (2, 5)$$

At each stage, check your screen display against the ones shown on the right.

Store the *x*-coordinates in list L_1 and the corresponding *y*-coordinates in list L_2.

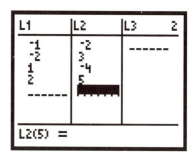

Set STAT PLOT to draw a scatterplot of L_1 against L_2.

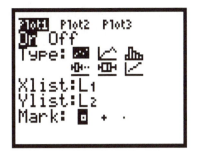

Display the plot using **ZoomStat** from the ZOOM menu.

To calculate the quadratic regression coefficients, you need to choose option 5 from the STAT CALC menu and specify the appropriate lists. At the same time, paste the regression equation onto the Y= screen. To do this press the following keys:

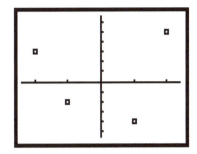

[STAT] [▶] **5** [2nd] [L1] [,] [2nd] [L2] [,]
[VARS] [▶] **1 1** [ENTER]

This means that the equation of the parabola which best fits the data points is:

$$y = 2.333333333\, x^2 + 0.2\, x - 5.333333333$$

It looks as if the three coefficients could have been expressed exactly as fractions. For example, the first one looks very much like $2\frac{1}{3}$ or $\frac{7}{3}$. To check this you could use the fraction facilities of the calculator. Press the following keys to paste a, b and c on to the Home screen and evaluate them as fractions.

[VARS] **5** [▶] [▶] **2** [MATH] **1** [ENTER]
[VARS] **5** [▶] [▶] **3** [MATH] **1** [ENTER]
[VARS] **5** [▶] [▶] **4** [MATH] **1** [ENTER]

```
a▶Frac
                7/3
b▶Frac
                1/5
c▶Frac
              -16/3
```

So the equation of the parabola could be written as:

$$y = \frac{7}{3}x^2 + \frac{1}{5}x - \frac{16}{3}$$

187

Finally, you can draw the parabola to see how well it fits the data points by pressing GRAPH.

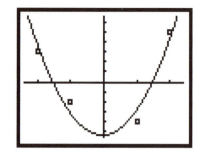

The curve appears to fit the four points quite well. However, with quadratic regression, the correlation coefficient *r* cannot be calculated. You have to judge the goodness of the fit by plotting the quadratic regression function on top of the data points and observing how closely the curve fits.

Exercise 11.11   *Fitting a quadratic function to three data points*

(a) Fit the best quadratic curve to the following three data points:

$$(^-1, ^-2)   (^-2, 3)   (1, ^-4)$$

Notice that these are the first three data points of the set used in the example above, so you need to delete only the fourth values in lists L_1 and L_2. Use the same viewing window as before but do not forget to recalculate the regression coefficients using option 5 in the STAT CALC menu. Leave Y_1 as it was and paste the new regression equation alongside Y_2 on the $Y=$ screen. You will then be able to compare the fit of the new parabola with the fit of the old one.

(b) Write down the equation of the quadratic regression function with the coefficients expressed as fractions.

You saw in the last exercise that with three data points the quadratic regression function appeared to fit the data exactly. You may recall that in Chapter 10, with two data points, the linear regression equation fitted the data exactly.

However, are you sure that the curve really passes through the three points? How could you check this? Would either the ZOOM or the TABLE facility help?

Brain stretcher	*Calculator stretcher*

If you have only three data points, will the quadratic regression equation *always* pass exactly through all three of them?

Make up some data points, enter their coordinates in L_1 and L_2, and test your theory.

What if you choose some very awkward data points? Make it as difficult as you can for your calculator!

Quadratic models from two data points

Suppose you only have two data points. Your calculator will produce an error if you try to fit a quadratic function to them – try it if you like. The problem is that there is a whole range of parabolas that could be drawn through the two points, as shown in the diagram below.

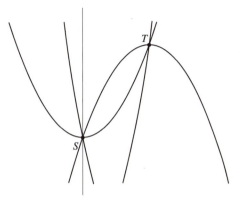

The calculator has just too much choice!

However, suppose you know that one of the two points is actually the vertex of the parabola. There is then only one possible parabola, as the next diagram shows.

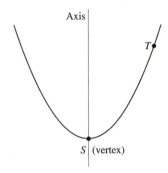

In a case like this, you can use the symmetry of the situation to obtain a further data point. Since a parabola is symmetrical about the axis through the vertex, you can be sure that there is another data point placed symmetrically on the opposite side of the parabola to the point T.

Suppose, for example, that you have two data points called S (the vertex) and T with coordinates $(2,1)$ and $(4,5)$ respectively. As you can see in the next diagram T is two units to the right of S and four units above it.

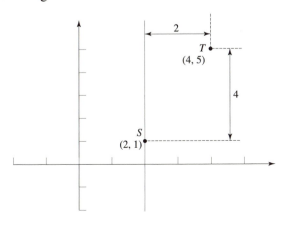

Because of the symmetry of the parabola, there must be another point on the curve two units to the left of S and four units above it. This point would have an x-coordinate of $2 - 2$ and a y-coordinate of $1 + 4$, so it is the point $(0, 5)$. Knowing this you could enter the data for three points into lists L_1 and L_2.

Exercise 11.12   Using two data points

In each case below, use your calculator to find the equation of the parabola with a vertical axis.

(a) The vertex is at $(2, 1)$ and the curve passes through the point $(4, 5)$.

(b) The vertex is at $(4, 0)$ and the curve passes through the point $(1, 9)$.

11.4   A program to solve quadratic equations

There is a formula which gives the solutions (if there are any) of all quadratic equations. The formula gives the solution of a quadratic equation in the form:

$$ax^2 + bx + c = 0$$

where a, b, and c are constants and $a \neq 0$, as

$$x = \frac{-b \pm \sqrt{(b^2 - 4ac)}}{2a}$$

In this section you will be asked to create a program which will produce the solutions of a quadratic equation using this formula. You will probably find that the program will save you a lot of time when you meet quadratic equations in the future, so it is well worth the effort needed to write it now.

First enter the general form of the quadratic function on the calculator by setting $Y_1 = AX^2 + BX + C$. (Note: use [ALPHA] A, ... to enter the constants.)

On the Home screen store some appropriate values for A, B and C. For $2x^2 + 4x - 8 = 0$, store 2 in A, 4 in B and ⁻8 in C.

Select **ZStandard** from the ZOOM menu. You should see the graph shown here. Notice that the curve cuts the horizontal axis twice, so there must be two solutions to the equation $2x^2 + 4x - 8 = 0$. From the graph, these values of x appear to be between 1 and 2 and between ⁻3 and ⁻4.

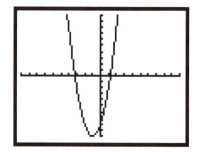

Now create a program which will calculate these values of x accurately.

Press [PRGM] [◄] [ENTER] and enter the name for this program. You could call it QUADRAT. Press these letters and then [ENTER].

Before you go any further it would be as well to think carefully about the formula which will be used:

$$x = \frac{^-B \pm \sqrt{(B^2-4AC)}}{2A}$$

Notice the $\pm$ sign which indicates that there will be two possible solutions, one formed by taking plus the square root and one by taking minus the square root. In the program it would be good to distinguish between the two solutions, perhaps by calling one S and the other T. It would also save time if the square root were to be worked out separately; call it D. In other words, instead of the full formula, you will have:

$$D = \sqrt{(B^2 - 4AC)}$$

$$S = \frac{^-B + D}{2A} \qquad T = \frac{^-B - D}{2A}$$

Make sure you understand how these three equations relate to the original formula before you go any further. Be careful also about the use of brackets. Notice that in the formulas for S and T you will need to divide by (2A).

Exercise 11.13   *Lines 1, 2 and 3*

Enter these three equations as the first three lines of the program. Remember that you will have to reverse the order; for example, in the first line enter the square root first and then store the result in D.

The last step of the program is to display the calculated values of S and T. This can be done on a single line by pressing

[PRGM] [▶] 3 [ALPHA] S [,] [ALPHA] T

Now try out the program. Press [2nd] [QUIT] to leave the program edit screen, press [PRGM] and select the program QUADRAT to be executed. Confirm your selection by pressing [ENTER]. You should see the two solutions of the equation displayed on the Home screen and, as expected, one should be between 1 and 2 and the other between $^-3$ and $^-4$.

One refinement you could make to your program would be to display the values of A, B and C as well. If you press the following you will find that an extra line is added at the beginning of the program. The line will display the values of A, B and C in the form of a list – that is, they will be side by side on the screen rather than underneath each other.

Press	*Comment*
[PRGM] [▶] followed by the number corresponding to the program QUADRAT.	This returns you to the program edit screen in order to edit the program.
[2nd] [INS] [ENTER] [▲]	Creates an extra line at the beginning of the program.
[PRGM] [▶] 3 [2nd] [{] [ALPHA] A [,] [ALPHA] B [,] [ALPHA] C [2nd] [}]	Displays a list consisting of the values of A, B and C.

Leave the program edit screen by pressing [2nd] [QUIT] and then execute the program.

You should see the display shown here. The values of A, B and C appear at the top of the screen, followed by the two solutions.

You have now built an extra facility into your calculator which enables you to investigate quadratic equations. For example, with a few keystrokes you can change the number stored in B to 6, draw the graph and solve the equation $2x^2 + 6x - 8 = 0$. Here are the two resulting screens.

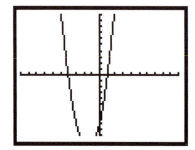 

Exercise 11.14 *Solving quadratics (sometimes!)*

Use your calculator to investigate the solutions of the following equations.

(a) $^-3x^2 + 15x - 10 = 0$

(b) $0.5x^2 - 6x + 18 = 0$

(c) $1x^2 + 2x + 3 = 0$

Comment on the graphs and solutions produced by the QUADRAT program in each case.

Chapter 12 Exponential functions

In this chapter you will be using your calculator to investigate **exponential functions**, that is, functions of the general form $y = ab^x$. Specific examples of such functions include

$y = 2^x$ (where $a = 1$ and $b = 2$)

$y = 3 \times 10^x$ (where $a = 3$ and $b = 10$)

$y = 200(1.1)^x$ (where $a = 200$ and $b = 1.1$)

exponential functions

There is nothing new in this chapter concerning the mechanics of drawing up tables of values, graphing and the use of the trace and zoom facilities: refer to previous chapters if you need any reminders of how to do any of those things. This chapter deals only with matters that are specific to exponential and related functions. You will be using the keys shown in the diagram below.

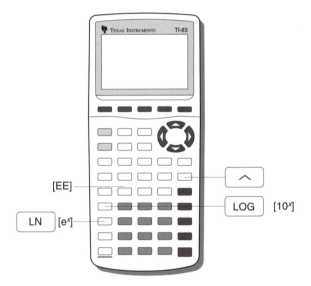

12.1 Storing and graphing exponential functions

Functions which have the general form $y = ab^x$ are known as exponential functions, because the power or **exponent** is a variable (in this case, x). To enter such a function into the calculator, you usually need to use the ⌃ key. For example, to enter 2^x you press **2** ⌃ X,T,Θ,*n*.

exponent

Be careful to do things in the right order. For example, you must take care never to confuse 2^x with x^2.

Notice also that $200(1.1)^x$ could be written as 200×1.1^x, and could be entered in either form on the calculator.

Exercise 12.1   Getting the feel of $y = 3^x$

(a) Enter the function $y = 3^x$ into your calculator. Use the Table facility to find the value of Y_1 corresponding to the following values of x:

$$0, 1, {}^-1, 5, 10, 15, 20, {}^-5, {}^-10, {}^-15, {}^-21$$

(b) Using the standard window setting on your calculator, draw the graph of the function $y = 3^x$.

An important point to emerge from the last exercise is that the value of 3^0 is 1. This is also true for other similar expressions. For example, 2^0, 5^0 and 10^0 all have the value 1. You could test this by entering them on the Home screen of your calculator.

Also in the last exercise, you will have found that the exponential function became very big very quickly; this is usually the case with exponentials. To see any reasonable amount of the graph, you need to reset the window.

Try making the x-range run from $^-3$ to 3. There is no point including negative values of y, because the y-value never becomes negative; so set the y-range to run from 0 to 28.

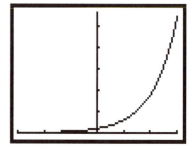

You should get the graph shown here.

Using TRACE you can check that the graph cuts the vertical axis at $Y = 1$.

For most exponential functions you must use the ⌃ key to enter them into the calculator. However, there is a special key for 10^x, because the familiar counting system is base 10, and scientific notation is based on powers of 10. You will find [10^x] on the keyboard in the second-function position, above the key marked LOG.

To enter, for example, 5×10^x you can use the following sequence:

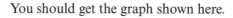

5 ⊠ 2nd [10^x] X,T,Θ,n ⟩

Notice that you still need the X,T,Θ,n key; all that 2nd [10^x] produces for you is **10^(**. You could have omitted the ⊠ key, but you may feel that it is best to include it for the sake of clarity. Try it for yourself.

logarithm   Log stands for **logarithm**, and the LOG key is used to find the logarithm of a number (to base 10). The reason that log and 10^x are on the same key is that they are inverse functions of each other. You saw in Chapter 1 the relationship that $\sqrt{x}$ has to x^2. Log and 10^x behave in a similar way. You can confirm this in the following exercise.

Exercise 12.2   Guess and press with inverses

On the Y= screen enter $Y_1 = \log(10^\wedge(X))$ by pressing

[LOG] [2nd] [10^x] [X,T,Θ,n] [ )] [ )]

What would you expect the resulting table to look like if log and 10^x really are inverses? Tabulate the values of this function to check this.

Now try a similar expression, but with log and $10^\wedge$ the other way round – $Y_1 = 10^\wedge(\log(X))$. You will find that the value of Y_1 is the same as x when x is positive, but you get ERROR when x is negative or zero. This is because the logarithm is defined only for positive values of the argument. This is somewhat similar to what occurs if you enter $Y_1 = \sqrt{(X)^2}$.

Growth or decay

All the exponential functions you have entered so far have had the form $y = ab^x$, with a value of b greater than 1. They are examples of exponential growth. If b is less than 1, a rather different shape of graph results and the function is an example of exponential decay.

Exercise 12.3   Getting the feel of exponential decay

(a) Think about the function $y = 100 \times (0.5)^x$. What will be the value of y when $x = 1$, $x = 2$, $x = 3$, ... ? Enter the function as Y_2 and check your predictions using TABLE. Look at the values of Y_2 when $x = {}^-1$, $x = {}^-2$, $x = {}^-3$, ... Can you explain these values?

(b) Make a sketch to show what the graph of $y = 100 \times .5^x$ will look like. Check your prediction by entering the function as Y_2 on your calculator. Choose a window setting to make the graph match your sketch as closely as possible.

Brain stretcher   More decay

Set up your Y= screen as shown on the right. Before you draw the graphs sketch what you predict the display will look like.

Will Y_1 be above or below Y_2? For which values of x?

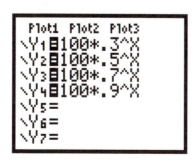

Brain stretcher   *On reflection*

On the same screen draw the graphs of $y = 3^x$ and $y = (1/3)^x$. What do you notice?

What about $y = 5^x$ and $y = (1/5)^x$, … ?

12.2 *e to the power x*

There is another key which produces an exponential function and its inverse: the one immediately below the $\boxed{\text{LOG}}$ key, marked **LN**. The second function of this key is marked e^x, which is the exponential of a special number, e. This number turns up in lots of mathematical applications. A symbol is used to represent it for just the same sort of reason that a special symbol is used for the ratio of the circumference of a circle to its diameter, namely π: like π, e is not a whole number, nor even a fraction, and when it is expressed as a decimal the decimal goes on for ever without repeating. So there is no short way of writing down e using the digits 0 to 9.

Just as log is the inverse of 10^x so ln is the inverse of e^x; that is to say, it is the logarithm associated with e. In ordinary mathematical notation (as opposed to calculator notation), it is usually written as ln, or as $\log_e$. The symbol ln comes

natural logarithm   from one of its names, **natural logarithm**.

One way of finding an approximation to the value of e is to enter e^1 on the Home screen of your calculator. Do this now by pressing $\boxed{\text{2nd}}$ $[e^x]$ **1** $\boxed{)}$ $\boxed{\text{ENTER}}$.

You should find that the value of e is given as 2.718 281 828 to nine decimal places. There would not be room on the calculator key to write $2.718\,281\,828^x$ instead of e^x; but in any case it would not be strictly correct to do so, because e is not exactly equal to 2.718 281 828 anyway.

e has a very important exponential function associated with it, which is used frequently in mathematics. As you will see in Exercises 12.4 and 12.5, the graph of $y = e^x$ looks much the same as that of $y = b^x$, where b is any other number greater than 1. However, it does have a rather surprising property which sets it apart from other exponential functions: you will discover this in Exercise 12.6.

Exercise 12.4 *Between 2 and 3*

Since e lies between 2 and 3, the graph of $y = e^x$ will lie between those of $y = 2^x$ and $y = 3^x$. Use your calculator to draw the graphs of $y = e^x$, $y = 2^x$ and $y = 3^x$, in that order.

Use $\boxed{\text{WINDOW}}$ to set the x-range from $^-1$ to 1 and the y-range from $^-1$ to 3.

The graph of $y = e^x$ certainly has the shape expected of an exponential graph: it passes through the vertical axis at $x = 0$, $y = 1$ and increases rapidly as x increases. It also lies snugly between the graphs of $y = 2^x$ and $y = 3^x$, as you would expect given that e lies between 2 and 3. In fact, since e actually lies between 2.7 and 2.8, you can repeat what you did in Exercise 12.4, this time using 2.7 and 2.8 as values of b. The two corresponding graphs should again lie one either side of the graph of $y = e^x$, and should approximate to that graph more closely than $y = 2^x$ and $y = 3^x$ do.

Exercise 12.5 Between 2.7 and 2.8

(a) Plot the graphs of $y = e^x$ with $y = 2.7^x$ and $y = 2.8^x$, using the same window settings as for the previous exercise.

(b) Use WINDOW to change the range so that x goes from 1 to 3, and y from 5 to 25 and graph the three functions again.

You could try the effect of changing the two approximating graphs so that they give even closer approximations to $y = e^x$: you could use $y = 2.71^x$ and $y = 2.72^x$, for example. You would have to zoom in a very long way in order to separate the graphs if you look at values of x close to 0. However, for larger values of x, the difference between the graphs again becomes noticeable.

In the last two exercises you have seen that the function $y = e^x$ has the shape of a typical exponential function. In the next exercise, you will investigate one of its properties that makes it rather special.

Exercise 12.6 Where's the other graph gone?

(a) Set up your $Y =$ screen as shown on the right. (You met **nDeriv** in Chapter 11. Look back to it now if you need to remind yourself what it means.)

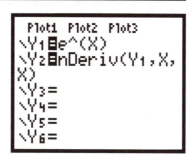

Write down, in words, which function has been allocated to Y_2.

Try to predict what its graph will look like.

(b) From the ZOOM menu choose option 4, **ZDecimal**, and draw the graphs.

Can you find the second graph? Perhaps using TRACE and/or TABLE will help.

(c) What does this tell you about the graph $y = e^x$?

12.3 Powers

When you do arithmetic with numbers expressed as powers, there are some simple rules which can be applied. The purpose of this section is to use the calculator to investigate these rules.

As you saw in Chapter 1, when you enter a large number on your calculator it appears in the display in a special form, which uses the letter E. For example, $400\,000\,000\,000\,000$ appears as 4E14. This stands for 4×10^{14}, and is a version of scientific notation or, as it is sometimes called, standard form. The calculator uses E numbers because of the difficulty of displaying 10^{14} clearly on the screen using pixels. This notation provides a convenient way of exploring the rules for manipulating powers of numbers.

The letter E is used because the superscript in an expression like 10^8 (the 8, in other words) is often called an exponent. However, it is not the same as e, which you were using in Section 12.2, so do not get them confused with each other!

You can force the calculator to use E numbers by using scientific notation mode. Press ⌷MODE⌷ and select and confirm **Sci** in the top row of the menu.

Now any number displayed on the Home screen will appear with an E number.

Produce the display shown on the right on your calculator.

The second line has been produced by pressing ⌷2nd⌷ [EE]. (This is the second function on the ⌷,⌷ key.)

You can think of the symbol E as being the name of a particular exponential function, namely the exponential function $y = 10^x$. Most of what follows will be true (with appropriate modifications) for other exponential functions, but cannot be demonstrated so easily in other cases, where there is no analogue of the E number notation at your disposal.

First, explore what happens when you multiply or divide E numbers. You can ignore the bit that comes before the E: that is, just consider what happens when, for example, you multiply E17 by E5. (Here, of course, E17 means the same as 1E17, which is how it appears on the calculator screen.)

In general, what happens when you multiply or divide Em by En, where m and n stand for whole numbers?

Exercise 12.7 *Multiplying and dividing with ease*

Using your calculator, evaluate the following, expressing your answers in scientific (E number) notation. Can you see patterns (or rules) appearing in the answers?

(a) E14 times E5

(b) E9 times E18

(c) E14 times E14

(d) E27 times E3

(e) E90 times E⁻9

(f) E2 times E⁻2

(g) E42 divided by E13

(h) E6 divided by E8

(i) E10 divided by E10

(j) E0 divided by E⁻2

All the answers to the last exercise are themselves E numbers. Parts (a)–(f) indicate that the product of two powers of 10 is itself a power of 10, but which power of 10?

In every case the E number in the product is the *sum* of the E numbers in the question, or in symbols:

E*m* times E*n* = E(*m* + *n*).

This was true even when negative numbers were used. For example, in part (e) you had 90 for *m* and ⁻9 for *n*. The answer was E(90 + ⁻9), or E81.

Similarly, parts (g)–(j) suggest that when you divide you can subtract the E numbers, or in symbols:

E*m* divided by E*n* = E(*m* − *n*).

Notice that the answer to part (i) was 1E0. Since the question was E10 divided by E10 this must mean that E0 is equal to 1, confirming the result from Section 12.1 that 10^0 is 1.

Notice also that in part (c) you had E14 times E14 = E28. Multiplying E14 by itself is simply squaring it, and 28 is just 14 times 2. So that could be written as $(E14)^2 = E(14 \times 2)$.

Exercise 12.8   *Powers of powers*

Using your calculator (or otherwise) evaluate the following:

(a) $(E17)^2$ (b) $(E^-5)^2$ (c) $(E9)^3$ (d) $(E2)^{17}$ (e) $(E99)^2$

Again, there is a general rule: the exponent of a power is the *product* of the exponents, or in symbols:

$(Em)^n = E(m \times n)$

Calculator-marked assignment

Finally in this section, if you feel you need more practice at using the rules for combining powers, here is a short program which will produce as many practice questions as you wish. However, this is optional – you can certainly leave it out if you wish.

Before entering this program, make sure that your calculator has been set back to **Normal** mode.

program: POWERS

:RandInt (⁻10,10) → M	The calculator randomly chooses two
:RandInt (⁻10,10) → N	whole numbers between ⁻10 and 10 and stores them in M and N.
:Disp 10^M * 10^N	It displays the values of $10^M \times 10^N$ and M.
:Disp "M", M	
:Input "N?", A	You are asked to input the value of N.
:If A = N: Disp "YES"	The calculator 'marks' your answer.
:If A ≠ N: Disp "NO"	

Enter this program now, either thinking out the key sequences for yourself or using the ones suggested below.

Press	**Display shows**
PRGM ◁ ENTER **P O W E R S** ENTER	PROGRAM:POWERS :randInt(-10,10) →M :randInt(-10,10) →N :■
MATH ◁ 5 (-) 1 0 , 1 0) STO▶ ALPHA **M** ENTER	
MATH ◁ 5 (-) 1 0 , 1 0) STO▶ ALPHA **N** ENTER	
	PROGRAM:POWERS →M :randInt(-10,10) →N :Disp 10^M*10^N :Disp "M",M :Input "N?",A :■
PRGM ▷ 3 1 0 ^ ALPHA **M** × 1 0 ^ ALPHA **N** ENTER	
PRGM ▷ 3 ALPHA ' ALPHA **M** ALPHA ' , ALPHA **M** ENTER	
PRGM ▷ 1 2nd [A-LOCK] '**N ?**' ALPHA , ALPHA **A** ENTER	
	PROGRAM:POWERS :Disp "M",M :Input "N?",A :If A=N:Disp "YE S" :If A≠N:Disp "NO " :■
PRGM 1 ALPHA **A** 2nd [TEST] 1 ALPHA **N** ALPHA : PRGM ▷ 3 2nd [A-LOCK] '**Y E S**' ALPHA ENTER	
PRGM 1 ALPHA **A** 2nd [TEST] 2 ALPHA **N** ALPHA : PRGM ▷ 3 2nd [A-LOCK] '**N O**' ALPHA ENTER	

Leave the programming screen by pressing 2nd [QUIT].

Here is an example of what appears on the screen when the program is executed. The program can be run repeatedly by simply pressing ENTER.

If you make a mistake, as here, you can press ALPHA **N** ENTER to see the correct answer (⁻10 in this case).

If you wish to make the questions easier or harder, you can edit lines 1 and 2 of the program and change the range for the random numbers.

Alternatively, you could change line 3 if you want to practise the division or 'powers of powers' law.

12.4 Fitting exponential curves to data

In Chapters 10 and 11, you used two of the data-fitting options from the STAT CALC menu: linear and quadratic regression. There is another option in that menu which allows you to fit an exponential function to data points.

Like all regressions, exponential regression is a method of finding a curve which passes through, or at least as close as possible to, a collection of points which represent some data. For example, you might have some population figures that show a marked increase over a period of time and might be interested in discovering whether there is evidence that the population is growing exponentially. Does an exponential model fit the population data? And if so, what are the values of the relevant parameters of the model? Since many exponential functions take the form $y = ab^x$, carrying out an exponential regression will produce values for a and b. The calculator will also calculate the value of a correlation coefficient, which it calls r. This is a measure of how well the exponential curve fits the given data: just as with linear regression the corresponding coefficient r that is calculated is a measure of how well the regression line fits the data.

In order to carry out exponential regression you follow almost the same procedure as for linear and quadratic regression.

◇   Enter paired data into two lists (say L1 and L2).

◇   Set up a scatterplot to display the data points and choose an appropriate viewing window.

◇   On the Home screen calculate values of a and b using option 0, **ExpReg**, from the STAT CALC menu followed by the names of the lists where the data are stored. Follow this with the name of the function (such as Y1) where the resulting exponential regression is to be pasted.

◇   On the Graphing screen display the data points together with the graph of the exponential function which is supposed to fit them.

Comparing the exponential graph with the data points will often bring to your attention unexpected facts about the data which will challenge you to find an explanation. For example, there may be isolated data points which do not lie close to the graph; there may be special circumstances which explain such a discrepancy, and it is of interest to try to work out what they might be.

Here is one example explained in full detail, and then in Exercise 12.9 there is another data list for you to use for practice.

The following data come from a population study of the robin (*erithacus rubecula*), a bird familiar from Christmas cards as well as its residence in British gardens. The aim of the study was to determine how long robins live. The project began with the ringing of 129 young birds. The numbers of these ringed birds known to be surviving one, two, three and four years later were counted. The results are given in the following table.

Year	0	1	2	3	4
Survivors	129	49	20	8	2

Source: D. Brown and P. Rothery (1993) Models in Biology

Do these data show exponential decay?

It is important to decide which of the data will be represented on the (horizontal) *x*-axis and which on the (vertical) *y*-axis. It is usual to assign times (in this case years) to the *x*-axis, so enter the data with the year numbers in list L_1 and the numbers of surviving robins in list L_2.

Look at a scatterplot of the data before carrying out the exponential regression. First of all, make sure that all other graphs and plots are turned off by executing the program CLEARGS. Set up a scatterplot of the data, remembering that the *x*-coordinates are in list L_1 and *y*-coordinates in L_2.

Press ZOOM **9** to view the scatterplot.

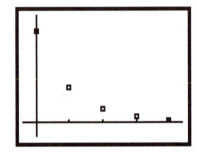

The plot certainly suggests exponential decay. The next move is to carry out exponential regression by pressing

STAT ▶ **0** [2nd] [L1] , [2nd] [L2] ,
VARS ▶ **1 1** ENTER

Again, notice the order of the lists: first L_1 (*x*-coordinates), then L_2 (*y*-coordinates).

The results of the exponential regression calculation are shown here.

Press VARS **5** ▶ ▶ **7** ENTER to calculate the value of the correlation coefficient, *r*. The coefficient *r* is very close to $^-1$ in value, which indicates a very good fit. The reason why it is negative, of course, is that there is an exponential decay, and the graph slopes down to the right. Note that *b* is less than 1, as you would expect for exponential decay. The value of *a* is more than 129, which shows that the exponential curve will actually lie a little above the first data point.

Now look at the graph in relation to the data points. Press GRAPH. The fit of the curve to the data is extremely close, as you will see.

Having seen how well the exponential graph fits the data, you will no doubt want to think about *why* an exponential model is appropriate in this case. You could ask yourself about the significance of the exponential growth factor *b*, and you could try to imagine a mechanism which would lead to exponential decay. You might also want to think about analysing the data in other ways. One obvious (but hard!) question to ask is what the *average* life expectancy of a robin is.

Here is another data list for you to practise on. The primary aim of the exercise is for you to master the use of exponential regression, of course. However, do not carry it out mindlessly: fitting a curve by regression, whether linear, quadratic, exponential or some other kind, is only one step in developing a model for a situation. A successful conclusion to the curve fitting should always be followed by consideration of questions such as 'How should I interpret the results?' and 'What kind of process would explain the observed relationship between the variables?'.

Exercise 12.9 Russian coal production

The following table gives the amount of coal mined in Russia in various years (roughly at intervals of 5 years) from 1869 until 1960. The figures for coal production are given in millions of tonnes. The middle column of the table gives the time, in years, since 1869.

Year	Time	Production
1869	0	1
1874	5	1
1879	10	2
1884	15	4
1889	20	5
1894	25	7
1899	30	11
1904	35	17
1909	40	24
1914	45	27
1919	50	28
1929	60	31
1934	65	73
1939	70	133
1950	81	261
1955	86	390
1960	91	509

Make a scatterplot of time since 1869 against production. Fit an exponential function to the data using exponential regression, drawing the graph of the exponential over the scatterplot.

Your results could be of great interest to economic and political historians. You might like to examine them from these points of view, paying particular attention to those years for which the data fail to fit the pattern of exponential growth.

Chapter 13 Power regression and more!

In the first section of this chapter, you will use another of the regression facilities of your calculator. Power regression allows you to fit a function whose equation has the form $y = ax^b$ to given data.

This power regression facility works in much the same way as the other regression facilities (linear, quadratic and exponential) that you have already met in Chapters 10, 11 and 12, respectively. In the second section of the chapter there is a review of all the regression facilities and you will see how they can be used to fit curves to data which do not fit the standard regression equations.

13.1   Using the power regression facility

Like the other curve-fitting facilities you have used in previous chapters, power regression allows you to find the curve which is the best possible fit for a set of data points. In this case the equation of the curve will have the form

$$y = ax^b$$

where a and b are numerical constants determined by the calculator.

Notice the subtle, yet important, difference between this equation and the one that you used in Chapter 12: exponential regression produces curves whose equations have x and b the other way round. Their general form is $y = ab^x$.

With power regression you might end up with an equation having one of the following forms:

$y = 3x^4$ (Here $a = 3$ and $b = 4$.)

$y = {}^-3x^2$ (Here $a = {}^-3$ and $b = 2$. This curve is a parabola.)

$y = x^{-2}$ (Here $a = 1$ and $b = {}^-2$.)

$y = x^{1/2}$ (Here $a = 1$ and $b = 1/2$.)

Exercise 13.1   *Getting the feel of $y = ax^b$ when x is positive*

In this exercise you are asked to look at the shape of graphs of the form $y = ax^b$, but only for values of x greater than zero. Consider cases where $a = 1$ and b has values of your own choosing. Enter equations on the Y= screen and look at the corresponding graphs. In each case concentrate on the general shape of the graph and think about the effect that the value of b has had. You do not need to worry about negative values of x at the moment, so you can use a window setting with Xmin = 0 and Ymin = 0.

Continue experimenting until you feel able to complete the following table.

Equation of the form	*Description*	*Sketch of typical graph*
(a) $y = ax^b$ with b a number greater than 1		
(b) $y = ax^b$ with b between 0 and 1		
(c) $y = ax^b$ with b less than 0		

Exercise 13.2 $y = x^b$ *(x any number, b any whole number)*

(a) Using **ZStandard**, or other window settings which allow you to see both positive and negative values of x, investigate the graphs of $y = x$, $y = x$, $y = x$ and so on. Can you predict the shape of $y = x^b$, when b is any positive whole number?

(b) Can you predict the shape of $y = x^b$, when b is any negative whole number?

One important fact to remember is that when b is negative, there is no defined value of y when $x = 0$. Check this by entering, for example, $Y_1 = X^{\wedge}{}^{-}2$. The graph, drawn using **ZStandard**, might make you think that when $x = 0$, y is some very large number. However, if you press $\boxed{\text{TRACE}}$ you will see no value of y displayed. Alternatively, if you look in TABLE, or enter $Y_1(0)$ on the Home screen, an error message appears.

In a similar way, many fractional powers are not defined for negative values of x. For example, as you saw in Chapter 1, the square root of x (which is another way of writing $x^{1/2}$) has no meaning or value when x is negative. The following Brain stretcher invites you to consider what happens for negative values of x when you have fractional powers.

Brain stretcher $y = x^b$ (x any number, b any number)

Try the following values and then some of your own choosing. Can you predict what the graph will look like in each case? However, this Brain stretcher comes with a health warning – non-integer powers are a mathematical minefield!

(a) $y = x^{1/2}$, $y = x^{1/3}$, $y = x^{1/4}$, ... (Compare $y = \sqrt{x}, \sqrt[3]{x}, \sqrt[4]{x}, ...$)

(b) $y = x^{0.51}$, $y = x^{0.33}$, $y = x^{0.251}$

(c) $y = x^{-2}$, $y = x^{-3}$, $y = x^{-4}$

(d) $y = x^{-3.4}$, $y = x^{-3.5}$, $y = x^{-3.6}$

If you have a batch of data to which you want to apply power regression, the method you need to use is very similar to that used for the other regression facilities in previous chapters. You need to carry out the following steps:

◇ Enter data as coordinates into two lists.

◇ On a suitable viewing window, draw a scatterplot to represent the data points.

◇ Calculate the power regression coefficients using the STAT CALC menu and paste the regression equation on the Y= screen.

◇ Draw the graph of the line of best fit.

Follow through these steps using the data below.

Suppose that you are doing an investigation into how the prices of the different UK sizes of egg are related to their weight and you have collected the following data.

UK egg size	1	2	3	4
Mean weight (in grams)	75	70	65	60
Mean price for six (in pence)	87	78	69	65

Notice that it is not the relationship between *egg size* and weight or price that is required here, but rather that between weight and price; the figures in the second and third rows of the table.

Enter the data in lists L_1 and L_2 of your calculator, putting the numbers for mean weight in L_1 and the corresponding prices in L_2.

Clear the Graphing screen by executing the program CLEARGS and use STAT PLOT to set up a scatterplot with L_1 (the weights) on the x-axis and L_2 (the prices) on the y-axis.

Press WINDOW and set the ranges as shown here.

```
WINDOW
 Xmin=0
 Xmax=80
 Xscl=10
 Ymin=0
 Ymax=90
 Yscl=10
 Xres=1
```

Now press GRAPH to see the graph. Check that the data points look sensible. You should see the display shown on the right.

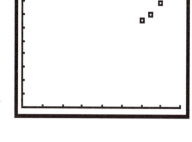

At first glance, it might seem likely that a straight line would be a good fit for these data. However, think again. Because eggs of zero weight cost nothing, any curve through the data points must also go through the origin. A straight line through the four data points would certainly not pass through the origin.

If you need to be convinced about this, carry out a *linear* regression calculation and plot the resulting graph.

You should get the display shown here.

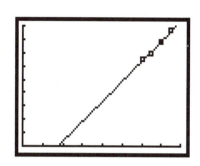

A power regression *might* be a more appropriate model because, as you saw in Exercise 13.1, the graphs of $y = x^1$, x^2, x^3 (or any other positive value of b greater than 1) all pass through the origin and increase steadily.

It is not clear yet whether a power law will be a good fit, but it seems well worth using power regression to see how good the fit is.

Press STAT ▶ to see the STAT CALC menu.

The option that you need, **PwrReg**, is option A, off the bottom of the screen. You can scroll up or down to find it or just press ALPHA **A** to paste **PwrReg** on to the Home screen.

Press 2nd [L1] , 2nd [L2] , VARS ▶ 1 1 ENTER.

You should see the display on the right.

This means that the best fit power law of the form $y = ax^b$ has $a = .27$ and $b = 1.33$, both to two decimal places. That is, $y = .27x^{1.33}$.

Calculate the correlation coefficient by pressing VARS 5 ▶ ▶ 7 ENTER.

You should find that $r = .9867570613$. The fact that r is close to 1 means that there is quite a good fit. Now check that this regression equation is a good fit graphically.

You should find that it is an excellent fit and, of course, the curve passes through the origin.

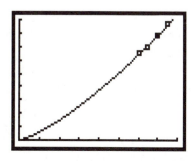

In order to look at the relationship in a little more detail, zoom in on the four data points. There are four ways to do this. You could:

◇ use **ZBox** and draw a box around the four points

◇ use **Zoom In** and move the cursor close to the four points

◇ use WINDOW and adjust the range manually

◇ use **ZoomStat**, which automatically focuses on the four data points – this is the most convenient method

Choose one of these methods and then comment on the graph.

The graph actually looks very much like a straight line over this limited range, so you might wonder whether linear regression might have been just as good as power regression. This would really depend upon the purpose of the investigation. Remember too that it is unwise to put too much reliance on a model which is based on only four data points.

Shortest stopping distances

In the exercises below you are asked to use your calculator to find the best fit power law for the way the braking distance of a vehicle varies with its speed at the moment of braking. You are then asked to consider the effect of a driver's reaction time (thinking distance) on overall stopping distances. The data used here are taken from the *Highway Code*.

Exercise 13.3   Braking distance

The *Highway Code* gives the following data for shortest braking distances of a car with good brakes on a dry road. This is the distance the vehicle takes to stop after the brakes have been applied. It does not take into account the driver's reaction time. The *Highway Code* indicates that the length of an average car is 4 metres.

Speed in miles per hour	x	20	30	40	50	60	70
Braking distance in metres	y	6	14	24	38	55	75

(a) Enter the data in lists L₁ and L₂ and draw the appropriate scatterplot.

(b) Use power regression to produce an equation which fits these data and use it to plot the graph.

(c) Using TRACE, TABLE or direct calculation, as appropriate, find the braking distance for speeds of 55 mph and 80 mph.

Exercise 13.4   Thinking distances

The *Highway Code* also gives the thinking distances for different speeds. This is the distance which a car is likely to have covered before the driver manages to apply the brakes.

Speed in miles per hour	x	20	30	40	50	60	70
Thinking distance in metres	y	6	9	12	15	18	21

(a) Leaving L_1 and L_2 as they are, enter the thinking-distance data in list L_3. Plot thinking distance against speed on your calculator, using **Plot 2** on the STAT PLOT menu and a different sort of mark from the one you used for the braking distance.

(b) Find a suitable equation for the thinking distance and enter this formula as Y_2 on the $Y=$ screen.

(c) Predict the thinking distance for speeds of 55 mph and 80 mph.

The *Highway Code* points out that the overall distance to stop a car in an emergency, called the stopping distance, is the total of the thinking distance and the braking distance.

You can set up list L_4 to give data for the total stopping distance without having to add the data and re-enter it. Can you remember how to do this?

You can add the data in lists L_2 and L_3 by pressing:

[2nd] [L2] [+] [2nd] [L3] [STO▸] [2nd] [L4] [ENTER]

Do this now and then check that the data are in fact in L_4.

Set up a third scatterplot using **Plot 3** in the STAT PLOT menu. This one will require the data in L_1 to be plotted against that in L_4. Redraw the graphs, making an appropriate change to the window setting so that the maximum value in L_4 will be included in the display.

In a similar way you can set up a formula in Y_3 for the stopping distance. Press [Y=] and move the cursor alongside Y_3.

Then press [VARS] [▸] 1 1 [+] [VARS] [▸] 1 2.

You should now have $Y_3 = Y_1 + Y_2$ and you can graph this and read off values from the table for this stopping-distance function.

Your graph should look something like this.

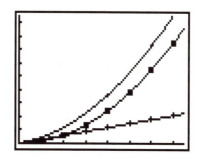

You can use the table to predict the overall stopping distance for cars travelling at 55 mph and 80 mph. You should find that the model predicts that the shortest stopping distance for a car travelling at 55 mph is 62.6 metres, and at 80 mph it is 121.9 metres or about 30 car lengths.

These formulas for thinking, braking and stopping distances contribute towards road safety in a number of ways. Not only are they used to provide advice to drivers on the distance to leave between vehicles, but they can be used by road designers in considering safe visibility distances and by government officers in devising safe speed limits for different types of road.

13.2 Overview of the regression features of the calculator

In Chapters 10–13 you have used four of the 10 available regression facilities of the calculator to find an equation which specifies a best fit curve for some given data. In this section all the regression facilities are reviewed and some techniques suggested for ways of tackling data where the curve of best fit does not appear to arise from any of the 10 types of equation offered by the calculator.

Throughout this overview, regressions are carried out on the batch of six data points shown below. As you can see from the scatterplot, it is far from obvious which type of regression facility will provide a best fit. These are not real data, but are provided purely for teaching purposes.

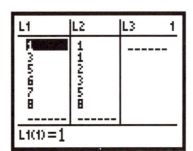

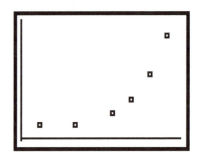

If you wish to follow the example through on your calculator, you should enter these data into L1 and L2 now. Alternatively, you may prefer to make up your own data. Begin by making a change to your calculator settings which will cause r, the correlation coefficient, and other coefficients which indicate goodness of fit to be displayed on the screen whenever you carry out a regression calculation. To do this you need to select **DiagnosticOn** from the CATALOG menu, as follows.

Press [2nd] [CATALOG] Note that CATALOG is the second function of the grey number 0.

You should see the screen shown here.

Hold your finger on the ⊡ key until the arrow cursor scrolls down to point to **DiagnosticOn**. Press [ENTER] to paste this command to the Home screen.

Press [ENTER] again to carry out the command.

```
CATALOG          ▯
▸abs(
 and
 angle(
 ANOVA(
 Ans
 augment(
 AxesOff
```

Linear regression: y = ax + b

In Chapter 10 you used option 4 of the STAT CALC menu to produce an equation of the form:

$$y = ax + b$$

An alternative form of the equation of the straight line is available using option 8. The two alternative linear regression calculations are shown below.

```
LinReg
 y=ax+b
 a=.9117647059
 b=-1.225490196
 r²=.7570903361
 r=.8701093817
```

```
LinReg
 y=a+bx
 a=-1.225490196
 b=.9117647059
 r²=.7570903361
 r=.8701093817
```

As you would expect, both options produce the same regression equation. The **regression coefficients**, a and b, have been interchanged, but so have their positions in the two equations.

regression coefficient

Notice the effect that setting **DiagnosticOn** has had. *r,* the **correlation coefficient**, has been displayed automatically. Also displayed is the value of r^2: this is known as the coefficient of determination but its use is beyond the scope of this book.

correlation coefficient

Both calculations produce the same value of r and it is 0.87, indicating only a moderate fit. This is confirmed by plotting the graph on the same screen as the data points, as is shown here.

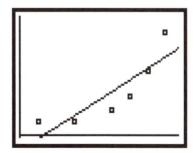

You may well have wondered how the calculator goes about calculating the equation of the line of best fit. It uses what is essentially a built-in program to carry out a series of calculations which is often called the **least-squares** method. This method minimizes the sums of the squares of the distances from the data points to the proposed line.

least-squares

median–median line

There is another method for producing a straight line of best fit using what is known as the **median–median line** (or resistant line) technique. Option 3 of the STAT CALC menu, **Med-Med,** is used for this calculation. The results are shown below. As you can see, this produces a line which is quite close to the lines produced using the **LinReg** options.

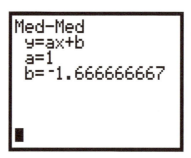 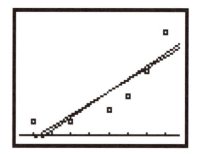

Exponential regression $y = ab^x$

As you saw in Chapter 12, option 0 of the STAT CALC menu, **ExpReg,** provides a means of fitting a line whose equation has the form

$$y = ab^x$$

The calculation for the data used above is shown on the right.

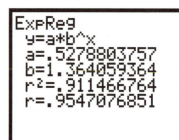

Notice that exponential regression also produces two regression coefficients, a and b.

In this case, r is nearer 1, indicating a rather better fit as is shown by plotting the graph.

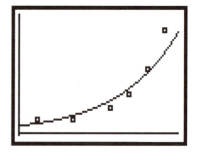

Power regression $y = ax^b$

Earlier in this chapter you used power regression. If you carry out this calculation on the data in L_1 and L_2 you will see the display shown on the right. Notice again that there are two regression coefficients and also a value of r is given. In this case, r is not as good as the previous values so power regression does not produce a very good fit.

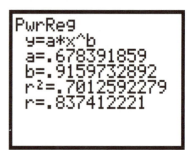

Drawing the graph confirms this.

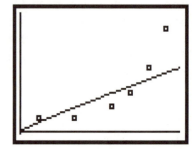

Logarithmic regression $y = a + b \ln x$

This regression facility has not been mentioned so far in this book, but it can be used in the same way as all the other regression facilities and it will calculate a regression equation which has the form $y = a + b \ln x$, where ln stands for the natural logarithm.

The results of this calculation on the data in L1 and L2 are shown below, together with the resulting graph.

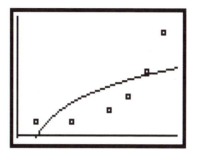

It obviously produces a very poor fit indeed for these data.

Quadratic regression $y = ax^2 + bx + c$

In Chapter 11 you met quadratic regression. This produces an equation of the form:

$$y = ax^2 + bx + c$$

The values of a, b and c for the data in L1 and L2 are shown on the right.

Unlike the other regression facilities you have used, quadratic regression produces *three* regression coefficients. Because it is not based on the least-squares method for linear regression, a value for r is not produced as part of the calculation. Instead, a different coefficient, known as the coefficient of determination (R^2) is displayed. Once again, a value of 1 would indicate a perfect fit, so the value produced here indicates a very close fit. However, R^2 and r are not directly related and should not be compared with one another.

Plotting the graph confirms that quadratic regression produces an equation which fits the data points quite well.

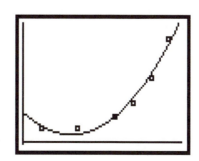

Cubic and quartic regression

Just as option 5 in the STAT CALC menu produces a model of the form $y = ax^2 + bx + c$, so options 6 and 7 can be used to produce models of data which take the forms:

cubic $\qquad y = ax^3 + bx^2 + cx + d \qquad$ (a **cubic**)

quartic $\qquad y = ax^4 + bx^3 + cx^2 + dx + e \qquad$ (a **quartic**)

Here are the corresponding calculations and graphs.

Cubic:

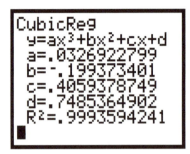 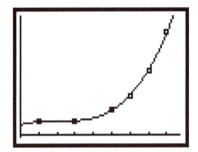

Quartic:

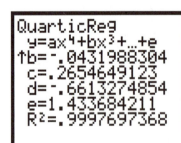 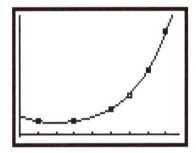

Like quadratic regression, both cubic and quartic regressions produce values of R^2 and notice how these values get ever closer to 1 as a regression model with a higher power of x is employed.

Regression model	Highest power of x	R^2
Quadratic	2	.9860
Cubic	3	.9994
Quartic	4	.99977

Other types of regression calculation

The TI-83 provides two other regression calculations; logistic and sinusoidal regression, which are options B and C in the STAT CALC menu. (Neither of these is appropriate for the data in L_1 and L_2.) Logistic regression is beyond the scope of this book but sinusoidal regression will be used in Chapter 15.

So for this batch of data, exponential, quadratic, cubic and quartic models seem to produce a good fit. The decision about which one to choose would need to be taken in the light of the situation from which the data were derived. If this were a real situation, you would need to use your discretion to decide whether, for example, when x is 0, y will be about 0.5, as the exponential model predicts, or about 2, as indicated by the quadratic model.

Fitting non-standard curves to data

Sometimes you are faced with the situation of fitting a curve to data where none of the standard curves which your calculator can deal with is appropriate. You may have a pretty good idea what sort of curve is the best fit, but no straightforward way of finding the coefficients in the regression equation. With your calculator, work through the following example, which shows one way of dealing with problems of this nature.

Imagine that you are faced with fitting a curve to the data shown in the following table.

L_1	x	5	8	11	14	17	20	23
L_2	y	383	227	145	106	89	77	73

The data points are shown in the scatterplot on the right. The y-values are falling rapidly at first, but it looks as though the decline levels off for values of x above 20. Suppose the data have been drawn from a real situation where you know that the y-values are likely to stabilize at some value. From the data and the scatterplot it looks as if that stable value will be about 70.

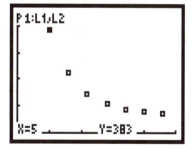

In order to get a clearer graphical picture of the way in which the curve is levelling off around 70, you can use one of the options on the DRAW menu.

Start on the Graphing screen and press [2nd] [DRAW] to see the menu.

Choose option 3, **Horizontal**.

A horizontal line appears on the Graphing screen which can be moved up or down using the cursor keys. When it appears where you want it, press [ENTER] to fix its position.

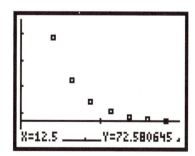

Now you need to decide which of the various regression facilities to use to produce a curve to fit these data. The best-fit curve will clearly not be a straight line, so linear regression is ruled out. Similarly, quadratic regression will not be suitable since this would produce a parabola with a minimum followed by increasing *y*-values, and what is required here is a curve which levels off at about 70. Cubic and quartic regression models are ruled out for similar reasons. However, both exponential and power regression might produce suitable curves.

The exponential and power regression calculations are shown below.

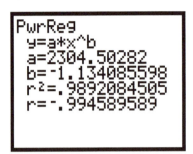 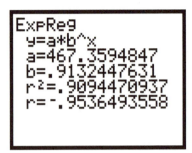

The values of *r* in both cases indicate a fairly good fit, and this is confirmed when the graphs of the regression equations are drawn. The graphs are shown below, with the horizontal line again drawn in.

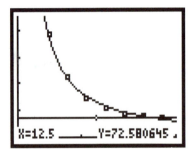 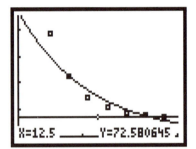

However, although either of these is quite a good fit, there is still a problem. Both curves, if continued off to the right, would get closer and closer to the horizontal axis, and the *y*-values would certainly not settle down around 70.

Rather than equations of the form:

$$y = ab^x \quad \text{or} \quad y = ax^b$$

it seems that they should be of the form:

$$y = ab^x + c \quad \text{or} \quad y = ax^b + c$$

where *c* is a number round about 70. Unfortunately, neither of these forms is available in the calculator's range of regression facilities, but it may be possible to adapt the basic models. The required forms of the equation are, in fact, the same as

$$y - c = ab^x \quad \text{or} \quad y - c = ab^x$$

This suggests that a way round the problem is to carry out the regression calculations again, this time using *y*-values which are 70 less than those used before. To do this you first need to subtract 70 from the *y*-values in L2 and store them in another list, such as L3.

So press:

2nd [L2] − 7 0 STO▶ 2nd [L3] ENTER

Now the two regression calculations can be repeated, operating this time on lists L1 and L3. The results are shown below.

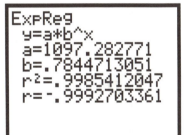

ExpReg
  y=a*b^x
  a=1232.627976
  b=.7738425706
  r²=.9962238043
  r=-.9981101163

PwrReg
  y=a*x^b
  a=61952.84111
  b=-2.970360438
  r²=.9313409323
  r=-.9650600667

Both values of *r* are close to ⁻1, indicating a good fit. The value for exponential regression is closer to ⁻1 than for power regression, indicating a better fit.

However, you do not know for sure that the *y*-values settle down to a value for *c* of *exactly* 70. What if *c* = 69 is a better value? It is fairly easy to change the values in L3 and try again.

Press 2nd [ENTRY] repeatedly until L2 − 70 → L3 appears; change 70 to 69 and press ENTER. Then, repeat the exponential regression calculation, again using 2nd [ENTRY].

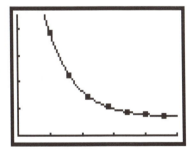

ExpReg
  y=a*b^x
  a=1097.282771
  b=.7844713051
  r²=.9985412047
  r=-.9992703361

This process should produce the display shown on the right, with a slightly better fit than before.

You could easily try other nearby values for *c*. For example, *c* = 68 produces an even better fit with an *r* value of ⁻.9995.

Now the particular graph of the form $y = ab^x + c$ can be entered on the Y= screen and the curve plotted by pressing

Y= CLEAR VARS 5 ▶ ▶ 1 + 6 8 GRAPH

The key point to be aware of here is that, although there are a range of regression facilities provided by the TI-83, it may turn out that none of them provides models that fit your data particularly well. This may require you to be a bit creative in trying to adapt one of the basic models in some way, or perhaps you might simply conclude that there is no model which satisfactorily describes the pattern of data.

There is, however, a slight complication, caused by the calculator's inability to deal with the lower-case letters *a*, *b* and *c* which are conventionally used for the lengths of sides in the normal statement of the cosine formula. In the program *A*, *B* and *C* stand for the lengths of sides and a reminder is displayed to indicate that *angle C* has been calculated. The program makes use of a programming command, **Prompt** which is option 2 in the PRGM I/O menu. Although similar to the command **Input**, which you have used before, **Prompt** provides a useful shortcut. Before, you might have keyed in:

Input "A=?",A

The same effect is achieved with:

Prompt A

and, when executed, this will produce the prompt A=?

More than one variable may be used after **Prompt**. For example, **Prompt L,M,N** can be used to replace the cumbersome lines below.

Input "L=?",L

Input "M=?",M

Input "N=?",N

Exercise 14.1 Program COSFOR1

(a) Press PRGM ◄ ENTER and enter a name for the program (COSFOR1, standing for Cosine Formula 1, is suggested). Using **Prompt**, enter a line which will allow you to enter the lengths of sides into locations A, B and C.

(b) On the second line enter a command to display the text 'ANGLE C' (note that a space is the third function of the 0 key).

(c) On the third line enter a command to display the result of the calculation suggested by the cosine formula. This will be a long instruction which will run over on to a second line. It should start **Disp** (Option 3 in the PRGM I/O menu) and should include the use of [COS⁻¹]. Notice that A, B and C will replace 6, 5 and 4 in the bracketed expression you entered on the Home screen before.

(d) Quit the program edit screen and run the program to test it. Input the values 6, 5 and 4 and check that you get the same angle as you did before.

The basic program which you entered in Exercise 14.1 can be used as it stands or it can be improved in a number of ways. For example, it is possible to make the program calculate all three angles rather than just one, to display the angles rounded to one decimal place, and to ensure that the calculator is operating in Degree mode. You are asked to make these additions to the program in the next exercise.

Exercise 14.2 Adding to COSFOR1

(a) Using the PRGM EDIT menu, enter the program edit screen to see the list of the instructions making up the COSFOR1 program. You will need two extra lines at the beginning of the program. To create two blank lines check that the cursor is alongside the colon on the first line and then press [2nd] [INS] [ENTER] [ENTER].

(b) On the first line enter **Degree** mode by pressing [MODE] [▼] [▼] [▶] [ENTER] On the second line enter the command to round numbers to one decimal place. Do this by pressing [MODE] [▼] [▶] [▶] [ENTER].

(c) Move to the beginning of the line of the program in which **Disp "ANGLE C"** appears and enter four more blank lines before that command. Enter the command **Disp "ANGLE A"** and follow it with a command to calculate that angle. It should be similar to the previous calculation command, but with the As changed to Bs, the Bs to Cs and the Cs to As. Add two similar commands for angle B.

(d) Enter an extra command at the end of the program which will reset the calculator to floating point mode.

(e) Test that the program works by entering the numbers 6, 5 and 4 once again.

You should now have a program which will calculate the three angles when you input the lengths of the three sides for *all* triangles, and, of course, the three angles should always add up to 180 degrees.

Exercise 14.3 Using COSFOR1

Use the following triples of numbers as input for the program COSFOR1. In each case draw a sketch or try to imagine what the triangle will look like.

(a) 5   12   13

(b) 6   7   12

(c) 3   8   5

(d) 8   8   8

(e) 4   7   4

(f) 2   5   8

The other form of the cosine formula

Earlier you saw an alternative form for the cosine formula:

$$c^2 = a^2 + b^2 - 2ab \cos C \tag{2}$$

This enables you to calculate the third side of a triangle if you know the lengths of two sides and the angle *between them*. Notice, by referring back to Figure 14.1, that the angle C lies between the sides of lengths a and b. It is important to be aware that it has to be this 'included' angle that is used – the others will certainly not do!

> ## Exercise 14.4 *Program COSFOR2*

Enter a program that will allow you to use this form of the cosine rule to calculate the third side of a triangle when you know two sides and the included angle. Include as an input prompt a reminder that it is the angle that has to be input.

When the program is complete, test it using some suitable values, such as $a = 3$, $b = 4$ and angle $C = 90°$.

14.2   How far is it to ...?

In Section 14.1, you produced programs based on the cosine formula, which can be used to calculate the lengths of lines or angles in 'normal' triangles – that is, triangles drawn on a flat plane. But what happens if you want to calculate lengths of lines drawn on the surface of a sphere, such as the Earth? The shortest distance between two points on any sphere is along what is known as a

great circle   **great circle**.

There is usually only one such circle through two points on the surface of the sphere, and the centre of a great circle is also the centre of the sphere. So, for example, the shortest distance from London to Vancouver on the west coast of Canada is on a circle passing near the North Pole. It is much further if you fly west (along the line of latitude).

How could you calculate the great circle distance from, say, London to any other place in the world? Once again there is a formula which enables this distance to

latitude
longitude   be calculated as long as you are able to specify the position of each of the places by means of its **latitude** and **longitude**.

meridian   Both latitude and longitude are defined in terms of the **meridian** on which a place lies; that is, the imaginary line running from the North Pole to the South Pole through the place in question. The latitude of a position is the angular distance along the meridian through that point measured in degrees north or south of the equator. For example, Prague is about 50° N, as shown in Figure 14.2.

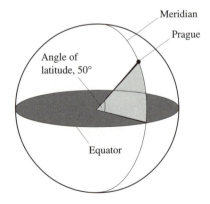

Figure 14.2   The angle of latitude of Prague.

Longitude is the angular distance of the meridian east or west of the standard meridian through Greenwich in the UK, measured in degrees. For Prague it is about 14° E, as shown in Figure 14.3.

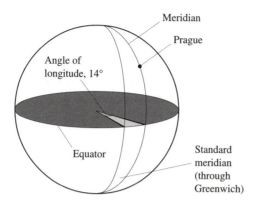

Figure 14.3   The angle of longitude of Prague.

The formula for calculating the shortest distance between two points on the surface of the Earth is derived from a spherical trigonometry version of the cosine rule. The angular distance around the great circle, *C*, is given by the following formula. The cosine formula for a spherical triangle is not usually presented in quite this way: this version uses latitudes directly:

$$\cos C = \sin(LT1)\sin(LT2) + \cos(LT1)\cos(LT2)\cos(LG1 - LG2)$$

where

   *LT*1 represents the latitude of the first point

   *LG*1 represents the longitude of the first point

   *LT*2 represents the latitude of the second point

   *LG*2 represents the longitude of the second point

Using this formula it is possible to evaluate cos *C* and then *C*, the angular distance around the great circle. But how far is the corresponding distance in kilometres?

When the metric system of measurement was developed in France in 1799 it was decided to define one metre as one ten-millionth of the distance from the equator to the pole. The circumference of the Earth would be 40 000 000 metres, or 40 000 kilometres. Since then, accuracy in measuring the Earth has improved, and it is now known that it is not exactly spherical. 40 011 kilometres is currently used as a reasonable figure for the circumference.

So, if an angular distance of 360° is equivalent to 40 011 km, 1° is equivalent to 40 011 ÷ 360 = 111.14 km and this can be used to convert the angle *C* into a distance in kilometres.

Exercise 14.5   Great circle program

Enter a program on your calculator which will allow you to input the latitude and longitude of two points on the Earth's surface and, using the formula given above, calculate the distance between them.

Test your program by inputting the latitude and longitude of the following pairs of points, each of which should produce an answer which is equal to one quarter of the circumference of the Earth, or about 10 000 km.

(a) The North Pole (latitude 90°, longitude anything you like) and any point on the equator (latitude 0°, longitude anything you like).

(b) Two points on the equator, 90° apart, with longitudes such as 30° E and 120° E, or 20° E and 70° W.

(c) Two points on the same meridian but whose latitudes are 90° apart, such as 10° N and 80° S.

Exercise 14.6   How far is it to Bethlehem?

Use your program to calculate the distance to Bethlehem from where you are now. An atlas gives Bethlehem's position as 31° 43′ N, 35° 12′ E. Either find the latitude and longitude of the place where you are now, or use as your starting point Milton Keynes (52° 3′ N, 0° 42′ W).

Notice that the latitude and longitude are usually given in degrees (°) and minutes (′), which are sixtieths of a degree. It would be possible to enter these angles by pressing, for example, 3 1 ⊞ 4 3 ⊟ 6 0. Alternatively, you could convert to a decimal value, or sacrifice some accuracy by rounding to the nearest degree.

Exercise 14.7   Around the world

A travel firm is advertising a round-the-world series of flights. The route is London, Rome, Bangkok, Sydney, Vancouver, New York and back to London. Try to estimate the total distance travelled, remembering that the circumference of the Earth is about 40 000 km. Which would be the longest and shortest parts of the journey?

Now calculate the distances using your program and the data which are given below.

London (51° 30′ N, 0° 5′ W)

Rome (41° 54′ N, 12° 30′ E)

Bangkok (13° 45′ N, 100° 35′ E)

Sydney (33° 53′ S, 151° 10′ E)

Vancouver (49° 15′ N, 123° 10′ W)

New York (40° 45′ N, 74° 0′ W)

Brain stretcher   *I can see for miles and miles*

Imagine that you are standing at the water's edge of a totally calm sea. How far away is the horizon?

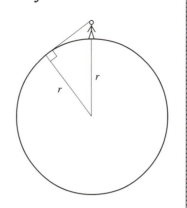

The popularly held view seems to be about 25 miles or 40 km. Check this for yourself with your calculator using Pythagoras' theorem. You can calculate the radius r of the Earth since you know the circumference is 40 011 km. Use an appropriate figure for your height.

Now try standing on a 50 m cliff.

Surprised?

14.3 Motorways in perspective

In this section, you will see how some of the drawing facilities of the calculator can be used to create a pictorial representation of a very simple scene in perspective. The instructions can be included within a short program which will allow you to try out the effect of changing the position of the point of view.

First, imagine yourself standing in the middle of a straight four-lane motorway (which is fortuitously empty of traffic!). The motorway stretches away from you across a perfectly flat plain and seems to disappear at the distant horizon. Now imagine viewing this scene through a small rectangular frame which just happens to have the same dimensions as the screen of your TI-83 calculator. If you looked through the frame at the vanishing point of the motorway what would you see? Can you imagine how the lines which define the lanes of the motorway would appear through the frame? The program that follows will produce on the Graphing screen a simulation of that view.

Imagine that the vanishing point of the motorway on the distant horizon is represented by the origin of the Graphing screen of the calculator. The x-axis then represents the distant horizon and the negative part of the y-axis can represent the central dividing line of the motorway.

The tricky mathematical part of the simulation is finding the correct equations for the straight lines which form the edges of the lanes of the motorway. It turns out that these equations are dependent on both L, the width of the lanes (as you might expect) and H, the height of your viewpoint above the road surface. Can you imagine how the view through the frame might change if you were lying down or if you were on a bridge over the top of the motorway rather than viewing from normal head height?

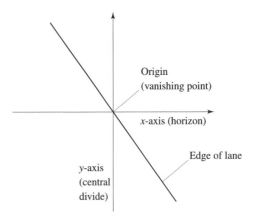

Figure 14.4

Figure 14.4 shows the right-hand edge of the lane on your immediate right. Notice that this is a straight line with negative gradient and it passes through the origin. Although it will not be derived here, it is possible to show that the equation of that line would be

$$y = \frac{^-H}{L}x$$

Notice that as H, the height of the viewpoint, increases, it has the effect of making the line steeper. Does this accord with what you imagined? As L, the width of the lane, increases the line becomes less steep, as you would expect.

Since the motorway has four lanes, each of which will be the same width, L, you need to draw the five lines given by the following equations.

$$y = \frac{^-H}{L \times 2}x \quad y = \frac{^-H}{L \times 1}x \quad y = \frac{^-H}{L \times 0}x \quad y = \frac{^-H}{L \times ^-1}x \quad y = \frac{^-H}{L \times ^-2}x$$

The third of these equations looks rather peculiar since it includes a division by zero. Rather surprisingly the calculator interprets this equation as representing the y-axis, which happens to be exactly what is needed here.

The easiest way to draw these five lines within a program is to use a variable such as C and to set up a loop which runs for values of C from $^-2$ to $+2$. You may remember using a similar loop within the program SCALE that you met in Chapter 9. Within the loop, the line

$$y = \frac{^-H}{L \times C}x$$

can be drawn.

The complete program is shown below.

PROGRAM:LANES :prgmCLEARGS	The first instruction within LANES is to execute the program CLEARGS to clear the Graphing screen.
:Prompt H,L	You are asked to input appropriate values for the height of the viewpoint and the width of the lanes.
:Shade(0, 10)	Shade the region *above* $y = 0$ and *below* $y = 10$ (that is, the part of the screen above the horizon). This will have the effect of obscuring the lines that are drawn above the horizon (the sky is very dark today!).
:For (C,⁻2,2) :DrawF ⁻HX/(LC) :End	This is the loop that draws the five lines.

Enter this program now, either thinking out the key sequences for yourself, or using the ones suggested below.

Press	*See*

[PRGM] [◀] [ENTER] **L A N E S** [ENTER]

[PRGM] [◀] (Enter the number of the program called CLEARGS – this number will vary depending on how many other programs you have stored on your calculator.) [ENTER]

[PRGM] [▶] 2 [ALPHA] **H** [,] [ALPHA] **L** [ENTER]

[2nd] [DRAW] 7 0 [,] 1 0 [ )] [ENTER]
[PRGM] 4 [ALPHA] **C** [,] [(-)] 2 [,] 2 [ )] [ENTER]
[2nd] [DRAW] 6 [(-)] [ALPHA] **H** [X,T,Θ,*n*] [÷] [( ]
[ALPHA] **L** [ALPHA] **C** [ )] [ENTER]
[PRGM] 7

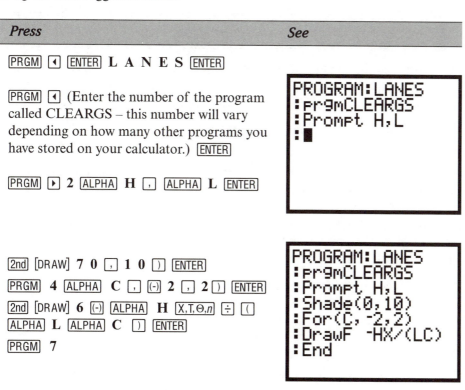

When you are convinced that the programming instructions are entered correctly, leave the program edit screen by pressing [2nd] [QUIT].

You will need to set a suitable viewing window before you run this program. Since the program simulates the perspective view through a frame that is the size of the Graphing screen, it may be sensible to use the dimensions of that screen in metres to define the viewing window.

The screen measures roughly 52 by 35 millimetres (that is, 0.052 by 0.035 metre), so the window settings shown on the right would be appropriate. These **Ymin** and **Ymax** settings will produce a horizon near the top of the screen. **Xscl** and **Yscl** have both been set to zero to ensure that no tick marks appear on the axes.

```
WINDOW
 Xmin=-.026
 Xmax=.026
 Xscl=0
 Ymin=-.028
 Ymax=.007
 Yscl=0
 Xres=1
```

Now run the LANES program. Choose suitable input values in metres for *H* and *L*. For example, if you want to produce the view from head height input the approximate height in metres of your eyes above ground level. Make an estimate for the width of a motorway lane in metres and input this figure for *L*.

The program takes a few seconds to run and during the drawing of the lines there appears to be a pause while the third line is drawn over the top of the *y*-axis. You can tell when a program is running by the appearance of a moving vertical barline in the top right-hand corner of the screen. When the program has finished this barline disappears. If you want to interrupt the program at any stage you can do so by pressing ON.

Exercise 14.8   *Other views, other motorways*

(a) Experiment by changing the value that you input for *H*. For example, input a value which could reasonably represent the height if you were viewing the motorway from a footbridge, from a helicopter or from waist height.

(b) Edit your program so that it will display a six- or eight-lane motorway.

Since you will probably always want to use the same window settings in this program, it is possible to include them as extra programming instructions. This will mean that whenever you use the program in the future, appropriate window settings will be set automatically. The variables which record the window settings are available within the VARS Window menu. Press VARS 1 if you want to see this menu now.

Now enter the program edit screen and ensure that the cursor is at the top line, beside the colon.

Press 2nd [INS] followed by ENTER six times to produce six blank lines at the beginning of the program.

Now move the cursor back to the top line and press the following keys to enter the instructions shown on the right.

(-) . 0 2 6 STO▸ VARS 1 1 ENTER

. 0 2 6 STO▸ VARS 1 2 ENTER

0 STO▸ VARS 1 3 ENTER

(-) . 0 2 8 STO▸ VARS 1 4 ENTER

. 0 0 7 STO▸ VARS 1 5 ENTER

0 STO▸ VARS 1 6 ENTER

```
PROGRAM:LANES
:-.026→Xmin
:.026→Xmax
:0→Xscl
:-.028→Ymin
:.007→Ymax
:0→Yscl
:prgmCLEARGS
```

Brain stretcher

Central reservation

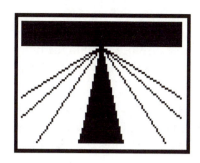

To produce the display shown on the right, change the eleventh line of the program LANES so that it becomes

:For(C,⁻3.5,3.5)

Why choose these values for C?

Also add the following extra lines at the end of the program.

:Shade(⁻10,⁻HX/.5L,0,1)

:Shade(⁻10,HX/.5L,−1,0)

For an explanation of these two shading instructions, have a look at p. 8–10 of the *TI-83 Guidebook*.

Chapter 15 Return of the sine wave

In Chapter 9, you first used the trigonometric functions of your calculator, and they were also used within the programs that you met in Chapter 14. In this chapter, the sine curve appears again and provides a unifying theme to the four sections.

In Chapters 10–13, you used the various regression facilities of the calculator to find a mathematical model which was the best fit for various batches of data. Section 15.1 explores the trigonometric regression function available on the calculator.

Section 15.2 provides a brief view of an alternative means of drawing graphs to that which has been used so far. There are a number of Brain stretchers in which intriguing shapes and curves can be produced.

Section 15.3 introduces a number of programming commands in a program which combines sine curves to produce other types of waveform.

Section 15.4 returns to a topic which you first met in Chapter 7: how the size of the pixels on the screen display affects the appearance of objects on the screen. In this case the object in question is a sine curve but which particular sine curve is it?

15.1 Modelling sunrise

In this section, the calculator is used to investigate and model sunrise data. Is it possible to find an equation which will give the time at which the sun rises for any particular week in the year at a particular location?

Exercise 15.1 *Here comes the sun*

Spend a few minutes thinking about how the time of year might affect the time of sunrise. If you were to draw a graph of sunrise times against the time of year, what would you expect its shape to be?

Also consider how the location of a place might affect the time at which the sun rises. Imagine two towns at the same latitude, one lying east of the other. At which will the sun rise earlier?

Now imagine two towns at the same longitude, one lying north of the other. It is rather harder to decide whether there is any difference in the time that the sun rises. Is dawn earlier or later in the north? Always?

Sunrise times

The data in Table 15.1 are the times of sunrise at four-week intervals during the year for four locations in the United Kingdom. The times are Greenwich Mean Time (with no allowance made for British Summer Time, when the clocks are one hour different) and are expressed in hours and minutes.

Table 15.1 Sunrise times (GMT) for 1996

Date	Week	Belfast	Glasgow	Liverpool	London
6 Jan.	0	08.45	08.46	08.26	08.05
3 Feb.	4	08.11	08.09	07.54	07.37
2 Mar.	8	07.10	07.05	06.57	06.43
30 Mar.	12	06.00	05.52	05.49	05.40
27 Apr.	16	04.53	04.42	04.45	04.40
25 May	20	04.03	03.48	03.57	03.56
22 Jun.	24	03.47	03.31	03.43	03.44
20 Jul.	28	04.15	04.01	04.09	04.08
17 Aug.	32	05.04	04.53	04.55	04.50
14 Sep.	36	05.55	05.47	05.44	05.34
12 Oct.	40	06.47	06.42	06.33	06.20
9 Nov.	44	07.43	07.41	07.26	07.09
7 Dec.	48	08.31	08.33	08.13	07.52

In order to draw a scatterplot representing sunrise times at any one location it will be necessary to enter the week numbers and the times into two data lists, say L_1 and L_2. However, there is a small problem with the sunrise times. They are expressed in hours and minutes, and you will need them in hours. For example, 08.45 or a quarter to nine will need to be entered in the list as 8.75 (hours).

There are a number of ways of overcoming this problem, all of them relying on a calculation which involves dividing the minutes by 60 and adding to the number of hours. One possible solution would be to use the sort of approach that you met in Chapter 6 which used list arithmetic. You could enter hours in list L_3 and minutes in list L_4. Then on the Home screen you could enter $L_3 + L_4/60 \rightarrow L_2$.

However, entering the hours and minutes data in two separate lists is rather awkward, and a short program might provide a better option.

A timely program

In Section 9.3, you created a program called SCALE which stored a sequence of numbers in a list. That program incorporated a loop, starting with the command **For** (option 4 in the PRGM CTL menu) and finishing with the command **End** (option 7). For the sunrise data you will need to go around a loop 13 times (once for each row of Table 15.1), so the relevant command is **:For(C,1,13)**. This means 'go around the loop for each of the whole-number values of C from 1 to 13'.

In the case of SCALE, each number in the sequence was calculated from the previous one; here the number to be stored will be calculated from the data that you input. So within the loop there will be a command to input H and M, the number of hours and minutes. Next will come a command which does the appropriate calculation and stores the result in L_2, with the position in that list determined by C, the count number for the loop. Finally, within the loop, the calculated number of hours will be displayed – a comforting feature indicating, as the program is executed, that all is well.

Exercise 15.2 *Saving HOURS (?)*

Enter the HOURS program shown on the right and add it to the library of short programs in your calculator's memory.

The key presses necessary to enter the program are given in the comments for this exercise.

```
PROGRAM:HOURS
:For(C,1,13)
:Prompt H,M
:H+M/60→L₂(C)
:Disp L₂(C)
:End
```

Exercise 15.3 *Plotting the sunrise*

Clear the lists L₁ and L₂.

Choose one of the four cities for which data are given in Table 15.1 and, using the HOURS program, enter the sunrise times, which will be stored in list L₂.

In list L₁, enter the corresponding numbers of the weeks of the year, perhaps using **seq** (option 5 in the LIST OPS menu).

Set up a statistical plot to show the data in L₁ and L₂. Choose an appropriate viewing window (or use **ZoomStat**) and draw a scatterplot.

Fitting a sine curve to the data

In Exercise 15.3, you should have found that the sunrise times for the city of your choice, plotted against week number appear to lie on a sine curve. This means that the trigonometric regression function available on the TI-83, **SinReg**, might be appropriate. This function works in radians, so first press MODE and check that line 3 is set to Radian mode. The regression model below uses the London sunrise data.

Press STAT ▶ and select Option C: **SinReg**.

Now press

> 2nd [L1] , 2nd [L2] , VARS ▶ 1 1
> ENTER

The screen on the right is displayed.

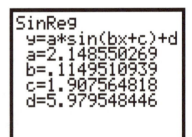

```
SinReg
 y=a*sin(bx+c)+d
 a=2.148550269
 b=.1149510939
 c=1.907564818
 d=5.979548446
```

Notice that the regression equation is in the form $y = a \sin(bx + c) + d$. The relevance of the values of a, b, c and d is explained later in the text. Now press GRAPH to display the regression line and the sunrise data plotted together. By looking at this graph you can see that the curve is a good fit for the data. Whichever set of data you have chosen in Exercise 15.3, your regression curve should look similar to this. You can now use the model to predict sunrise times in any week. For example, to find the sunrise time in week 33, you could press:

TRACE ▼ 3 3 ENTER

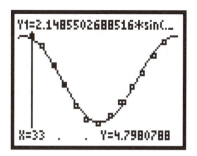

The sunrise time appears on the Graphing screen as 4.7980788 hours. To convert this to hours and minutes you can use the **fpart** function as follows:

2nd [QUIT] VARS ▶ 1 1 ENTER
MATH ▶ 4 2nd [ANS]) × 6 0 ENTER

This indicates that sunrise time in London in week 33 would be 04:48.

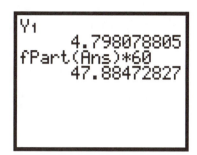

A general sine function

In order to understand how the sine regression fitted the data points, it is useful to investigate more fully various members of the family of sine curves. You have seen that the function has the general form $y = A \sin (Bx + C) + D$: but what effect do particular values of A, B, C and D have on the graph?

◇   First, ensure that your calculator is operating in Radian mode. (Either degrees or radians are possible here, but radians are more commonly used for this type of application.)

◇   Switch off the statistical plot. On the Y= screen, deselect the regression equation in Y_1 and enter the function $Y_2 = A \sin(BX+C)+D$. The calculator will evaluate this using the values that are currently stored in A, B, C and D. Enter $Y_3 = \sin(X)$ for purposes of comparison.

◇   On the Home screen, store 1 in memories A and B and 0 in memories C and D. This will have the effect of producing the graph of the function $y = 1 \sin (1x + 0) + 0$ or just $y = \sin x$.

◇   Choose the **ZTrig** window settings to check that the expected identical graphs appear for Y_2 and Y_3.

◇   Now try changing A, B, C and D on the Home screen, as suggested in the next exercise, and, in each case, see their effect on the graph.

Exercise 15.4   *Modifying the sine curve*

(a)   Store some different values in A; for example 2 or 1.5 or 0.8. What effect does changing A have on the shape of the sine curve?

(b)   Store 1 in A again and try changing B to 2 or 0.5. What effect does changing B have on the shape of the sine curve?

(c)   Store 1 in B again and try changing C to 1 or 2. What effect does changing C have on the sine curve?

(d)   Store 0 in C again and try changing D to 1 or ⁻1. What effect does changing D have on the sine curve?

amplitude
phase shift
vertical displacement

In Exercise 15.4, you found how to change the **amplitude** and period of a sine curve, how to produce a **phase shift** to the left or right and how to create a **vertical displacement** of the curve. This means that the most general form of the sine function could be expressed as $y = A \sin (Bx + C) + D$. This is summarized in the box below.

For a sine curve of the general form $y = A \sin (Bx + C) + D$:

◇   A is the amplitude

◇   B determines the period, since the period is $2\pi/B$

◇   C gives rise to a phase shift, moving the curve in the negative x direction if C is positive

◇   D is the vertical displacement of the curve

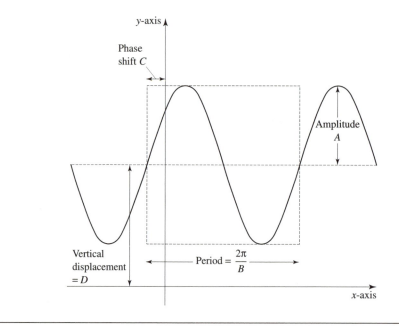

In the following exercise you are asked to build up, step by step, to the regression equation that you used to model the sunrise data in Exercise 15.3.

Start by setting up the Y= screen as shown here. The regression equation remains in Y₁ but is deselected.

Notice that **Plot 1** is now highlighted, indicating that the scatterplot of sunrise times is now on.

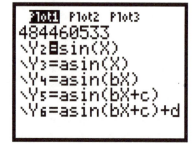

The regression coefficients a, b, c and d need to be pasted on to the Y= screen from the VARS Statistics EQ menu, which is found by pressing

VARS 5 ▶ ▶

Notice that only Y₂ is selected.

Select **ZoomStat** so that you can see the scatterplot. However, the graph of Y₂=sin(X) does not show up with these settings, so on the WINDOW screen change **Ymin** to ⁻2. This should produce the Graphing screen shown on the right.

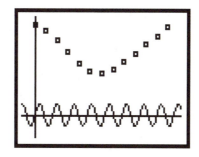

In the exercise you will transform the graph of $y = \sin(x)$, step by step, until it fits the scatterplot of sunrise times.

Exercise 15.5   *Step by step transformations*

(a) Select Y₂ and Y₃. What transformation has been applied to Y₂?

(b) Select only Y₃ and Y₄. What transformation has been applied to Y₃?

(c) Select only Y₄ and Y₅. What transformation has been applied to Y₄?

(d) Select only Y₅ and Y₆. What transformation has been applied to Y₅?

15.2   Parametric graphing

In previous chapters you have seen how the TI-83 plots graphs of functions, using X for the input variable and Y for the output variable. You have seen that formulas stored on the calculator usually take the form:

Y = expression involving X

For each value of X the calculator computes a value of Y and a corresponding point is plotted on the screen.

There is an alternative means of drawing graphs which involves using a third variable or parameter. The TI-83 insists that the letter used to represent this variable is always T. Then formulas are stored in the form:

X = expression involving T

Y = expression involving T

For each value of T the calculator computes values of both X and Y and a corresponding point is plotted on the screen. One of the most frequent uses for parametric graphing is when you know how X and Y vary with time. (This is why T is used as the third parameter.) For example, you may be interested in recording the motion of an object over a period of time and you know that its coordinates are given by the equations x = cos T and y = sin T. In this section, you will see how parametric graphing can be used to investigate this motion and others of a similar type.

In order to make your calculator carry out this type of graphing, it is necessary to change one of the settings on the Mode menu. First, clear the graphing screen, perhaps by using the program CLEARGS.

Press [MODE] and ensure that the settings are as shown here. In particular, select and confirm the second option, **Par**, on line 4.

Once this option has been selected there are a number of differences in the way in which your calculator operates. For example, if you press [X,T,Θ,n] the calculator will now produce the letter T, rather than X.

Another obvious difference occurs when you press [Y=].

You should see the display shown on the right, which replaces the familiar Y$_1$ =, Y$_2$ =, Y$_3$ =, Y$_4$ = ...

Notice that there are spaces for six pairs of equations to represent six graphs.

In order to investigate what happens when $x = \cos T$ and $y = \sin T$ enter these as X$_{1T}$ = cos(T) and Y$_{1T}$ = sin(T).

Press [ZOOM] **6** to select **ZStandard**. The graph is drawn automatically but, because the values of cos T and sin T can never exceed 1, the graph is confined to the centre of the screen. You need to change the window settings to see the graph more clearly so press [WINDOW].

You will immediately notice another difference when using parametric mode for graphing. As well as the usual window settings produced by **ZStandard**, the calculator has also chosen a range of values for T.

It may not be immediately obvious from these numerical values but **Tmax** is actually equal to 2π and **Tstep** is $\pi/24$. This means that the calculator will carry out 48 pairs of calculations of the values of x and y corresponding to the 48 values of T.

In order to see the graph more clearly you need to reset the range of values on the x- and y-axes. So change **Xmin** and **Ymin** to $^-$1 and **Xmax** and **Ymax** to 1. Then, before drawing the graph, square up the axes using **ZSquare**, option 5 in the ZOOM menu.

At last you should be able to see clearly the graph formed by $x = \cos(T)$ and $y = \sin(T)$. Is this what you expected it to look like?

Press [TRACE] and hold [▶] down to move the cursor around the circle. Notice that with parametric graphing the current value of T is displayed along with the current x- and y-coordinates.

For the display on the right, the cursor has moved four steps from its starting position so T has increased by 4 lots of $\pi/24$; that is, $\pi/6$ radians. The x-coordinate is cos $\pi/6$ or 0.866 and the y-coordinate is sin $\pi/6$ or 0.5.

Finally, see if you can predict what the Table screen will look like in parametric mode. Recall that, normally, values of X appear in the left-hand column and corresponding values of Y_1, Y_2, ... in the right-hand column. Press [2nd] [TABLE] and see whether your prediction was correct.

The following optional activities will provide further practice of using parametric graphing.

Brain stretcher   *Lissajous figures*

The graph shown on the right was produced by plotting $X_{1T} = \cos(3T)$, $Y_{1T} = \sin(5T)$. Can you find a way of describing the drawing that includes a mention of 3 and 5?

Investigate what happens when you change the 3 or the 5 to other whole numbers.

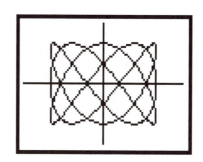

Brain stretcher   *Black-out*

What happens when $X_{1T} = \cos(3.1T)$, $Y_{1T} = \sin(5T)$, and **Tmax** = 1000?

Brain stretcher   *Spirographs*

Press [MODE] and change to degree mode. Check that parametric mode is still selected.

Set $X_{1_T} = 10\cos(T)$ and $Y_{1_T} = 10\sin(T)$.

Select **ZStandard** and then **ZSquare** to produce a circle.

Press [WINDOW] Notice that the standard **Tstep** is 7.5.

Try changing **Tstep** to other values such as 45, 120, 1 and so on. What shape are the graphs produced?

Now set **Tmax** to 100 000 and experiment with **Tsteps** of 100, 80, 90, 110 and so on. Can you explain and predict what happens?

By changing the settings of T, can you produce patterns like those shown below?

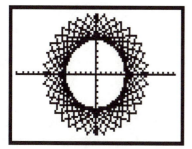 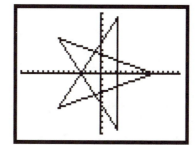

Brain stretcher   *Polar graphing mode*

Try changing from parametric to Polar graphing mode by selecting **Pol** in the fourth line of the Mode menu.

How does this change the way the calculator functions? Try drawing graphs of some of the following functions.

$r = \theta$ $r = \sin(2\theta)$

$r = .5$ $r = \sin(8\theta)$

$r = \sin(\theta)$ $r = \sin(2\theta) + .2$

You should find that, with an appropriately chosen Window, one of the above functions produces the shape shown on the right.

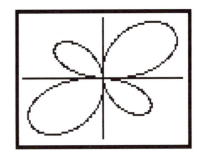

When you have finished working on this section, it is advisable to use the Mode menu to reset your calculator to normal function graphing.

15.3   A program for Fourier series

In Section 9.2, you saw that a simple function such as $y = \sin x$ has a period of 2π radians, and that any member of the family of sine curves such as $y = \sin nx$ has a period of $2\pi/n$. You also saw that adding two sine curves together produced a more complicated curve which was also periodic.

Early in the nineteenth century, the French mathematician, Jean-Baptiste Joseph Fourier, developed a method of representing any periodic function in terms of sines and cosines. For example, Figure 15.1 shows the graphs of two functions which are certainly periodic (they repeat themselves over and over again) but are certainly not very curvy! They are known as the square wave and the sawtooth wave.

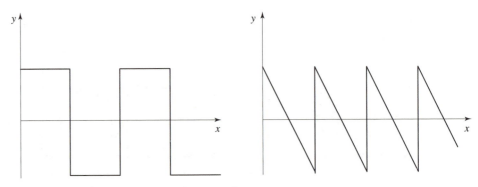

Figure 15.1   Square wave and sawtooth wave.

Using Fourier's ideas it can be shown that, unlikely as it may seem, such waves can be produced by forming the sum of a series of sine curves.

Fourier analysis suggests that the square wave is formed from the series

$$y = \sin x + \tfrac{1}{3}\sin 3x + \tfrac{1}{5}\sin 5x + \tfrac{1}{7}\sin 7x + \cdots \qquad (1)$$

and that the sawtooth wave is formed from the series

$$y = \sin x + \tfrac{1}{2}\sin 2x + \tfrac{1}{3}\sin 3x + \tfrac{1}{4}\sin 4x + \cdots \qquad (2)$$

Approximations to both of these waves could be produced on your calculator by entering the first few terms of the series as Y₁ and drawing a graph using the **ZTrig** viewing window. To see the effect of each additional term of the series you would need to return to the Y= screen, enter the extra term on the end of the series and then redraw the graph. This is fine for the first few terms, but becomes pretty tedious if you want to see the effect of having 10 or 20 terms in the series. It would seem an ideal opportunity to use a program to investigate these Fourier series, and such a program, using several new programming commands, is developed in the next subsection.

Using Goto and Lbl

Rather than entering a long series of terms, each of which is very similar to the others, it is possible to create the same effect using a loop in a program. The only slight problem is that you are not adding *exactly* the same term each time: in the case of the square wave, equation (1), you need to add a term such as

$$\frac{1}{N}\sin(Nx)$$

where N goes up 2 for each successive term. The program will need to use a variable, N, which starts at 1 and increases by 2 for each loop of the program.

In the HOURS program in Section 15.1 you used the commands **For** and **End** to control a program loop, but there is a different method which is appropriate here. Rather than the structure shown on the left of the diagram below, the FOURIER program uses the commands **Goto** and **Lbl** (short for label) as shown on the right.

A loop using For...End	A loop using Goto...Lbl
	: 1→N
:For(N,1,?,2)	:Lbl 1
...	...
: *Commands within the loop*	: *Commands within the loop*
...	...
:End	:N+2→N
	:Goto 1

The two structures have almost the same effect, but, since it is not possible to say in advance how far N should increase in order to achieve an acceptable square or sawtooth wave, there is no way of knowing which number would be appropriate as the third argument in the **For** command. **Lbl** is option 9 in the PRGM CTL menu and must be followed by a single letter or digit. **Goto** is option 0 and creates a branch (back, in this case) to the corresponding label.

Using a line graph to draw curves

Next, which commands should be included within the loop? Unfortunately it is not possible to make the appropriate changes to what is stored in Y_1 from within a program. However, there is another way of drawing graphs. As you saw in Chapter 6, the STAT PLOT facilities allow you to draw a line graph connecting points whose coordinates are stored in lists. In that chapter, the points were some distance apart from each other on the screen, so the line graphs you produced consisted of a series of straight-line segments. However, if the points are very close together (for example, with x-coordinates just one pixel-width apart), the line graph will look just like a graph drawn on the $Y=$ screen. So, if appropriate x-coordinates are stored in list L_1, and if list L_2 holds the corresponding y-coordinates, then a STAT PLOT which draws a line graph of L_1 against L_2, with appropriate window settings, will appear just like a normal graph drawn using a function entered on the $Y=$ screen.

Before you begin to enter the FOURIER program, try out this approach with the graph of the simple function $y = \sin x$ by following these steps.

◇ Check that your calculator is set to Radian mode, and run the program CLEARGS to clear the Graphing screen.

Set the viewing window settings to those shown on the right. With these values of **Xmin** and **Xmax** the pixel width will be 0.2. You can check this using **ΔX**, one of the options from the VARS Window menu. First press GRAPH then return to the Home screen and press

VARS 1 8 ENTER

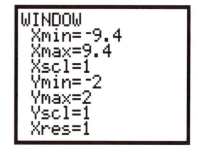

◇ Press 2nd [STAT PLOT] 1 and set **Plot 1** as shown here. Notice the choice in the last line of the menu of a single pixel as the mark.

◇ The x-coordinates need to have values from ⁻9.4 to 9.4 in steps of .2, Use **seq** (option 5 in the LIST OPS menu) to enter these values in list L_1.

The corresponding y-coordinates, in list L_2, will need to be $\sin x$. Enter $\sin(L_1) \rightarrow L_2$ to set this up.

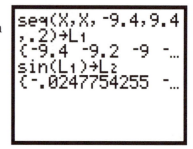

◇ Finally, press GRAPH and you should see the sine curve drawn as you would expect it to be. If you want to check that it is exactly the same as what would be produced by the usual graph-drawing procedure you could enter $y = \sin x$ on the $Y=$ screen and see its graph superimposed on the line graph.

Other commands in FOURIER

As was explained above, in order to see the Fourier series for a square wave built up term by term, it is necessary, within the loop of the program, to increase each y-coordinate by $(1/N)\sin(Nx)$.

Since L_1 contains all the x-coordinates, these increases can all be calculated by using $(1/N) \sin(N L_1)$, or $\sin (N L_1)/N$. Since the y-coordinates are stored in L_2 each time the calculator goes around the loop, for values of N starting at 1 and going up in steps of 2 it should carry out the command

$$:L_2 + \sin(N L_1)/N \rightarrow L_2$$

This will have the effect of adding $(1/N) \sin(N L_1)$ to every one of the 95 values in L_2 each time the loop is executed. However, before entering the loop for the first time it will be necessary to set all of the L_2 values to zero. An easy command to achieve this is:

$$:L_1 \times 0 \rightarrow L_2$$

Two further commands are necessary inside the loop. Since you want to see the graph displayed each time the loop is executed there must be a command which tells the calculator to do this. Option 4 of the PRGM I/O menu, **DispGraph**, is what is needed. However, since you are likely to want to study the graph for a while, it is necessary to make the calculator pause before it rushes around the loop again. The **Pause** command, which is option 8 in the PRGM CTL menu, has the desired effect. When you want to continue with the execution of the program you simply press ENTER or, if you wish to break out of the loop and the program at that point, you can press ON.

Exercise 15.6   *Programming the series*

Enter the program as shown on the right. The comments on this exercise give you the necessary key presses, but you should try to enter the commands for yourself, using the comments only if you get stuck.

As you enter each command, make sure that you understand what its purpose is. If necessary re-read the relevant section above, which explains the various commands.

```
PROGRAM:FOURIER
:L1*0→L2
:1→N
:Lbl 1
:L2+sin(NL1)/N→L
2
:DispGraph
:Pause
:N+2→N
:Goto 1
:
```

Various waveforms

You should now be ready to execute the program FOURIER. Leave the program edit screen by pressing 2nd [QUIT]. Now press PRGM and select the program FOURIER from the EXEC menu. There will be a pause and you should see the basic sine curve as before. While the calculator is working (calculating values for L_2 or drawing the curve) there is a moving vertical line in the top right-hand corner of the screen, but once the curve is drawn the moving line becomes dotted, indicating that the calculator is pausing and waiting for you to press ENTER. When you do this you will see the effect of adding the term $\frac{1}{3}\sin 3x$. Successive presses of ENTER will add further terms in the series, and you will see graphs produced, which become closer and closer to a square wave.

When you have had enough, you will have to interrupt the execution of the program: the looping structure has no natural exit. To do this you can press ON, which will always interrupt a program's execution and produce an error message. You can either choose option 1: **Quit,** to return to the Home screen or 2: **Goto,** if you want to edit the program on the program edit screen.

Exercise 15.7   *A sawtooth wave*

Look back at the Fourier series for square and sawtooth waves, labelled (1) and (2). By comparing the two series, decide how you could change the FOURIER program to make it produce successive approximations to the sawtooth wave.

Edit the program and test it.

Brain stretcher   *Another wave, another series*

Change the penultimate command of FOURIER to :N+2→N and change the fourth command to

 :L2+($^{-}$1)^((N−1)/2)SIN(NL1)/N²→L2

How would you describe the wave that is produced? Write down the first few terms of the series.

The FOURIER program should be working very well now, and can be left in your library of programs stored in the calculator's memory. In Chapter 16 you will return to it again and build in some extra commands which will automatically set the window, set up **Plot 1** and store appropriate x-coordinates in L1. This will make the program easier to use whenever you wish to do so in the future.

15.4   *Mistaken identity*

In Chapter 9, you saw that the period of $y = \sin x$ is 2π radians but that $y = \sin 2x$, $y = \sin 3x$, ... all have shorter periods.

Check that your calculator is set to Radian mode and use the **ZTrig** window settings for the following exercise.

Exercise 15.8   *Sines of difference*

(a) What would you expect the graph of $y = \sin 49x$ to look like? Write down a brief description of the graph or draw a sketch. What will its period be?

(b) Plot the graph of $y = \sin x$. Now check your answer to part (a) by entering the equation $y = \sin 49x$ on the Y= screen and drawing the graph. Can you explain this? Write down any ideas that you have.

(c) Now try graphing the equation $y = \sin 48x$. Use TRACE to help you identify the graph.

So what is wrong with the graphs of $y = \sin 48x$ and $y = \sin 49x$? According to the theory developed in Chapter 9, they should both be oscillating very frequently, with very short periods. Perhaps it would be worth taking a closer look at their graphs. If you press WINDOW you will see that **ZTrig** has set **Xmin** to ⁻6 and a bit and **Xmax** to +6 and a bit. Change these to 0 and 0.8 respectively and set $Y_1 = \sin 49X$ and $Y_2 = \sin 48X$.

When you draw the graph and press TRACE you should get the display shown on the right.

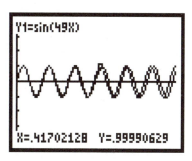

This is certainly much more how you would expect the graph to behave. The point whose coordinates are shown is roughly at the end of the third period of $y = \sin 49x$. The expected period length for this curve is $2\pi/49$. Enter this fraction on your calculator's Home screen and you should find that it is close to 0.128. Therefore three periods would be roughly 0.4, the same as the x-coordinate displayed on the Graphing screen.

If you wish, you can trace the graph off to the right of the screen – keep your finger on the ▶ key. You will see the two curves separating more and more. Again this is what you would expect, since one has a slightly shorter period than the other.

So taking a closer view of the two graphs confirms what was previously believed – they do oscillate very frequently with a very short period. But this does not explain what you saw on the screen when you used the larger range for the x-axis provided by the **ZTrig** window settings.

Select **ZTrig** once again and have another look at the graph of $y = \sin 49x$ as it appears on the screen. It is shown enlarged below, with one apparent cycle marked. Now you know that there should be 49 oscillations within the marked area, not the single one that is shown. Try to imagine 49 complete oscillations squeezed into that space. The problem lies in the resolution of the screen: the marked area is only 48 pixels wide so there is a width of less than one pixel for each cycle.

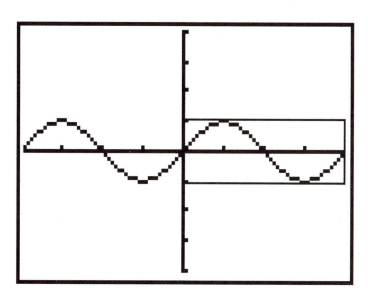

You can check in various ways that there are 48 pixels in one cycle of the sine curve, that is that the pixel width is $2\pi/48$. One method is to use option 8 from the VARS Window menu. It is labelled ΔX and is the distance between the centres of two adjacent pixels.

Press $\boxed{\text{VARS}}$ **1 8** $\boxed{\text{ENTER}}$ and you will see the current value displayed on the Home screen. The display on the right shows what happens if you multiply the value of ΔX by 48 and then compare the result with 2π.

```
ΔX
            .1308996939
Ans*48
           6.283185307
2π
           6.283185307
```

After working through the next two exercises, you should find that you can explain why the graphs of $y = \sin 48x$ and $y = \sin 49x$ appear as they do on the **ZTrig** viewing window.

Exercise 15.9   *The disappearance of $y = \sin 48x$*

◇ Store the value of ΔX, the width of a pixel, in store location P.

◇ Choose any whole number between $^-47$ and 47 to represent a pixel a number of steps along the x-axis away from the origin. You can make the calculator choose this number using **RandInt** (option 5 in the MATH PRB menu). Store that number in store location N.

◇ Multiply N by P to calculate the x-coordinate of the pixel chosen and store the result in X.

◇ Finally evaluate $\sin 48X$, the y-coordinate corresponding to the pixel chosen.

Repeat the above procedure several times. How do the results explain the graph of $y = \sin 48x$ as it appears on the **ZTrig** viewing window?

Exercise 15.10   *$\sin 49x$ or $\sin x$?*

Use a similar technique to the one in the previous exercise to calculate the y-coordinates of points on the graph of $y = \sin 49x$ as they appear on-screen with **ZTrig** window settings.

Compare each result with the corresponding y-coordinate of points on the graph of $y = \sin x$.

Explain the result.

You have seen that when **ZTrig** is used the graphs of $y = \sin 49x$ and $y = \sin x$ appear identical. There are other sine curves, such as $y = \sin 97x$, which are also indistinguishable from $y = \sin x$. It is not an effect which is restricted to the **ZTrig** window settings: which pairs appear identical depends on the range of x-values set on the Graphing window.

The effect has important implications in digital communication – or any digital processing. Suppose one person digitizes a particular sound wave, choosing to **sample** the wave at some particular interval. (This corresponds precisely to what the calculator does – ΔX corresponds to the sampling interval). A second person can be sent a string of numbers (corresponding to a series of y-coordinates on the calculator) and the sampling interval. The second person can then construct an image of the sampled wave, but would be unable to tell unambiguously which sound wave the sampled sequence represents. The 'real' sound wave is said to have several aliases.

sample

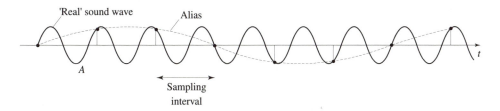

It is necessary to take special precautions to ensure that the reconstructed signal from a sample sequence has a frequency within an expected range. Otherwise 'aliasing' errors will occur and these can lead to distortion in hi-fi and communication systems or to disaster in computer-based industrial control systems.

Brain stretcher   *Alias sin 0 and sin x*

You have seen that, with sampling intervals determined by **ZTrig**, $y = \sin 48x$ and $y = \sin 49x$ provide aliases of $y = \sin 0$ and $y = \sin x$.

Find aliases of $y = \sin 0$ and $y = \sin x$ with sampling intervals determined by **ZDecimal** or another window setting of your choice.

Hint: for **ZTrig** you know that ΔX is $2\pi/48$.

Brain stretcher   *Straight sine curves*

On the **ZTrig** screen, plot the graph of $y = \sin(48x + C)$ where C is 1 or π.

Can you explain why this occurs?

Brain stretcher   *Aliasing the Fourier series*

It has been suggested that because aliasing works on sine wave components it will work on any waveform produced by the Fourier series.

For example, the square wave $y = \sin x + (\sin 3x)/3 + (\sin 5x)/5 + \cdots$ would appear the same as $y = \sin 49x + (\sin 51x)/3 + (\sin 53x)/5 + \cdots$ when drawn with the **ZTrig** settings. Is this true?

Could you check this conjecture by making appropriate changes to the FOURIER program? Remember that the pixel width, ΔX, was set at 0.2 for that program.

Chapter 16 Personal programming

The main theme of this, the final chapter of this book, is programming on the TI-83. In earlier chapters, a number of short programs have been suggested and in most cases you have been told which commands to use. The emphasis in this chapter is on *you* writing and editing your own programs to meet your individual requirements.

In Section 16.1, a final calculator facility is introduced. The MEMORY facility can be used to review the contents of your program library and delete programs that are no longer required. The section also includes a listing of all the programs you have met so far in this book.

Section 16.2 provides an overview of all the commands that can be used in programs. This is followed in Section 16.3 by an analysis of the various uses that programs have – providing ideas for future additions to your library.

Section 16.4 returns to the theme of improving your programs, both those that are already written and those which you may include in the future. Improvements are judged by whether they make the program more helpful to you and whether they make the calculator a more powerful *personal* tool.

16.1   Your own program library

Checking the catalogue

If you have entered all the programs that have been suggested in this book so far you will have a library of 11 programs stored in your calculator's memory. It is quite possible that you have written other programs too or copied some of the ones from the *TI-83 Guidebook*.

As each program is stored in the calculator's memory, its name is added to a list which appears like a menu when you press PRGM. No doubt you have realized that this is arranged in alphabetical order. The digits 1–9 and 0 are used to precede the first 10 programs, and then the rest of the programs are simply listed in alphabetical order. Check this on your calculator now. How many programs do you have stored? Remember that these menus can be scrolled from the bottom through to the top; so if you want to access a program at the bottom of the list, you can simply press the ▲ key at the top of the list.

You may well be wondering whether there is a limit to the size of this library. There is a way of assessing how much more space is available using the MEMORY menu.

Press [2nd] [MEM] and choose option 1. You should see a display similar to the one on the right, but obviously yours will display different values.

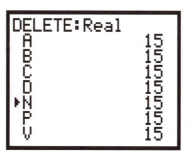

```
MEM FREE 24869
  Real          180
  Complex         0
  List         1047
  Matrix          0
  Y-Vars        331
  Prgm         1037
↓Pic            0
```

TI-83 Plus: Choose option 2: **Mem Mgmt/Del...**. This displays options leading to sub-menus, which is slightly different to that shown.

Unless you have entered some very long programs or have large amounts of data stored in lists, you will probably find that you still have a lot of memory free. The display shown here was produced by a calculator which had 14 short programs stored, but little in the data lists, L_1 to L_6.

However, if you were going to use a lot of data in lists you could find yourself running out of memory space. Any list can contain up to 999 values although the calculator does not have sufficient memory for every list to be full. If the calculator finds that it does not have enough memory available to perform a task, it produces a warning error message and you are given the chance to remove any data or programs which are no longer needed.

To see how to do this, press [2nd] [MEM] and choose option 2: **Delete**. Now be very careful to keep your fingers well clear of the [ENTER] key. Within the DELETE FROM menu are displayed all of the different forms in which the data can be stored. Suppose you wish to delete a program. Press **7**, and a list of all of your programs is displayed along with the number of memory units that they occupy. On the left of the screen is an arrowhead which can be moved up and down using the cursor keys. If you press [ENTER] the item beside the arrowhead will be deleted – permanently!

TI-83 Plus: Press [2nd] [MEM] and choose option 2: **Mem Mgmt/Del...**. This menu displays all the different forms in which data can be stored.

TI-83 Plus: Press [DEL] to permanently delete the item beside the arrowhead.

There are nine data forms within the DELETE FROM menu from which stored data can be deleted. Option 6: **Y-Vars** allows you to delete any formulas which you have stored on the Y= screen, such as Y_1, Y_2, ... as well as X_{1T}, Y_{1T} .... Pressing [ENTER] when the arrowhead is beside any of these will cause that list or formula to be cleared.

TI-83 Plus: There are 13 data forms within the **Mem Mgmt/Del...** menu from which data can be deleted.

TI-83 Plus: Press [DEL] to cause a list or formula to be cleared.

Within Option 2: **Real**, there is a list of all the store locations, A, B, C, ... which are currently in use. You saw in Chapter 1 how to store a number in these locations – you may remember entering 0.175, a VAT rate, in location V, for example. Unless you have reset your calculator since then, or stored something else in V, that number will still be there. If you have never used a store location, it will not appear in the list.

```
DELETE:Real
  A            15
  B            15
  C            15
  D            15
 ▶N            15
  P            15
  V            15
```

Once again, pressing [ENTER] will clear the store location beside the arrowhead. Apart from resetting the calculator, there is no other way of clearing these values, and indeed, there is very little point in doing so – there is no reason why a value should not remain in R, say, until you want to store something else there.

TI-83 Plus: Press [DEL] to clear the store location besides the arrowhead.

If you are unsure about the category title of the data you wish to delete, Option 1: **All** in the DELETE FROM menu gives a complete list of the variables of all types.

TI-83 Plus: Option 1: **All** in the **Mem Mgmt/Del...** menu lists all variables.

Spend a moment or two looking at the catalogue of programs that are stored in your calculator, but do not delete any yet. Later in this chapter you may wish to return to the catalogue and delete programs for which you have no further use. In the next section, however, you will need to look again at some of the programs that have appeared in earlier chapters of this book.

Press [2nd] [QUIT] to return to the Home screen.

Programs from this book

All the programs that have appeared in this book, along with samples of what they produce when they are executed, are listed below. In the next sections, you will be asked to do some analysis of the commands that have been used in these programs and also to classify the purposes for which the programs have been used. For a variety of reasons some of these programs may differ from those in your calculator – do not worry if this is the case. There is no need to make your programs exactly the same as these; indeed, in Section 16.4, you will be encouraged to do just the opposite and make your programs more individual.

Program	Sample display	Position in book, purpose and comments
PROGRAM:CLEARGS :PlotsOff :FnOff :ClrDraw :GridOff :	prgmCLEARGS Done	Section 7.4 Clears the Graphing screen at a stroke.

PROGRAM:CTOF
:Input C
:Disp 32+1.8*C
	prgmCTOF
	?0
	          32
	        Done
	?100
	        212
	        Done
		Section 7.4 (optional Brain stretcher)
		
		Converts degrees C to F.
		
		Probably the simplest possible example of a program to evaluate a formula.

PROGRAM:SCALE
:1→L
:For(C,1,13)
:L→L₁(C)
:L*R→L
:End
	12ˣ√.5→R
	    .9438743127
	prgmSCALE
	        Done
	L₁
	{1 .9438743127 …
		Section 9.3 (first version)
		
		Calculates string lengths using the equal temperament method and stores values in L_1. This is an example of a program which does a one-off job (setting up data values in a list). Requires an appropriate value to be stored in R before it is executed.

```
PROGRAM:SCALE
:1→L
:For(C,1,13)
:L→L₂(C)
:2/3*L→L
:If L<.49
:2L→L
:End
```

```
prgmSCALE
                 Done
L₂
{1 .6666666667 ...
```

Section 9.3 (second version)

This is the revised version which uses the Pythagorean method to calculate string lengths and store them in L2.

```
PROGRAM:QUADRAT
:Disp {A,B,C}
:√(B²-4AC)→D
:(-B+D)/(2A)→S
:(-B-D)/(2A)→T
:Disp S,T
:
```

```
prgmQUADRAT
           {8 13 5}
              -.625
                 -1
              Done
```

Section 11.4

Calculates solutions of quadratic equations.

Values of A, B, C are assumed to have been stored already.

```
PROGRAM:POWERS
:randInt(-10,10)
→M
:randInt(-10,10)
→N
:Disp 10^M*10^N
:Disp "M",M
:Input "N?",A
:If A=N:Disp "YE
S"
:If A≠N:Disp "NO
"
```

```
prgmPOWERS
              1E14
M
                 4
N?10
YES
              Done
```

Section 12.3

Provides practice at using the rule for multiplying powers: a 'calculator-marked assignment'.

By changing command 3 (**Disp**...) other rules can be practised. Similarly, the range of random numbers chosen can be changed in commands 1 and 2.

```
PROGRAM:COSFOR1
:Degree
:Fix 1
:Prompt A,B,C
:Disp "ANGLE A"
:Disp cos⁻¹((B²+C
²-A²)/(2BC))
:Disp "ANGLE B"
:Disp cos⁻¹((C²+A
²-B²)/(2CA))
:Disp "ANGLE C"
:Disp cos⁻¹((A²+B
²-C²)/(2AB)
:Float
```

```
ANGLE A
                52.0
ANGLE B
                99.7
ANGLE C
                28.2
              Done
```

Section 14.1

Uses the cosine formula to calculate the angles of a triangle.

```
PROGRAM:COSFOR2
:Prompt A,B
:Input "ANGLE C?
",C
:Disp √(A²+B²-2A
Bcos(C))
:
```

```
prgmCOSFOR2
A?3
B?4
ANGLE C?90
                5
              Done
```

Section 14.1

Uses the cosine formula to calculate the third side of a triangle.

```
PROGRAM:GRTCIRC
:Input "LT1 ",J
:Input "LG1 ",K
:Input "LT2 ",L
:Input "LG2 ",M
:cos⁻¹(sin(J)sin(
L)+cos(J)cos(L)c
os(K-M))*40011/3
60→D
:Disp "DISTANCE"
,D
```

```
LT1 31+43/60
LG1 35+12/60
LT2 52+3/60
LG2 -42/60
DISTANCE
      3671.846832
              Done
```

Section 14.2

Uses a formula to calculate the great circle distance between two points on the Earth's surface.

The calculator must be in Degree mode so it would be useful to include this mode setting at the beginning of the program.

```
PROGRAM:LANES
:-.026→Xmin
:.026→Xmax
:0→Xscl
:-.028→Ymin
:.007→Ymax
:0→Yscl
:prgmCLEARGS
:Prompt H,L
:Shade(0,10)
:For(C,-3.5,3.5)

:DrawF -HX/(LC)
:End
:Shade(-10,-HX/(
.5L),0,1)
:Shade(-10,HX/(.
5L),-1,0)
```

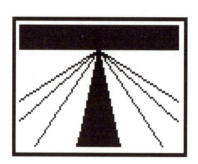

Section 14.3 (including optional Brain stretcher)

Produces a perspective view of a motorway.

Commands 8–12 make up the main program. The first seven commands set and clear an appropriate viewing window. The final two commands shade the central reservation.

```
PROGRAM:HOURS
:For(C,1,13)
:Prompt H,M
:H+M/60→L₂(C)
:Disp L₂(C)
:End
:
```

```
prgmHOURS
H?8
M?45
              8.75
H?7
M?57
              7.95
H?
```

Section 15.1

Allows you to input 13 times, in hours and minutes, converts them to hours alone and stores the values in list L_2.

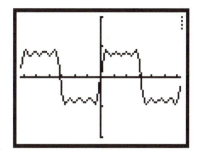

```
PROGRAM:FOURIER
:L₁*0→L₂
:1→N
:Lbl 1
:L₂+sin(NL₁)/N→L
₂
:DispGraph
:Pause
:N+2→N
:Goto 1
:
```

Section 15.3

Plots graphs (using a line graph) which are successive approximations to a square wave. The *y*-coordinates of the points are stored in L_2.

Requires a particular set of window settings and other starting conditions to run properly.

16.2 Program commands

There is a wide range of commands that can be used when writing programs for the TI-83. Some of these are special program commands which are useful only in the context of programming. Examples are **If** and **Input**. Others are familiar commands which might appear equally well on the Home screen such as $1 \rightarrow N$ or **PlotsOff**. There is also a third group of commands which carry out familiar tasks in rather a special way. An example is the way in which a mode setting such as **Radian** is set within a program.

One important thing to remember with all commands is that the command word itself (**If, Disp, Lbl, Fix,** and so on) must be pasted to the program edit screen from a menu: you must never spell out the word letter by letter.

Commands in the PRGM menu

There are 30 special program commands on the TI-83: that is, commands that can *only* be accessed by pressing PRGM when you are working on the program edit screen. Eighteen of these are in the PRGM CTL submenu and the other 12 in the PRGM I/O menu. You have already met many of the most useful of these commands.

Exercise 16.1   *Special program commands*

Look at the list of special program commands in the PRGM submenus. (One way of doing this is to refer to the *TI-83 Guidebook*, p. A-50. There you will find 'Menu Maps' showing the contents of all the TI-83's menus and submenus.)

Identify which of the commands have been used in the 11 programs listed in Section 16.1 and write a sentence summarizing the purpose of each command.

The two PRGM submenus are headed CTL, standing for control, and I/O, standing for input/output. The commands in the CTL submenu are used to control the order in which program commands are carried out. In particular, many of them are used to define the beginning and end of loops or branches.

If, Then, Else (options 1–3 in the CTL menu)

branches   The **If** command is used to create alternative **branches** of commands in a program. It tests to see whether a particular condition is true or false and always includes one of the symbols such as = or < which are in the TEST menu. In its simplest form, such as in the program SCALE, if the condition is true the next command (and only the next) is carried out; if not it is skipped.

If can also be used in conjunction with **Then, Else** and **End**. If the condition is true the calculator carries out commands following **Then** (up as far as **Else**). If the condition is false it carries out those following **Else** (up as far as **End**). So the effect of the three commands is to control the order in which commands are carried out, creating two alternative branches. The use of these commands is described in more detail on p. 16-10 of the *TI-83 Guidebook*.

For, While, Repeat and *End* (options 4 and 7 in the CTL menu)

loop   The **For** command is used to set up a **loop** in a program. It must be followed by three (or four) arguments. The first of these must be a variable and the second and third are, respectively, its starting and finishing values. The variable's value is usually increased by 1 each time the loop is executed. However, as explained on p. 16-10 of the *TI-83 Guidebook*, it is possible to include a fourth argument which allows the increment to be set to values other than 1.

While and **Repeat** are also used to set up loops in programs. The details are on p. 16-11 of the *TI-83 Guidebook*.

The **End** command is used to mark the end of either a program loop which has been set up using **For, While** or **Repeat** or a branch set up by **If…Then…Else**. Some care is necessary when using **End** in programs in which both loops and branches occur.

Pause (option 8 in CTL menu)

When the calculator meets the **Pause** command it will pause in its operation until you press ENTER to make it continue again. It can be used to slow down the calculator if, for example, it is displaying a large number of values so quickly that they are scrolling off the screen before you can read them. It was used in FOURIER to give you time to look at each displayed graph before starting to draw the next version.

Lbl and *Goto* (options 9 and 0 in the CTL menu)

The **Goto** command is used, in conjunction with **Lbl**, to control the order in which commands are carried out. The labels themselves may be either single digits or single letters. They label a location in the program to which a **Goto** command can refer. In the FOURIER program **Goto** was used to loop back to the beginning of the program. These commands are also used in BOXPLOTS, a program you will meet later in this chapter.

IS> and *DS<* (options A and B in the CTL menu)

IS> (increment and skip) and **DS<** (decrement and skip) are commands which can sometimes be used to replace **If** when you want to be able to omit the next command under certain circumstances. Details are on pp. 16-13 and 16-14 of the *TI-83 Guidebook*.

Menu *(option C in the CTL menu)*

This powerful branching command, used in conjunction with **Lbl** allows you to create menus on your TI-83. For example the program TEMPS, shown on the right, produces a menu allowing you to choose a conversion from degrees Celsius to Fahrenheit (C TO F) or vice versa.

You may want to add the TEMPS program to your library.

```
PROGRAM:TEMPS
:Menu("CONVERT",
"TO F",A,"TO C",
B)
:Lbl A
:prgmCTOF
:Stop
:Lbl B
:Prompt F
:Disp (F-32)/1.8
```

prgm *(option D in the CTL menu)*

prgm is a command which is used to execute one program from within another. For example it was used to execute program CLEARGS as part of the LANES and program CTOF as part of TEMPS above. There is another example on p. 16-22 of the *TI-83 Guidebook*, where a program to calculate the area of a circle is used within a program to calculate the volume of a cylinder.

Return *and* Stop *(options E and F in the CTL menu)*

None of the programs used in earlier chapters of this book has included these commands. **Return** has a very limited usefulness. When you call one program from within another (using the **prgm** command) on rare occasions **Return** is needed to force control to return to the calling program. See p. 16-11 of the *TI-83 Guidebook* for more details.

Stop is rather more useful. Sometimes, as in program TEMPS above, when a program has a branching structure the final command to be executed will not be the last command in the program listing. In such a case the command **Stop** can be used to make the execution terminate. The program called GUESS on p. 17-13 of the *TI-83 Guidebook* includes another example of this.

DelVar *and* GraphStyle *(options G and H in the CTL menu)*

These commands can be used to delete variables or change the graphing style from within programs. Details are on p. 16-15 of the *TI-83 Guidebook*.

The I/O menu

The commands in the I/O menu are used to input data or output results. Within the programs described so far you have used **Input, Prompt** and **Disp** very frequently.

Input *(option 1 in the I/O menu)*

Input, followed by the name of a variable, was first used in the program CTOF in the form **Input** C. When the program runs, a question mark appears, prompting you to input a value which will be stored in C. It is possible to improve the prompt by including in the command, before the name of the variable, words, letters or numbers within quotation marks. (For example, the command could be changed to Input "DEGREES C?", C.)

You can also use **Input** to take values of X and Y from the Graphing rather than the Home screen by using the command **Input** without a named variable. When this command is executed a cursor and its coordinates are displayed on the current Graphing screen. You are then able to move the cursor to any position on the screen. When you press ENTER execution restarts with the current values of X and Y. The next Brain stretcher 'Revising boxplots' includes a program that uses this form of **Input** command.

Page 16-17 of the *TI-83 Guidebook* shows how to use **Input** if you wish to input a list of values or a function to store on the Y= screen.

Prompt (option 2 in the I/O menu)

Prompt is like **Input** in that it allows you to enter the values of variables as the program is executed. However, it automatically displays the variable name followed by a question mark and also allows you to input more than one variable in one command line, as in the program COSFOR1, where the following command occurred:

> :Prompt A,B,C

Lists, but not Y= functions, can be entered using **Prompt.**

Disp (option 3 in the I/O menu)

Disp is used to display the values of variables or text on the Home screen. For example, in CTOF, line 2 could be replaced by:

> :Disp "F IS",F,"DEGREES"

Notice that items in the command must be separated by commas and text to be displayed on the screen must be entered in quotation marks. The resulting display shows each item on a separate line, with text on the left and values on the right of the screen. In the program QUADRAT you entered the command:

> :Disp {A,B,C}

This is an example of including variable names within a list in order to have more than one value displayed on a single line.

Disp may also be followed by an expression to be evaluated such as the following which appeared in COSFOR1.

> :Disp $\cos^{-1}((A^2+B^2-C^2)/(2AB))$

DispGraph, DispTable, ClrHome and ClrTable (options 4,5,8 and 9 in the I/O menu)

These four commands are fairly self-explanatory. If you want to display a graph or table or clear the Home screen or the values in a table from within a program these are the commands to use. The first three have the same effect as pressing GRAPH TABLE and CLEAR on the Home screen.

DispGraph appeared in FOURIER and **ClrHome** is in the program OWNER, below. It may have occurred to you to wonder why **DispGraph** was not necessary in LANES, which also produces a display on the Graphing screen. In that case, the drawing command, **DrawF** was used, and this displays the graph automatically, just as it would if you used it from the Home screen: you would not need to press GRAPH.

Output *(option 6 in the I/O menu)*

Output allows you to display text or values in a particular row and column on the Home screen.

The program on the right uses this feature, and you may like to add it to your personal program library.

```
PROGRAM:OWNER
:ClrHome
:Output(3,1,"THI
S CALCULATOR")
:Output(4,4,"BEL
ONGS TO")
:Output(6,1,"CHA
RLES BABBAGE")
:Pause
:ClrHome
```

getKey, GetCalc, Get *and* Send *(options 7,0,A and B in the I/O menu)*

These four commands in the I/O menu are beyond the scope of this book. **getKey** is chiefly useful in programs which simulate video games and **GetCalc** in those where two calculators are linked together. **Get** and **Send** are used to transfer data between the TI-83 and Texas Instruments' Calculator-Based Laboratory.

Familiar commands used in programs

In the last section the special program commands were discussed. Of course you have used a lot of other commands within programs too, but these are the familiar commands like **PlotsOff**, which are normally entered on the calculator's Home screen and appear exactly the same in a program listing.

The most common of these are commands which include the use of the STO▶ key. These may include calculations which use expressions pasted from the MATH or other menus. Here are some examples:

◇ :1→N   Store 1 in N

◇ :C+1→C   Increase the number in C by 1

◇ :randInt(1,100)→L₁(C) Store a random integer in the Cth location in list L₁

◇ :0→Xmin   Set the **Xmin** window setting to 0. **Xmin** is pasted from the VARS Window menu

Other examples of these familiar commands that you have used in programs are

◇ **PlotsOff, FnOff** and **ClrDraw,** in CLEARGS

◇ Drawing commands, such as **DrawF** and **Shade** in LANES

To enter any of these commands in a program when you are working on the program edit screen you need to use the normal keys and menus, exactly as if you were working on the Home screen.

Commands to do familiar things in a special way

You saw in program COSFOR1 that it is possible to change mode from within a program. To do this, special commands need to be entered, and the MODE menu operates in a rather different way to allow you to do this. When you are working on the program edit screen, the MODE menu no longer highlights the current settings, but instead allows you to select settings such as **Degree** or **Par** and paste them into your program.

The only exception is if you wish to fix the number of decimal places that are displayed. In that case, as in COSFOR1, when you select a digit such as 1 from the second row of the MODE menu, the calculator pastes **Fix 1** into the program.

The FORMAT menu behaves in a similar way, as you saw when you pasted **GridOff** into the CLEARGS program.

One menu that appears in a totally different form when you use it from the program edit screen is the STAT PLOTS menu.

It contains three submenus, the first of which is shown on the right.

In order to set up a statistical plot from within a program it is necessary to enter the number of the plot (for example, **PLOT1**) using the submenu shown above. This must be followed by several arguments. These are, first, the type of plot, chosen from the second, TYPE submenu. This must be followed by the list or lists of data that are to be displayed. Finally, the mark to be used for a scatterplot or line graph must be entered from the MARK submenu. The full details are given on pp. 12-41 and 12-42 of the *TI-83 Guidebook*.

Here are some examples of completed commands.

◇   :PLOT1(Boxplot ,L$_1$)   Set up PLOT1 to be a boxplot of values in L$_1$

◇   :PLOT2(Scatter,L$_1$,L$_2$, □)   Set up PLOT2 to be a scatterplot of values in L$_1$ against those in L$_2$, using □ to mark the points

You will use this command in Section 16.4 as part of an addition to the FOURIER program and it is also used in the next Brain stretcher.

Another familiar thing that you may wish to do within a program is to assign functions to Y$_1$, Y$_2$ and so on. In order to assign a particular function such as $3X + 5$ to Y$_1$ you would need to include in the program the command

:"3X+5"→Y$_1$.

Note that it is essential to use quotation marks.

Brain stretcher   *Revising boxplots*

The program below allows you to investigate the effect on a boxplot of adding one extra value to a list.

Start with a very small data set in L1 and a window suitable for the boxplot. When the program runs it will pause, showing the boxplot. Move the cursor so that its *x*-coordinate defines an extra value for the list. Press ENTER to see the effect this has on the boxplot. Repeat the process. (Note that **dim** is in the LIST OPS menu.)

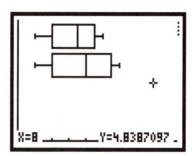

```
PROGRAM:BOXPLOTS
:dim(L₁)→N
:L₁→L₆
:Lbl 1
:Plot1(Boxplot,L
₆)
:Plot2(Boxplot,L
₁)
:Input
:L₁→L₆
:N+1→N
:X→L₁(N)
:Goto 1
```

Brain stretcher   *Calculator speed check*

Write a two-line program which counts from 1 to 1000 using only a **For** and an **End** command. How long does the program take to run? How many times does it count per second?

Try putting a command in the loop which consists of just C, or 2C or 2C+1. Compare the time taken to complete these programs and so estimate the time the calculator takes to carry out one single calculation.

Investigate the effect of putting various extra commands within the loop. For example **Disp C** will slow things down considerably.

Which functions seem to be particularly tough Brain stretchers for your calculator?

16.3   What are programs used for?

Programs can have a wide variety of uses and in the next exercise you are asked to try to classify the programs that you have entered on your calculator so far, both those from this book and any others you have entered. Five headings are suggested for the classification, but you may prefer to use other ones. The point of the exercise is for you to decide which types of program are useful to you, an important stage in personalizing your program library and making it more suitable for your own needs.

Exercise 16.2 *Program classification*

Here are five types of program. Which of your programs fall into each of these categories? You may feel that some programs fall into more than one category, or that you need other categories for some programs.

(a) Programs to evaluate a particular formula.

(b) Utility programs, which provide an additional feature to help you use the calculator more easily.

(c) Programs which help you practise or develop a skill.

(d) Programs which produce lists of numbers.

(e) Programs which draw pictures or plot graphs.

Programs to evaluate a particular formula

This category includes the largest number of programs from this book: CTOF, QUADRAT, COSFOR1, COSFOR2, GRTCIRC, HOURS and TEMPS could all fall into this category. There is also a short program to calculate the volume of a cylinder on p. 16-2 of the *TI-83 Guidebook*. In each case, a general formula which contains variables is stored in the program. Particular values are input to the variables, a numerical evaluation is carried out and the result displayed. This is an example of 'moving from the general to the particular' – a very important process in mathematics.

There are lots of other such formulas which could be programmed and you may wish to add programs to your collection which would carry out frequently occurring calculations. For example, you could write a program which calculates the cost of a telephone call when you input the time taken.

Utility programs

The first program you met, CLEARGS, is a good example of a utility program in that it provides an additional feature to help you use the calculator more easily. However, the choice of which commands to include in CLEARGS is a very personal one. For example, some people have suggested that **ZStandard** would be a useful command to include, as they almost always want to start plotting graphs with the standard window settings. Such a decision is best taken by you, the owner of the calculator.

Programs which help you practise or develop a skill

The POWERS program is an example of a program which falls within this category and there is another example, GUESS, on p. 17-13 of the *TI-83 Guidebook*. What these two programs have in common is the use of the random number generator by the calculator. You are then required to provide an answer which is assessed by the calculator.

Perhaps you could write a similar program which plots the graph of a quadratic function of the form $y = Ax^2 + Bx + C$, having chosen at random values of A, B and C. You then have to work out what these values are.

Such programs can be thought of as producing puzzles or games. They can be made as hard or as easy as you wish, allowing you to practise a skill while, it is hoped, enjoying yourself.

The BOXPLOTS program in the Brain stretcher above provides a way of allowing you to develop your understanding of this means of displaying statistical information.

In a different way many of the other programs allow you to develop your skills too. For example, the main purpose of COSFOR1 is to calculate angles of triangles when three sides are known. However, suppose you set yourself the puzzle of producing, as accurately as possible, three particular answers (for example, 50°, 60° and 70°). As you experiment by inputting different lengths for the three sides you will certainly be developing your understanding of how the sides and angles are related. By removing from you the chore of carrying out the actual calculation, the program allows you to concentrate on and get a feel for the underlying mathematical principles.

Programs which produce lists of numbers

There are two programs in this book which fall within this category: SCALE and HOURS. Both were introduced as a means of inputting data into lists.

The versions of SCALE that appeared in Chapter 9 were used to generate sequences of string lengths and store them in lists L_1 and L_2. As such they fulfilled their function at the time but it is fairly unlikely that you will ever want to use either version again. The first version probably no longer exists because you edited it to produce the second version. It may be sensible to remove this program from your library – you could use it to try out the MEMORY Delete facility. However, it is not necessary to get rid of it. The choice is yours – another example of personalizing your library of programs.

HOURS was also written for the specific purpose of inputting sunrise times into list L_2 and it may also be a candidate for deletion from your library. Alternatively, it might just be worth editing it, removing the loop and all reference to L_2 so that it just converts times given in hours and minutes into hours alone. Is it worth the effort? Will such a program be useful to you?

At the end of this section is a Brain stretcher in which a program produces successive terms of a sequence of numbers known as the Fibonacci sequence.

Programs which draw pictures or plot graphs

There have been three examples of this type of program in this book: LANES, FOURIER and BOXPLOTS.

Such programs often rely on particular window settings for their success so they often need to include these settings as part of the program. You saw how this was done in the LANES program. In the next section, these and other initial conditions will be added to FOURIER.

The next Brain stretcher contains another, very short, program which draws graphs. Perhaps it fits into other categories too?

Brain stretcher   *Family pictures*

This short program draws families of curves like the one shown.

```
PROGRAM:FAMILY
:For(A,-10,2,1)
:DrawF Y1+A
:End
```

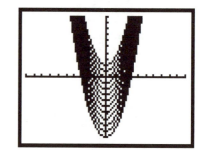

Experiment with:

◇   different functions in Y1

◇   different values for A in line 1

◇   different window settings

◇   different options from the DRAW menu in line 2

◇   a different graphing mode

◇   different ...?

Brain stretcher   *Fibonacci sequence*

Investigate this program.

How does it work? What does it display?

The sequence of numbers stored in A is called the Fibonacci sequence. It is interesting to note what happens to B/A as you move through the sequence. Can you modify the program to show more terms?

What happens if you change the numbers that go in A and B in the first line?

```
PROGRAM:FIBONACI
:0→A:1→B
:For(N,1,10)
:A+B→B
:B-A→A
:Pause {B,A,B/A}

:End
```

16.4   Improving your programs

In this section, there are a number of suggestions of how some of your programs might be changed. Whether or not these are improvements is very much a subjective matter. You need to decide for yourself and, if necessary, make the appropriate changes.

Initial settings and starting conditions

In Chapter 15, you entered the program FOURIER, which plotted graphs which were successive approximations to a square or a sawtooth wave. However, you might well have a problem if you ever wanted to use it again, because it only works for those particular calculator settings which you established as you worked through Section 15.3 before creating the program. For example, you needed 95 values stored in L1, and these were determined by the range of values of *x* chosen in the window settings. If you return to the program at some stage in the future you may well not remember what these settings should be.

It is possible to include all the necessary settings and starting conditions within the program, and there are advantages and disadvantages associated with this. The main disadvantage is that it makes the program much longer – as you will see, 10 extra commands are needed. Quite apart from the effort required to enter these commands, the final product is a long, complicated looking program which is less easy to understand and adapt if necessary. However, the advantage is that the program becomes foolproof and can be used much more easily.

It is always a matter of judgement to decide how many of these initial settings should be included in a program. In this book we have tried to keep programs short in order that their underlying purpose should be as transparent as possible. You have created programs like QUADRAT which fulfil a particular purpose at a particular time. QUADRAT works only if you have previously stored appropriate values in A, B and C. At the end of this section you will be encouraged to go through your library of programs and carry out some 'maintenance work', making them more robust and foolproof. First, have another look at the FOURIER program and remind yourself why its commands are as they are. Then, work through the next section in order to include all the necessary initial conditions as part of the program.

Giving FOURIER a fresh start

Below is a list of the settings that were necessary before the FOURIER program was entered in Section 15.3. If you look back at the subsection headed 'Using a line graph to draw curves', you will see that you made all these settings to your calculator before entering FOURIER. Now you can build them into your program by pressing the keys shown in the list.

First press PRGM ▶ and select FOURIER to enter the program edit screen with the program displayed. All of the initial settings will go at the beginning of the program so you will need extra blank lines.

Press 2nd [INS] [ENTER] [ENTER]... and create the 10 blank lines that you need. Take the cursor back to the top line and press the following keys. What appears on the screen can be checked against the complete listing of the program below.

◇	Set the calculator to radian mode	MODE ▼ ▼ ENTER ENTER
◇	Use the program CLEARGS to clear the Graphing screen	PRGM ◀ (followed by the number corresponding to CLEARGS on your calculator) ENTER
◇	Set the window settings as follows:	
	Xmin=⁻9.4	(-) 9 . 4 STO▸ VARS 1 1 ENTER
	Xmax=9.4	9 . 4 STO▸ VARS 1 2 ENTER
	Xscl=1	1 STO▸ VARS 1 3 ENTER

Ymin=‾2   (-) 2 STO▶ VARS 1 4 ENTER

Ymax=2   2 STO▶ VARS 1 5 ENTER

Yscl=1   1 STO▶ VARS 1 6 ENTER

◇ Set up Plot 1 to display a   2nd [STAT PLOT] 1 2nd [STAT PLOT] ▶ 2
line graph of the values in   , 2nd [L1] , 2nd [L2] , 2nd [STAT PLOT]
L₁ plotted against the   ◀ 3) ENTER
values in L₂, with a single
pixel used to mark the
points

◇ Enter as x-coordinates, the   2nd [LIST] ▶ 5 X,T,Θ,n , X,T,Θ,n , (-)
values from ‾9.4 to 9.4 in   9 . 4 , 9 . 4 , . 2) STO▶ 2nd [L1]
steps of .2 into list L₁   ENTER

Here is the completed list of commands in the FOURIER program. Notice that
this is the version of the program that draws a sawtooth wave. Check that the
program runs in the way that you have come to expect.

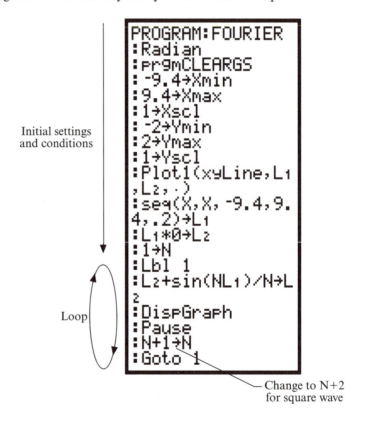

Initial settings
and conditions

Loop

— Change to N+2
for square wave

Inside or outside the program?

In the earlier chapters of this book, most of the programs were deliberately kept
short in order to clarify the essential calculations, but often this meant that
before using a program you needed to set up the window, put data in lists, put
values in variables, clear lists, set up Y= or a STATPLOT. This can be a
disadvantage, particularly if you come back to use a program a long time later
and cannot remember what these initial settings should be.

However, it is fairly easy to edit and extend programs so that individual decisions can be made according to what suits you best.

Here are some suggestions for this sort of maintenance work that you may wish to carry out on your programs.

◇ You need to remember to store appropriate values of A, B and C before you run QUADRAT. If you find that you keep forgetting, put in an extra **Prompt** command at the beginning. However, if you are using the program in conjunction with plotting a graph, A, B and C may have been already stored (as in Chapter 11). In this case, it will be a nuisance to have to input them again when the program is executed.

◇ The first version of SCALE only works if the appropriate value of R is stored first. If you are likely to use SCALE again, insert an appropriate input command in the program.

◇ It may be better to include **ZStandard** in the CLEARGS program. Also what about setting the graphing mode to **Func** (using the Mode menu) – or will you want to use CLEARGS when you are working in parametric mode?

◇ GRTCIRC only works in Degree mode, since angles of latitude and longitude are entered in degrees. Is it worth setting Degree mode within the program?

◇ Is it necessary to clear the lists before running FOURIER and HOURS?

Error trapping

Sometimes errors will occur when programs are running, errors caused by inputting inappropriate values, for instance. QUADRAT provides a good example of this. In the second line of that program there is the command:

$$:\sqrt{(B^2-4AC)}\to D$$

Now if B^2-4AC turns out to be negative, the calculator will have trouble with the square root and produce a 'Domain' error message. This is actually useful information, indicating that the quadratic equation has no real solutions. It would be possible to 'trap' this error by inserting these extra lines:

```
:If B²−4AC<0
:Then
:Disp "NO REAL SOLUTIONS"
:Stop
:Else
```

However, once again a decision has to be made about whether it is worth adding these extra lines and making the program more complex in order to get a more informative message displayed. Is a 'Domain' error message just as good for you?

Another example occurred in Exercise 14.3(f) where the numbers input in the COSFOR1 program could not actually have produced a triangle. The result was that the calculator produced a 'Domain' error message, indicating a problem when it was trying to evaluate the Cos^{-1} part of one of the **Disp** commands. In order to trap this and similar errors at least three **If** commands would be necessary. Is it worth it?

However, there are cases where inappropriate input values can cause the program to behave in unexpected ways, and to make the program totally robust an error trap would be necessary. For example, what happens if you input a negative value for H in the LANES program? Do you think it is worth trying to trap this potential error?

Who is the program for?

For software writers who are producing programs for other people to use, making them robust and foolproof is a prime concern. As many sources of error as possible must be anticipated and trapped. The program must be self-contained and not require special setting up, if possible.

In addition, software writers try to make the structure of the program as clear and obvious as possible. The program itself would be documented, with explanations included of what the various loops and branches are designed to do.

However, the TI-83 is essentially a personal tool – you are writing programs for yourself, rather than other people. They can therefore be tailored to suit your own circumstances and easily edited should those circumstances change.

You may feel that you can leave out error traps and initial settings. However, you should still do what you can to make the structure of the program clear and obvious so that when you come to edit it in a few months' time it will be easy to work out why the commands are as they are. Obvious points such as using sensible letters for variables can make all the difference. For example, in the POWERS program, A is used for the *A*nswer that is input, in the SCALE program memory location L is used for the *L*ength of the strings, while C is used to *C*ount the number of times around the loop.

Other devices that can sometimes help to make the structure of a program clear are to leave blank lines between different sections of the program and to run short, linked commands together on the same line (see, for example, the first line of FIBONACI at the end of Section 16.3).

Exercise 16.3   *A programming programme*

You should now be in a position to look through all your programs, discard those that have served their purpose and are no longer needed, and make improvements to others using the suggestions in this section. You should also be able to create other programs which will be of use or of interest to you in the future.

There is no need to do all (or any) of this now unless you wish to. But you will probably want to continue improving and updating your program library, just as you will want to continue using your calculator both as a mathematical tool and for the enjoyment it can give. Spend some time now planning the developments you want to make to your program library.

16.5 The story so far

We hope you have enjoyed working through this book and that you will now feel confident at using the calculator to carry out a wide range of activities. The aim was that you should not only learn *how* to use the calculator but also appreciate *when* it might be useful. The phrase *mathematical tool* was used in describing the calculator in the introduction to the book. In Chapter 16, stress has been put on ways in which it can be made a personal tool, using programs which are tailored to be helpful to you.

Here are reminders of some of the things you have used the tool for:

◇ VAT and percentage calculations

◇ calculating summary statistics relating to people's earnings

◇ producing displays which help to interpret statistics

◇ calculations involved in map work

◇ plotting conversion graphs

◇ drawing distance–time graphs

◇ exploring the graphs of various mathematical functions

◇ using linear programming to solve supply and demand problems

◇ finding functions of best fit for mathematical models of data

◇ finding solutions of quadratic and other equations

◇ setting yourself randomly chosen practice problems

◇ producing perspective drawings

◇ plotting sunrise times

◇ calculating great circle distances on the Earth's surface

◇ producing approximations to various waveforms

◇ evaluating frequently used formulas using programs

There are other very powerful facilities of the TI-83 calculator which are beyond the scope of this book. These include the financial functions contained in the FINANCE menu, the use of matrices and advanced statistical functions. All of these functions are covered in the *TI-83 Guidebook*.

TI-83 Plus: [FINANCE] is option 1 on the [APPS] menu.

We have certainly enjoyed discovering what the calculator can do and we hope that you have shared that enjoyment. As well as thinking of the calculator as a *tool*, you may have also come to think of it almost as a *toy*, as something to have some fun with. Many of the Brain stretchers were written with this in mind, and may have inspired you to set yourself some further mathematical investigations. Perhaps you will want to explore them further in the future.

Certainly the end of the book does not represent the end of the story as far as the calculator is concerned. You have reached the point where you are aware of very many of the things that it can do. Now you should be able to move onwards with your mathematical tool/toy – and make it do them!

Comments on exercises

Exercise 1.1 Press and see the operation keys

You should have noticed several things. Read the list which immediately follows the exercise in the text and see whether you had additional points or whether you missed some important ones.

Exercise 1.2 Guess 'n' press

Key sequence	See	Comment
(a) **2** + **3** ◄ **4** ENTER	6	The 3 was overwritten by the 4
(b) **2** + ◄ − **3** ENTER	⁻1	The + was overwritten by the −
(c) **2** + (-) **3** ENTER	⁻1	Remember to use the (-) key to enter negative numbers
(d) **3** + **4** × **5** ENTER	23	The multiplication is done first
(e) **4** + **6** ÷ **2** ENTER	7	The division is done first
(f) **3** − **4** ÷ **2** + **1** × **9** ENTER	10	$3 - 2 + 9$
(g) 2nd [ENTRY] ENTER	10	2nd [ENTRY] recalls the last entry, even if the display has been cleared
(h) 2nd [ENTRY] 2nd [ENTRY] 2nd [ENTRY] ENTER	7	Using 2nd [ENTRY] three times has recalled the third-last entry, **4** + **6** ÷ **2**
(i) × **6** ENTER	42	The previous answer was multiplied by 6
(j) **4** ÷ **0** ENTER	ERR	You cannot divide by zero. See the comment in the text after the exercise

Exercise 1.3 Ups and downs

Original price	Percentage change	Final price
£100	77% increase	£177.00
£2750	11% decrease	£2447.50
£100	18% decrease	£82.00
£1080	35% increase	£1458.00
£51	100% increase	£102.00
£2	250% increase	£7.00
£3	$33\frac{1}{3}$% decrease	£2.00

Exercise 1.4 *Pinta or Fiesta?*

(a) For the car, increase in price = £7990 − £4704 = £3286.

Method 1

$$\frac{\text{increase in price}}{\text{original price}} \times 100 = \frac{3286}{4704} \times 100$$

$$= 70\%$$

Method 2

$$\frac{\text{new price}}{\text{original price}} \times 100 = \frac{7990}{4704} \times 100$$

$$= 170\%$$

So the percentage price increase is 170% − 100% = 70%.

The above calculations appeared on the calculator (set to two decimal places) as shown here.

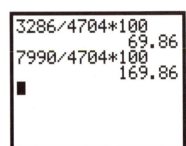

```
3286/4704*100
           69.86
7990/4704*100
          169.86
■
```

(b) The percentage increase of the pint of milk was very slightly more than that of the car.

Exercise 1.5 *Water, water everywhere*

Comments are given following the exercise in the main text.

Exercise 1.6 *Nor any drop to drink*

(a) If the tap drips once per second then there will be

60	drops per minute
60 × 60	drops per hour
60 × 60 × 24	drops per day
60 × 60 × 24 × 7	drops per week

With 12 drops per teaspoon this is

60 × 60 × 24 × 7 ÷ 12 teaspoons

Each teaspoon is 5 millilitres, so this is

60 × 60 × 24 × 7 ÷ 12 × 5 millilitres

Since 1000 millilitres = 1 litre, this is

60 × 60 × 24 × 7 ÷ 12 × 5 ÷ 1000 litres

Entering this on the calculator gives an approximate figure of 252 litres of water wasted in a week.

(b) Since one cubic metre of water (or 1000 litres) of water is approximately 90 buckets full, and since 252 litres is about $\frac{1}{4}$ of this it seems that the dripping tap wastes about 90 ÷ 4 buckets or about 23 buckets full per week.

Alternatively, since an average bath uses 90 litres, this is the same as $252 \div 90$ baths. That is about 3 average baths or probably about one bath full to the brim.

(c) The weekly cost of the nurse will be £15 000 ÷ 52, which is about £290 per week.

The hospital pays about £0.91 per cubic metre for water, so the dripping tap costs the hospital roughly

$$252 \div 1000 \times 0.91 = £0.23 \text{ per week.}$$

(d) On the basis of these calculations the claim looks pretty suspect!

The cost of the dripping tap is less than a thousandth of the cost of employing a nurse.

Exercise 1.7   *The sky's the limit*

(a) $300\,000\,000 = 3 \times 10^8$

(b) $E = 1 \times 300\,000\,000 \times 300\,000\,000$

$= 9 \times 10^{16}$ joules

(c) 149 million $= 149\,000\,000$

$= 149 \times 10^6$

$= 1.49 \times 10^8$

(d) The calculator cannot handle numbers with exponents of 100 or more. Notice that the calculator produces a message saying **ERR:OVERFLOW**.

Exercise 1.8   *Small is . . . ?*

(a) $0.1 = 1 \times 10^{-1}$ $0.0045 = 4.5 \times 10^{-3}$ $0.000\,000\,6 = 6 \times 10^{-7}$

(b) $3.78 \times 10^{-4} = 0.000\,378$ $8.91\text{E}^-7 = 0.000\,000\,891$
$0.7 \times 10^{-3} = 0.0007$

Exercise 1.9   *Pieces of gold*

(a) The number of minutes in a year is $60 \times 24 \times 365$ (ignoring leap years).

This is $525\,600$ or about half a million. So an eighty-year-old would receive about 40 million gold pieces. Not bad! 40 million is 4×10^7.

(b) Probably the largest number on the calculator that can be obtained with five key presses is 10^{99}. To get this you press [2nd] [EE] **9 9** [ENTER].

(c)   Let us assume that the month has 31 days.

Day	1	2	3	4	5	...	30	31
Gold on that day	1	2	$4=2^2$	$8=2^3$	$16=2^4$	...	2^{29}	2^{30}
Total so far	1	3	7	15	31	...	?	?

The numbers in the third row of the table are one less than a power of 2:

Total	1	3	7	15	31		?	?
so far	$=2-1$	$=4-1$	$=8-1$	$=16-1$	$=32-1$	...		
	$=2^1-1$	$=2^2-1$	$=2^3-1$	$=2^4-1$	$=2^5-1$	...	$=2^{30}-1$	$=2^{31}-1$

The figure you want is the total so far in the final box (corresponding to day 31). Entering $2^{31} - 1$ on the calculator gives $2\,147\,483\,647$, which is the same as $2.147\,483\,647 \times 10^9$.

So part (b) produces far and away the largest number, 10^{99}. However, you might be wondering whether it would be possible to deal with that many gold pieces. Is it possible to imagine a pile of that many coins? In fact, scientists have estimated that the total number of particles in the whole universe is only about $10^{80.}$.

Well, the exercise did start off with the word 'Imagine'!

Exercise 1.10   *Where did I come from?*

Using the pattern established in the question gives a pattern similar to that in the previous exercise.

Generations back	1	2	3	4	5	...	30
Number of ancestors	2	$4 = 2^2$	$8 = 2^3$	$16 = 2^4$	$32 = 2^5$	...	2^{30}

Suppose one generation is approximately 25 years. Then 30 generations is about 750 years.

And 2^{30} is over 10^9, or one thousand million. It does not seem possible that you had that many ancestors in the 13th century, since the population of the entire world was probably only about four hundred million at that time.

There must be something wrong with the assumptions in the question. What is wrong is the implicit assumption that no one appears more than once in each generation in a family tree. For example, it is quite possible for one of your mother's grandmothers to be the same person as one of your father's grandmothers, and the further back you go the more likely this sort of double counting becomes.

Exercise 1.11   *A colossal cash cache*

Using the figures given in the exercise:

$$1240 \text{ tons} = 1240 \times 2240 \text{ pounds}$$
$$= 1240 \times 2240 \times 16 \text{ ounces}$$

This was worth

$$1240 \times 2240 \times 16 \times 391.25 \text{ dollars}$$

or

$$1240 \times 2240 \times 16 \times 391.25 \div 1.497 \text{ pounds sterling.}$$

The calculator produced an answer of £1.16 × 10¹⁰, which is nearly £12 billion.

(In fact, you will find that the price of gold is usually given per troy ounce, and 1 troy ounce = 1.01 ordinary (or avoirdupois) ounces. Using this, the calculation above comes to a little less: £1.15 × 10¹⁰.)

Exercise 1.12 *Speakeasy*

Press	Say	Key sequence	Value
$\sqrt{\pi}$	The square root of pi	[2nd] [√] [2nd] [π] [)] [ENTER]	1.7725
2^9	Two to the power 9	2 [^] 9 [ENTER]	512.0000
$(2.5 \times 7.2)^{-1}$	The reciprocal of (2.5 times 7.2), or 2.5 times 7.2 all to the power minus 1	[(] 2.5 [×] 7.2 [)] [x⁻¹] [ENTER]	.0556
$\left(\dfrac{1}{\sqrt{2}}\right)^3$	The reciprocal of the square root of 2 to the power 3, *or* one over root 2, all cubed	[2nd] [√] 2 [x⁻¹] [^] 3 [)] [ENTER]	.3536
$\dfrac{^-6 + \sqrt{(6^2 - 15)}}{2}$	Minus 6 plus the square root of (6 squared minus 15), all divided by two	[(] [(-)] 6 [+] [2nd] [√] 6 [x²] [−] 15 [)] [)] [÷] 2 [ENTER]	$^-$.7087

Notice the importance of brackets in the last example. An extra pair of brackets is necessary in the key sequence to ensure that *everything* is divided by 2.

Exercise 1.13 *Explaining to others*

Many different answers are possible, but you should have included something equivalent to the following.

The 'square' ([x²] key) of a number is the number multiplied by itself, for example $4^2 = 4 \times 4 = 16$.

The 'square root' ([√] key) of a positive number is the number whose square gives the original number, for example $\sqrt{16} = 4$.

The 'reciprocal' ([x⁻¹] key) of a number is 1 divided by the number, for example the reciprocal of $2 = \frac{1}{2}$.

The 'power' ([^] key) is the number of times a number is multiplied by itself, for example 2^3 is 2 to the power 3, which is $2 \times 2 \times 2$.

You might like to try out your explanations on someone else.

Exercise 2.1 *Practice at finding the mean and the median*

Mean price   = £3.40 (to the nearest penny)

Median price = £3.39 (this is the price charged by Dixons)

Exercise 2.2 *Practice at summarizing frequency data*

The 1976 statistics are calculated using 1-Var Stats L_1, L_2 and the 1992 statistics by using 1-Var Stats L_1, L_3.

The calculations are summarized below.

Year	Mean
1976	2.14
1992	1.90

From these results it seems that not only has the overall number of homes built by local authorities been greatly reduced over the period (from 124 000 in 1976 to 3900 in 1992) but, in general, the size of home is smaller (the mean number of bedrooms per dwelling dropped from 2.14 in 1976 to 1.90 in 1992).

Exercise 2.3 *Temperature sequence*

The temperature values run from 12 to 24 in steps of 1°, so you need to produce **seq(X, X, 12, 24)** on the screen. To do this and store the result in L_1 you need to press the following key sequence:

[2nd] [LIST] [▶] 5 [X,T,Θ,n] [,] [X,T,Θ,n] [,] 1 2 [,] 2 4 [)] [STO▶] [2nd] [L1] [ENTER]

Exercise 3.1 *Practice at finding the median and quartiles*

The median is £181, the lower quartile, Q_1, is £142 and the upper quartile, Q_3, is £238.

Exercise 3.2 *Finding the rules for quartiles*

(a)

	Q_1	**med**	Q_3
(i)	2.5	4.5	6.5
(ii)	2.5	5	7.5
(iii)	3	5.5	8

(b) The median of a data batch which has been sorted into ascending order is either the middle value if the batch size is odd, or the average of the two middle values if the batch size is even.

   Q_1, the lower quartile, is the median of the data values below the median.

   Q_3, the upper quartile, is the median of the data values above the median.

(c) $Q_1 = 3$, **med** = 6, $Q_3 = 9$

(d) There is no comment.

Exercise 3.3 *Sketching boxplots*

Here is one attempt at sketching the two boxplots.

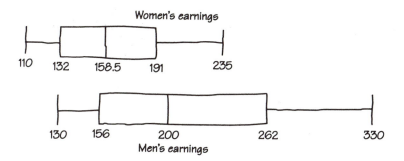

Exercise 4.1 *Extreme values*

List	L_1	L_2
min	220	58
max	1280	465

Exercise 4.2 *Shorter strings*

(a) On the occasions when the tenth digit of the decimal string is zero, this zero is suppressed and only the first nine digits are displayed. Note that this only occurs when the calculator is set to Float mode.

(b) If the numbers are truly random you would expect a zero to occur in the tenth place, on average, as often as any of the other digits. So you would expect a nine-digit display one in ten times on average.

(c) An eight-digit display would occur if the final two digits calculated are both zeros. This would occur, on average, once in a hundred times.

Further comments follow the exercise itself.

Exercise 4.3 *Standard deviation practice*

Using **1-Var Stats** first for L_1 and then for L_2 produces these screen displays.

The standard deviation in both cases is $1.414213562 \approx 1.414$.

```
1-Var Stats
 x̄=3
 Σx=15
 Σx²=55
 Sx=1.58113883
 σx=1.414213562
↓n=5
■
```

It should come as no surprise that the answers are the same since the standard deviation is a measure of how far the data are spread around the mean. For both batches, the data are spread in exactly the same way around their respective means.

```
1-Var Stats
 x̄=8
 Σx=40
 Σx²=330
 Sx=1.58113883
 σx=1.414213562
↓n=5
■
```

Exercise 4.4   *1-Var Stats with a joined list*

Using **1-Var Stats** for L3 produces the screen displays shown here.

```
1-Var Stats
 x̄=5.5
 Σx=55
 Σx²=385
 Sx=3.027650354
 σx=2.872281323
↓n=10
```

Notice that $n = 10$ for L3 and this is the sum of the n values for L1 and L2, (5 + 5).

Similarly, $\sum X$ for L3 (55) is the sum of the $\sum X$ values for L1 and L2, (15 + 40).

$\bar{x}$, the mean, for L3 (5.5) is the mean of the means of L1 and L2, $\frac{1}{2}$ (3 + 8).

All of the above relationships would be true whatever the data lists in L1 and L2, provided that the batch sizes are equal.

```
1-Var Stats
↑n=10
 minX=1
 Q₁=3
 Med=5.5
 Q₃=8
 maxX=10
```

The values of σX, Q1, Q3 and **med** for a joined list are generally not so easily predicted from the corresponding values of the constituent lists.

Exercise 6.1   *Hill profile*

There are comments following the exercise in the main text.

Exercise 6.2   *Looking through different windows*

The window settings for the two displays are shown below.

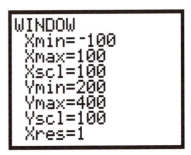

```
WINDOW
 Xmin=-800
 Xmax=800
 Xscl=100
 Ymin=0
 Ymax=800
 Yscl=100
 Xres=1
```

```
WINDOW
 Xmin=-100
 Xmax=100
 Xscl=100
 Ymin=200
 Ymax=400
 Yscl=100
 Xres=1
```

There are other comments following the exercise in the main text.

Exercise 6.3   *Finding the gradient using* TRACE

Near the bottom, the gradient is about 0.1, although the value obviously depends on which points are used for the calculation. For example, if you take the first and third points, you find that the height rises from 230 metres to 270 metres over a distance of 350 metres. So the gradient over this section of the slope is 40/350 = 0.11.

Higher up, the slope gets steeper. The fourth and ninth points on the line graph indicate that the ground rises steadily from 290 metres to 380 metres over a distance of 275 metres. The gradient here is 90/275 = 0.33. Again, you may well have chosen other points, giving a slightly different gradient, but you should still agree that the upper slope is about 3 times as steep as the lower slope.

You could have calculated the gradients directly from the numerical data in lists L_1 and L_2, but the graph provides a visual indication of the steepness of the slope that is far from obvious when you look at the data lists alone.

Exercise 6.4   *From screen points to map points*

Do not worry if your coordinates differ slightly from those given below.

Easting	Northing	Map feature
155	850	Where the final section of the walk crosses a road
154	838	Losehill Hall, the National Park Study Centre
151	830	The centre of Castleton
132	833	Blue John Cavern
125	853	Railway station
138	853	Backtor Farm

Exercise 6.5   *As the crow flies*

The crow moved east a distance of 566 − 462 = 104 km.

It moved south a distance of 370 − 272 = 98 km.

Using Pythagoras' theorem, the straight-line distance is 143 km (to the nearest kilometre). Of course, this is the very minimum distance the crow flew – crows do not really fly in straight lines despite what the phrase 'as the crow flies' seems to suggest!

Exercise 6.6   *Time for a walk*

The two list operations which are required are shown on the right, together with the calculation of the sum of the times in minutes.

Both of the operations could equally well have been carried out on the List screen.

```
L₁/5+L₂/600→L₃
{.4 .1 .3 .3 .3…
L₃*60→L₄
{21.4 5.6 17.2 …
sum(L₄)
            103.9
■
```

This should enable you to complete the route card as shown overleaf. Notice that times have been rounded to the nearest minute.

Date:	11 April 1995				
From:	Mam Farm	grid ref: 133840		Starting time:	10 am
To:	Losehill Farm	grid ref: 158846		Est. arrival time:	11.44am

Path to ...	Grid reference	Compass bearing (degrees)	Distance (kilometres)	Height climbed (metres)	Estimated time (minutes)
A625 road	128831	212	1.0	90	21
Footpath	125831	287	0.3	20	6
Mam Tor	127836	352	0.5	107	17
Hollins Cross	136845	24	1.3	0	15
Back Tor	145849	91	1.0	40	16
Lose Hill	153853	35	0.9	76	18
Losehill Farm	158846	156	0.9	0	10
Totals			5.9	333	104

Exercise 6.7   *Modified Naismith*

The map scale is 1:25 000, so 1 km on the ground is represented by 1/25 000 km on the map.

1/25 000 km is the same as $1/25\,000 \times 1\,000\,000$ mm = 40 mm.

Thus 1 km on the ground is represented by 40 mm on the map. (You could check this by measuring the distance between the 1 km grid lines on the map.)

Therefore, in Naismith's rule, the first term on the right-hand side needs changing like this:

$$\text{Time in hours} = \frac{\text{(actual) distance in kilometres}}{5} + \frac{\text{total ascent in metres}}{600}$$

$$= \frac{\text{map distance in millimetres} \div 40}{5} + \frac{\text{total ascent in metres}}{600}$$

$$= \frac{\text{map distance in millimetres}}{200} + \frac{\text{total ascent in metres}}{600}$$

Exercise 7.1   *Walking speed*

Near the beginning of the walk, the gradient of the distance–time graph is less, and hence the speed of a walker is lower. This is because, over these sections, the path climbs relatively steeply to Mam Tor, making walking difficult. From there to Hollins Cross, the path slopes down and the walk becomes easier, so the average speed increases.

The speed drops again for the climb up to Lose Hill but picks up for the last stretch downhill to Losehill Farm.

Exercise 7.2 *Steam train, steam train...*

There are several ways of setting up the lists in order to display a distance–time graph and to work out the speed of the train at each stage of the journey from Bridgnorth to Kidderminster. Here is one alternative.

L_1 time (minutes)	L_2 distance (km)	L_3 cumulative time (minutes)	L_4 cumulative distance (km)	L_5 average speed (km per hour)
0.0001	0	0	0	0
17	7.2	17	7.2	25.4
3	0	20	7.2	0
8	3.3	28	10.5	24.8
2	0	30	10.5	0
8	3.5	38	14	26.3
3	0	41	14	0
13	6	54	20	27.7
4	0	58	20	0
11	4.5	69	24.5	24.5

Note the following.

◇ The journey consists of nine stages (five when the train is moving between stations and four where it is waiting at intermediate stations).

◇ The timetable has been used to give the *cumulative* time of the journey in minutes past 11.00. These are in list L_3. They have been used to work out the actual times for each stage which have been entered into list L_1. This can be done automatically using option 7 in the LIST OPS menu to store **ΔList**(L_3) in L_1.

◇ The distances given in Table 7.1 are in list L_2, with appropriate zeros to represent the intermediate stations. These have been added to produce the cumulative distances for list L_4 using option 6 in the LIST OPS menu to store **cumSum**(L_2) in L_4.

◇ To avoid getting an error when L_2 is divided by L_1 (to find the average speeds), 0 at the top of L_1 has been replaced by 0.0001.

◇ The values of list L_5 (average speeds in kilometres per hour) were found from $L_2 / L_1 \times 60$.

◇ The distance–time graph is shown here.

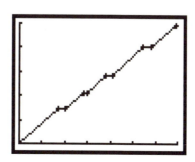

Exercise 7.3 Conversion tables

Miles (X)	Kilometres (Y₁)
30	48.3
1.4	2.254
10.86	17.485
4	6.44
105.59	170
3.1056	5.0

With the last two questions, a trial and improvement approach is needed, gradually reducing the value of **ΔTbl** and changing **TblStart** until the required Y_1 value is found.

No doubt you will have realized that it is easier to multiply or divide by 1.61 in each case.

Exercise 7.4   *Converting pounds to kilograms*

(a) The formula is

mass in kilograms = 0.454 × mass in pounds

This is entered on the calculator as

$Y_1 = 0.454 \times X$

For a range of masses from 0 to 10 pounds, the equivalent range is 0 to 4.54 kilograms. One possible window is shown below. Notice that **Ymin** has been set to ⁻1 in order to leave some space for the TRACE coordinates at the bottom of the screen.

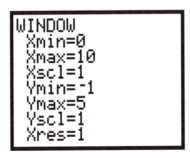
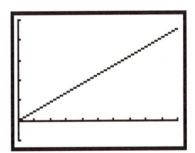

(b) (i) Using TABLE, with **TblStart** = 0 and **ΔTbl** = 1, you can see that 6 pounds is equivalent to 2.724 kg.

   (ii) After some trial and improvement and setting **TblStart** = 5.5064 and **ΔTbl** = .0001, you can see that 2.5 kg is equivalent to 5.5066 pounds.

(c) Using TRACE with the above window gives the nearest equivalence as

   (i) 5.9574 pounds = 2.7047 kg

   (ii) 2.5115 kg = 5.5319 pounds

The step size in the *x*-direction is 10/94 = 0.1064.

Exercise 7.5 *Trace or Table*

Using both TRACE and TABLE gives the answers 2.5, 5 and 40.

Notice that when $X = 5$ the corresponding value of Y is 2.5 on the graph of Y_1, because the slope of Y_1 is 0.5. So $Y = 0.5 \times 5 = 2.5$.

The slope of graph Y_2 is twice that of graph Y_1. So the corresponding value of Y for the same value of X is $2 \times 2.5 = 5$.

The slope of graph Y_3 is 16 times that of graph Y_1. So the corresponding value of Y is $16 \times 2.5 = 40$.

Exercise 7.6 *Degree conversion*

The calculator formula is $Y_1 = 1.8 \times X + 32$.

Suitable window settings and the corresponding display are shown below.

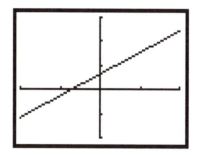

```
WINDOW
 Xmin=-50
 Xmax=50
 Xscl=25
 Ymin=-100
 Ymax=150
 Yscl=50
 Xres=1
```

The following table indicates the conversion values using Table. The nearest values that can be achieved using Trace and these window settings are given in round brackets.

Temperature in °Celsius	Temperature in °Fahrenheit
37.78 (38.298)	100 (100.936)
20 (20.213)	68 (68.383)
0 (0)	32 (32)
⁻17.75 (⁻18.085)	.05 (⁻0.553)
⁻40 (⁻40.426)	⁻40 (⁻40.766)

This is a clear case where the Table facility is more useful than Trace.

Notice that at ⁻40 °F the equivalent temperature is ⁻40 °C. Is this the only temperature for which the value in both scales is numerically the same? Stop and think how you would tackle this question.

When using Trace, if you try to move the cursor to the left of ⁻50 (or to the right of 50), you will find that the window is recalculated so that the graph shifts to the right (or to the left).

Exercise 8.1 *Entering formulas*

Here are the keystrokes required for each function:

(a) **4** 2nd [π] X,T,Θ,*n* x^2

(b) **1 . 8** X,T,Θ,*n* + **3 2** (for example)

(c) **. 5** ((X,T,Θ,*n* − **1 . 9**)) x^2 − **5**

   (Notice that there is no need to enter the 0 in 0.5.)

Exercise 8.2 *Evaluating functions on the Home screen*

(a) $Y_1(5) = {}^-1.765045216$

(b) 59, 64.4 and 86

(c) The answers are given in millions of square miles, to the nearest whole number.

	Radius	Area
Mercury	1.52	29
Venus	3.76	178
Earth	3.96	197
Mars	2.10	55
Jupiter	42.9	23 127
Saturn	35.5	15 837
Uranus	16.0	3217
Neptune	15.8	3137
Pluto	1.09	15

Exercise 8.3 *Investigating Y₄ with a table*

The variable *y* has a value of 0 when *x* is about $^-1.262$, and again when *x* is about 5.062.

The variable *y* has a minimum value of $^-5$ when *x* = 1.9, but no maximum value.

Exercise 8.4 *Alternative temperature conversion*

You should have entered $Y_5 = 2X + 30$ on the Y= screen.

Here are tables for the two functions.

The values of Y_5 and Y_3 are both 50 when X = 10. The rule of thumb is a reasonable approximation (within two or three degrees) for the normal range of atmospheric temperatures in the UK.

X	Y3	Y5
0	32	30
5	41	40
10	50	50
15	59	60
20	68	70
25	77	80
30	86	90

X=0

Exercise 8.5 *Graphing areas of spheres*

You should have produced a graph something like the one shown, which used 300 for **Ymax** and 50 for **Yscl**.

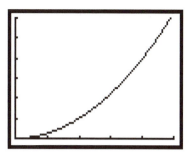

The value of **Ymax** needed in this exercise is (more or less) the value of the function when $x = 5$. This can be found, either as described in Section 8.2, or by using [TABLE]. In this way, the computational facilities of the calculator are used to help choose the window settings to produce the best graph. To get the most benefit from the calculator you often need to use the graphical and the computational facilities in tandem.

There is, however, a much more convenient method of producing this graph. This is through using the **ZoomFit** option within ZOOM. **ZoomFit** automatically calculates the **Ymin** and **Ymax** values, based on the given values of **Xmin** and **Xmax**.

Firstly, set **Xmin** to 0 and **Xmax** to 5 within WINDOW (the current values of **Ymin** and **Ymax** can be ignored.)

Press [ZOOM] **0** to select **ZoomFit**.

A graph is drawn which exactly fills the screen.

Pressing [WINDOW] will reveal the **Ymax** value which has been used (**Ymax** = 314.16).

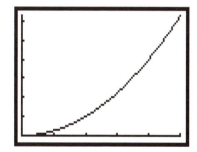

Exercise 8.6 *The graph of Y₁*

Below is one possible window setting and the corresponding graph.

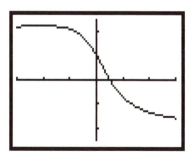

Exercise 8.7   *Investigating ZOOM, option 4*

ZDecimal provides the window settings shown here.

```
WINDOW
 Xmin=-4.7
 Xmax=4.7
 Xscl=1
 Ymin=-3.1
 Ymax=3.1
 Yscl=1
 Xres=1
```

Since the graphing area is 95 by 63 pixels, these settings ensure that each pixel represents 0.1 on both axes. Therefore, when you use TRACE, the step size along the *x*-axis is 0.1 – a very convenient, discrete step size.

ZDecimal also provides a convenient window setting for viewing graphs where the required range of *x* and *y* is small.

Exercise 8.8   *Another solution*

The solution is about $^-1.262$ (confirming the answer in Exercise 8.3).

Exercise 8.9   *Solving simultaneous equations*

You should find that the solutions to the equation are $x = 4.456$ and $x = {}^-1.904$.

Exercise 8.10   *Solving equations with CALC*

(a) Using option 1, when $X = 0$, $Y_1 = 1$ and $Y_4 = {}^-3.195$

(b) Using option 2, $X = -1.262$ and $X = 5.062$

(c) Using option 5, $X = -1.904$ and $X = 4.456$

Exercise 9.1   *Calculations with sin, cos and tan*

(a) (i) 2.050   (ii) 0.017   (iii) 23.578°   (iv) 66.422°

(b)

Angle in degrees	Sine	Cosine	Tangent
0	0.000	1.000	0.000
30	.500	.866	.577
45	.707	.707	1.000
60	.866	.500	1.732
90	1.000	0.000	–
180	0.000	$^-1.000$	0.000
270	$^-1.000$	0.000	–
360	0.000	1.000	0.000

Exercise 9.2   *Describing y = sin x*

There are comments immediately following the exercise in the main text.

Exercise 9.3   *Exploring cosine and tangent.*

The graphs of $y = \cos x$ and $y = \tan x$ are shown below.

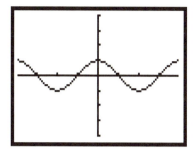 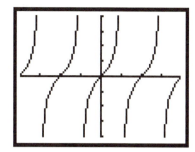

The graph of $y = \cos x$ is essentially the same shape as that of $y = \sin x$, but it is moved a bit along the x-axis. It has the same basic cycle which repeats at intervals of 360° on the x-axis.

The graph of $y = \tan x$ is very different, although it does repeat itself at intervals of 180° on the x-axis. However, unlike $y = \sin x$ and $y = \cos x$, there are no peaks and troughs. Instead the graph appears to shoot off the top of the display as x increases towards 90°, only to reappear at the bottom of the screen beyond 90°. If you use TRACE you will find that there is no calculated value of y when x actually equals 90°, confirming what you found earlier in Exercise 9.1.

Exercise 9.4   *The equivalent of 180°*

(a) By zooming in on the graph, you can see that the x-value corresponding to 180° is 3.1416.

(b) The table facility confirms that the required x-value lies between 3.141 and 3.142.

You will probably have recognized this number. It is the number known as π.

Exercise 9.5   *Exploring y = sin 2x*

The two curves are very similar; $y = \sin 2x$ produces a very regular, repetitive curve also. The maximum and minimum values of the two curves look the same.

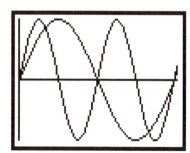

The major difference is that $y = \sin 2x$ has two full cycles in the same space as only one of $y = \sin x$. This means that $y = \sin 2x$, crosses the x-axis at the same points as $y = \sin x$, but it crosses at two other places in between as well.

However, this can be made more general because 2π is the same as $2\pi/1$ and a pair of coefficients such as 2, 3 have a common factor of 1. So the above generalization could be changed to the following:

The period of the sum of two sines is 2π divided by the highest common factor of the two coefficients.

Or a formal mathematical statement might be:

The period of $y = \sin Ax + \sin Bx$ (where A and B are positive integers) is $2\pi/C$ (where C is the highest common factor of A and B).

Exercise 9.10 *Comparing the lists of string lengths*

There are comments following the exercise in the main text.

Exercise 10.1 *Estimating and predicting*

(a) 1985: 11%; 1990: 8%

It is not appropriate to give more accurate figures than these, since the original data were only given to the nearest whole number.

(b) 1970: 21%

In 1972 the level fell below 20%.

(c) If the present trend continues the percentage of unqualified school-leavers will reach zero by 2003 (where $x = 103$).

Exercise 10.2 *Fitting a straight line to two data points*

(a) The value of a is .5 and this is the gradient of the line.

The value of b is 1 and this is the intercept where the line cuts the vertical axis.

The value of r is 1.

(b)

Points		a	b	r
(8, 5)	(4, 3)	.5	1	1
(2, 6)	(4, 3)	⁻1.5	9	⁻1
(2, 6)	(8, 3)	⁻.5	7	⁻1
(2, 6)	(8, 9)	.5	5	1

In each case a is the gradient of the line and b is the intercept where it cuts the y-axis. With two data points r is either ⁻1 or 1 and the sign is always the same as the sign of a. That is:

$r = 1$ if a, the gradient, is positive (an upwards sloping line)

and

$r = {}^-1$ if a, the gradient, is negative (a downwards sloping line)

There are exceptions: if the line is horizontal or vertical, then r cannot be calculated.

Exercise 10.3   *Supply and demand*

(a) The regression coefficients for the demand model are shown on the right.

```
LinReg
 y=ax+b
 a=⁻.7085714286
 b=40.48571429
 r²=.9984415584
 r=⁻.9992204754
```

(b) The regression coefficients for the supply model are shown on the right.

```
LinReg
 y=ax+b
 a=.9428571429
 b=⁻3.428571429
 r²=.9985329177
 r=.9992661896
```

(c) The two scatterplots and their corresponding regression lines are shown here. The viewing window used runs from 0 to 50 on the x-axis and 0 to 40 on the y-axis.

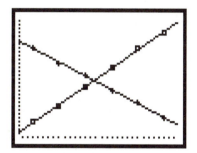

(d) $x = 27$ is the nearest whole number to the point of intersection. This represents a selling price of 27p.

The corresponding values of demand and supply, taken from the table are 21.354 and 22.029 million respectively. Since the predictions are based upon survey evidence they should not be given to a high degree of accuracy: about 21 to 22 million, or even just over 20 million, would be appropriate.

Exercise 10.4   *The four regions*

The four regions of the Graphing screen represent the following:

◇ Horizontal shading only: points where $y > x + 5$ and $y > 3 - x$

◇ Vertical shading only: points where $y < x + 5$ and $y < 3 - x$

◇ Vertical and horizontal shading: points where $y < x + 5$ and $y > 3 - x$

◇ No shading: points where $y > x + 5$ and $y < 3 - x$

Exercise 10.5   Rearranging inequalities

(a)	$x + y > 30$	Subtract x from both sides.	$y > 30 - x$
(b)	$x + 0.5y > 20$	Subtract x from both sides.	$0.5y > 20 - x$
		Multiply both sides by 2.	$y > 40 - 2x$
(c)	$y - x < 30$	Add x to both sides.	$y < 30 + x$
			(or $y < x + 30$)
(d)	$x - y < 30$	Add y to both sides.	$x < 30 + y$
		Take 30 from both sides.	$x - 30 < y$
			(or $y > x - 30$)
(e)	$x - 0.5y < 20$	Add $0.5y$ to both sides.	$x < 20 + 0.5y$
		Subtract 20 from both sides.	$x - 20 < 0.5y$
		Multiply both sides by 2.	$2x - 40 < y$
			(or $y > 2x - 40$)

Exercise 10.6   Unshaded feasible region

(a) Suitable window settings are shown below (left).

(b) The necessary entries on the Y=screen and resulting display on the Graphing screen are shown below (centre and right).

 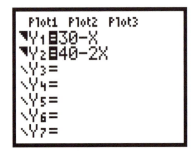 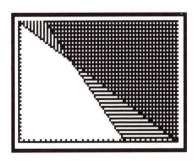

Exercise 11.1   The effect of a

(a) 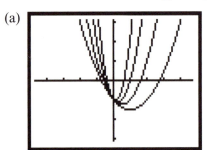   (b)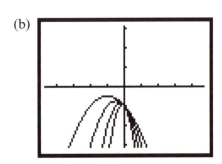

As the value of a increases the parabolas get steeper with sharper points at the vertices.

When a is negative the parabolas are the other way up. They have a shape like a hill rather than a valley. The vertices are maximum values rather than minimum ones.

Exercise 11.2   *The effect of c*

The graphs are shown on the right, again using
the **ZDecimal** window setting.

Increasing the value of   moves the graph
upwards.

Each graph cuts the vertical axis where y is
equal to the particular value of   .

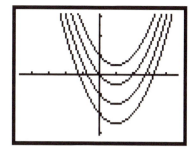

Exercise 11.3   *Zooming in on the vertex*

As you zoom in you should find that the vertex does not lie *on* the y-axis (as
seems likely initially) but rather a little to the left of it. It soon becomes clear
that the y-value is $^-3.032$ and further zooming does not allow you to improve on
the accuracy of this value. After zooming in a few times you probably get a
value of $x = ^-.125$; but how accurate is this? You cannot be sure about all three
decimal places in this value of x. With further zooming it becomes increasingly
difficult to decide exactly which x-value to choose for the vertex because the
curve is nearly horizontal close to the vertex.

There are a number of pixels which give a y-value of $^-3.032$ ranging from about
$x = ^-.11$ to $x = ^-.13$. Because the parabola is symmetrical about the vertex you
might say that a good estimate for x is $^-.12$, but no further accuracy is possible.
(Notice that you would not be able to use this procedure for other graphs
without the symmetrical property of the parabola.)

All in all, because of the flatness of the graph at the point of interest,
zooming in on a vertex cannot be used to produce accurate values for the
coordinates.

Exercise 11.4   *Locating the vertex using TABLE*

(a) The extreme value of Y_1 is $^-3.03$. The corresponding value of X is $^-.1$

(b) There are two values of Y_1 which are both $^-3.0312$. The corresponding
     values of X are $^-.12$ and $^-.13$. Either value will do.

(c) The next extreme value of Y_1 is $^-3.03125$, with corresponding value of X of
     $^-.125$. Repeating the procedure once again with Δ**Tbl** $= .0001$ does not
     change the extreme value of Y_1. Also, since the values of Y_1 on either side of
     $^-3.03125$ are exactly equal, it must be that this value lies on the axis of the
     parabola.

Exercise 11.5   *Solving for a particular value of y*

$x = 1.611555$ and $x = ^-1.861555$. Notice how, for this example, the guess allows
you to identify which of the two points of intersection will be evaluated.

Exercise 11.14 *Solving quadratics (sometimes!)*

(a)

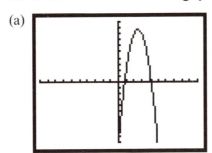 

The curve cuts the *x*-axis at two points and there are two solutions to the equation

(b)

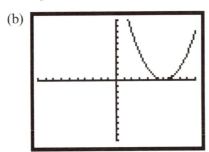 

There is only one solution to this equation: the curve touches the *x*-axis at a single point and both *S* and *T* are 6. This must mean that *D*, the square root, is zero. Check this by entering *D* on the Home screen.

(c) This curve does not cut the *x*-axis at all so the equation has no solution. If you try to run the program an error message appears. Use the **Goto** option in the error message and you will find that the error has occurred on the second line of the program. This indicates that the calculator cannot work out the square root. Try working out the value of $B^2 - 4AC$ on the Home screen and you should see why.

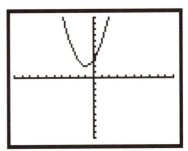

Exercise 12.1 *Getting the feel of* $y = 3^x$

(a) The three displays show the required values of *x* and Y1.

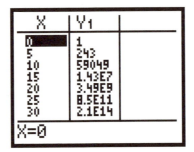

(b) If you use **ZStandard** you get the graph shown here.

Not very much of the graph is displayed!

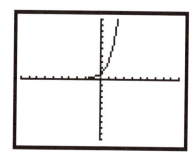

Exercise 12.2   *Guess and press with inverses*

You would expect the values of X and Y1 to be equal, and using Table should confirm this.

Exercise 12.3   *Getting the feel of exponential decay*

(a) The tabulated values are shown below.

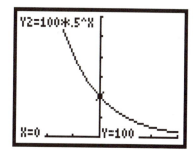

When $x = 1$, $y = 100 \times 0.5^1$, which is equivalent to 50.

When $x = 2$, $y = 100 \times 0.5^2$, which is equivalent to 10×0.25 or 25.

When $x = {}^-1$, $y = 100 \times 0.5^{-1}$, which is equivalent to $y = 100 \div 0.5$ or 200.

When $x = {}^-2$, $y = 100 \times 0.5^{-2}$, which is equivalent to $100 \div 0.25$ or 400.

(b) Here is one possible version of the graph.

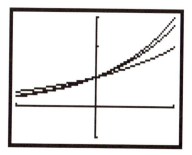

Exercise 12.4   *Between 2 and 3*

As is shown on the right, the graph of $y = e^x$ does lie between those of $y = 2^x$ and $y = 3^x$.

293